THE EVANGELICAL REVIVAL AND CHRISTIAN REUNION

THE
EVANGELICAL REVIVAL
AND
CHRISTIAN REUNION

BY

ARCHIBALD W. HARRISON

THE EPWORTH PRESS
(EDGAR C. BARTON)
25–35 City Road, London, E.C.1

Published for the
Fernley-Hartley Trust

Made in Great Britain

CONTENTS

DEDICATED TO

THE MEMBERS OF THE FELLOWSHIP OF
THE KINGDOM, WHO STILL BELIEVE IN
THE QUEST AND THE CRUSADE

Chapter I

THE BREATH OF THE SPIRIT

MR. JOHN STRACHEY in a recent book, *A Faith to Fight For*, deplores
the absence in this country of any faith with fighting quality in it.
He says: 'To-day all we have to live by is the remains of that
Protestant Puritan faith which was young and strong three
hundred years ago; and it is not enough.' He regards this Puritan
variant of Protestantism, first appearing in these islands during the
Reformation, as 'the essential faith of the British people'. Gradually that virile faith has lost its original impetus. 'It grew milder
and more civilized, less narrow and bigoted, but also thinner and
weaker.' He admits that he has recently discovered that there is
more that is still sound and valid for our day in that faith than
'some of us had realized'. Still, it is but the shadow of its former
courageous self. There is much truth in this diagnosis, however
much the present-day spokesmen for the Cavaliers may protest.
Mr. Strachey clearly does not consider that Caroline divines and
Royalist preachers were as characteristically British as the
Puritans; or he may not find in their view of Christianity the same
fighting qualities that he finds in the religion of Drake and
Cromwell. He fails, however, to remember the remarkable
reinforcement of that Puritan faith that came to the English-
speaking people on both sides of the Atlantic through the
Evangelical Revival in the eighteenth century. His words about
Puritanism as 'the essential faith of the British people' become
much more intelligible when we take the eighteenth and nineteenth centuries into account. The story of the revival of religion
has been told often enough, and our secular historians have
acknowledged its importance. Yet it needed the Frenchman,
Halévy, looking at the English people from the outside, to see that
the Revival is the chief element in helping us to understand the
British Empire and the United States of America to-day. The
greatness of the forces that swept through the mind and spirit of
the English-speaking people in the eighteenth century have even
now not been fully appreciated. It was the one religious
awakening in our history that really got home.

It was a discerning and detached critic of Methodism who said in the middle of the nineteenth century that it had 'so given an impulse to Christian feeling and profession on all sides, that it has come to present itself as the starting-point of our modern religious history. The field preaching of Wesley and Whitefield, in 1739, was the event whence the religious epoch, now current, must date its commencement'. Isaac Taylor, who made this observation, was in some ways unsympathetic, but he had no doubt that 'that great religious movement' was the work of God. If we believe in God at all and in His manifestation in history, we must agree that God's work is seen in times of revival; such times are marked by the renewal of the Holy Ghost. The leading actors in the drama of the Anglo-American revival were very conscious that they were the instruments of a Power greater and wiser than themselves. Whenever they reviewed their career, the text that rose habitually to their lips was, 'What hath God wrought?' So the Apostle Paul must have felt as he was swept along the great highways of the empire that led to Rome. God was working through him the signs of an apostle everywhere. In the words of an earlier lecturer in this series, 'When a revival of religion shakes the land, one of the truths which is most quickly demonstrated is that the Lord has poured out His Spirit as a free gift "upon all flesh". The experiences of the Day of Pentecost repeat themselves, and the weary Church, finding its lost youth, walks in the morning light of Apostolic days'.

It seems vain labour to search for the laws that regulate these Pentecostal visitations. 'The wind bloweth where it listeth, and thou hearest the voice thereof, but knowest not whence it cometh and whither it goeth.' When men's souls are dried up within them, the quest for the eternal source of refreshment begins anew. That search is never completely disappointed. 'Ye shall seek after me and find me,' says the Almighty, 'when ye shall search for me with all your heart.' When God is lost the search begins again. Still there is something mysterious in the simultaneous emergence of a company of great seekers in different parts of the world. The wonder grows as we see them converging to share the joy of their discoveries until the open secret is shouted across continents and sundering oceans and a dead Church comes to life again. The story can be told in such a way that the mystery and wonder of it depart. The tide of that great spiritual movement is now on the ebb and the psychologists are at work explaining it away. It may be, however, that the last word will not be with the psychologist. If religion begins with God and not with man (*von oben nach unten*, as the Germans say) the mystery of God's providential dealings with us remains. God fashions His prophets. God whispers in their ear. God sends them forth on their missions and prepares their way. God overrules their weaknesses for His large designs. God buries His workmen, but He carries on His work. God called to Spener in Saxony and through the Pietists to Zinzendorf. Not only Moravians, but humbler Palatines and Salzburghers were led by Divine Providence to England, to Ireland, and to the English colonies in America. So the heirs of the German Reformation were the heralds of the Anglo-American revival. Presently the drama will begin in the Puritan state of Massachusetts; then we are carried to the hills and valleys of Wales; the next scene takes us to the University of Oxford, whence the players are scattered far and wide on both sides of the Atlantic.

We must never lose sight of the American part of this history, or it will be thrown out of perspective. Indeed, it is in America that we must begin; not with the Wesleys and Whitefield in Georgia, but with Jonathan Edwards in Massachusetts. Jonathan Edwards was probably the greatest philospher and theologian the United States has yet produced. His *Treatise Concerning Religious Affections* and his *Freedom of the Will* must be regarded as classics. The latter book was a reply to Daniel Whitby, the English Arminian, and Edwards is the very personification of the completely logical Calvinist. It is unfortunate that he should be chiefly remembered as the author of a sermon on *Sinners in the Hands of an Angry God,* for if we find him saying, 'there is nothing that keeps wicked man at any moment out of hell, but the mere pleasure of God', we also learn from his autobiography how he struggled against the doctrine of divine sovereignty, and revelled in the beauties of God's world in which 'God's excellency, His wisdom, His purity and love seemed to appear in everything'. That such a God should be the sovereign of all mankind seemed to him, not only unutterably true, but unutterably sweet. He belonged to the Puritan aristocracy of New England and was born in the same year as John Wesley. His father was a distinguished graduate of Harvard and a minister of high repute. His mother was a daughter of Solomon Stoddard, the revered pastor of

Northampton, Mass., to whom he went as a colleague in 1727. Two years later Stoddard died and was succeeded by his grandson. The strong and serious personality of the young scholar from Yale was almost too much for his Northampton congregation. The absorbing passion for the will of God in their minister was a check to all frivolity and triviality among his people. In 1734 the Great Awakening broke out among them like a flash of lightning. It spread like fire throughout New England with the same ecstasies of sudden conversion, accompanied by strange physical effects, that were to be seen later in Old England. By 1740 the fire began to penetrate even into the conventional and worldly life of Episcopalian Virginia. The Establishment there was just as ineffective as a religious force as it was in any dull parish in the Old Country at the same time. The Awakening came in Presbyterian circles and from a few wandering Moravians, who carried the torch from Germany to the Middle Colonies. Then, in Virginia, the Baptists took up the story and, later, the Methodists with even greater effectiveness. We shall see how Whitefield and Wesley were to make their distinctive contributions to this movement, but for the moment it is enough to point out that it had begun before Whitefield's stirring eloquence was let loose on the American continent.

A few years before New Jersey and Massachusetts began to glow with a new warmth of love for God and man, similar signs were to be seen in a few obscure parishes in Cardiganshire and Carmarthenshire, South Wales. The names of Griffith Jones and Daniel Rowlands, rectors of Llanddowror and Llangeitho, are treasured in the story of the Revival in Wales as the pioneers of a great quickening of the Welsh people that was destined to change the whole character of their national life. Griffith Jones, by his circulating schools that moved round from parish to parish, laid the foundations of Welsh education. He was, however, an even greater influence as a wandering evangelist than as the organizer of hundreds of schools in which within a quarter of a century upwards of 150,000 adults, as well as children, learned to read the Bible. 'Fourteen years before Wesley took orders', says Miss M. G. Jones, 'and twenty-five years before Whitefield became a priest, Griffith Jones faced in Wales the problems which they later faced in England and met them in a manner which anticipated theirs. He was possessed, as they were, with the passion for saving souls, and consecrated his life to this end. Pastor, teacher, and doctor in his own parish, he found it too small for his missionary spirit and powers of organization, and travelled, as did his two great contemporaries, outside its confines to the villages around, preaching with passionate conviction the doctrine of faith and repentance, and in his early years, when the churches could not hold those who came to hear him, he taught in the fields and churchyards. Such was the conduct of the Methodists. His friendship with Whitefield and the Countess of Huntingdon in England, and with the leaders of the Methodist movement in Wales, established also his sympathy with Methodist ideas. Howell Harris, Daniel Rowlands, and Howell Davies, the remarkable trio of Methodist leaders in Wales, looked to Llanddowror as their spiritual home, and to the schools as agents of regeneration.'[1]

Rowlands was converted under the preaching of Griffith Jones, and a revival began in his own parish. There is a story of Daniel Rowlands, in the early days of his new-awakened devotion, preaching at his morning service unconscious of time and place as the hearers hung on his words; they lingered on till the rays of the setting sun began to pour in through the western windows, reminding them of the existence of an earthly home as well as the heavenly one to which they seemed for the time transported. But Howell Harris is the name at which we should pause, although he came on the scene rather later than Griffith Jones and Daniel Rowlands. On Whit-Sunday, 1735, as he received the sacrament in the parish church of Talgarth, Brecon, he saw the Lord crucified for him and, in recounting this experience, said, 'I was convinced by the Holy Ghost that Christ died for me'. Three weeks later he tells us that as he was praying his heart was filled 'with the fire of the love of God'. This experience made him the evangelist he continued to be all his days. He spoke to his neighbours and friends about his great discovery; he gathered them together and, though he was not ordained, he began to preach. In November of the same year he went to Oxford and kept a term there, but he soon found his religious activities were checked and so returned to Wales to set up a school at Trevecca. There he gathered religious groups or societies together until he was turned out of his school. So in 1737 he began his work as a preaching evangelist, at first in private houses and then in the fields and streets. This was two

[1] *The Charity School Movement in the Eighteenth Century*, p. 205.

years before Whitefield and Wesley went out into the open air to proclaim the gospel in Bristol. The importance of this irregular evangelism of Howell Harris lies in the fact that he led the way in the lay open-air preaching of the Revival. Three times he was refused ordination, though he was in every way fitted for the Christian ministry. The spirit of prophecy was, however, as a fire in his bones until he was weary with forbearing and could not keep silence. He travelled through seven counties, speaking at fairs and in the villages three or four times a day. Great crowds gathered to hear him and, by bitter opposition and persecution, clergy, magistrates, and mobs tried to silence him. There were many conversions and the converts were gathered into religious societies. After two years, Whitefield heard of his work and wrote to him from London. In his reply, Harris sent him the good news that there was a great revival in Cardiganshire and Carmarthenshire, where Daniel Rowlands was preaching. 'We have also a sweet prospect in Brecknockshire and part of Monmouthshire. And the Revival prospers in the county where I am now [Glamorgan]. There is also here a very useful dissenting minister, who is a man of great charity. There is another of the same character in Montgomeryshire. There are two or three young curates in Glamorganshire, who are well-wishers to the cause of God; and we have an exceedingly valuable clergyman in Brecknockshire. But enemies are many and powerful.' There in a few sentences we have a picture of the Methodist movement at any time during the next fifty years. Here we see a number of young men, Churchmen and Nonconformists, who are alive to God and the needs of men. One warm heart sets another on fire. At first the number of the evangelists could be counted on the fingers of two hands and the opposition was violent. The numbers of the 'well-wishers to the cause of God' steadily increased and the outrages of mobs diminished, though the opposition never disappeared. When Howell Harris met Whitefield at Cardiff later in the same year (1739), both of them were twenty-five years of age. Whitefield recognized him at once as a brother and kindred soul. Their friendship remained steadfast to the end. For three or four years Harris had been 'going about doing good', and so he continued. It was an accident that Whitefield was ordained and Harris was not. Both men were called of God to a noble prophetic ministry, and the layman was first in the field.

The only answer that we can give to the question why so many young men of like mind appeared simultaneously on widely separated parts of the earth is that God willed it. In the fullness of the times He sent forth His Spirit. Some new beginning for mankind is decreed and the instruments of the divine purpose must be prepared. To the English-speaking world, apathetic and listless after the fierce contentions of the seventeenth century, there came the stirrings of new life. First of all we perceive these tokens on the circumference of our civilization in the American colonies and in Wales. Soon we shall find them at the centre, in the heart of England, at London, at Oxford, and at Bristol. 'It looks as though there were seasons in the course of history', says Rufus M. Jones, 'which are like vernal equinoxes of the Spirit when fresh initiations into more life occur, when new installations of life seem to break in and enlarge the empire of man's divine estate.'[1]

[1] *The Eternal Gospel*, p. 80.

Chapter II

THE QUEST

THE Quest began with the study of the Greek Testament. It was Charles Wesley who invited two or three friends to join him in serious study in the 1729 Autumn Term at Oxford. He had come up to the University from Westminster School three years before and had enjoyed the freedom of undergraduate life. Perhaps he was rather relieved to escape from the strict supervision of his brother Samuel at Westminster. He might also have considered it fortunate that his brother John had just moved on from Christ Church to become Fellow of Lincoln. He was an attractive, cheerful, sociable young man in no hurry to become a saint. His first year was spent in diversions. The next year he began to settle down and do some work. The third year he began to be serious. He thought that somebody's prayers—perhaps his mother's—had influenced him. John had already moved into that world of earnest inquiry and achievement which he never after-wards left. He, too, had social gifts and graces, which he indulged for a time, but soon brought under such strict daily and hourly survey that he became a pattern of rectitude and precision. For some time he was away at Epworth, sustaining the failing strength of his father. When summoned back to Oxford in November, 1729, he was attracted to his brother's study circle. It soon became *his* study circle, for all the young men looked up to him as the acknowledged leader. He had been in the University for nine years and was now Greek Lecturer and Moderator of the classes at Lincoln College. The Greek Testament and the study of theology were his main occupations, but he read widely outside this field. He seemed marked out for distinction in the academic world.

At first, only William Morgan of Christ Church and Robert Kirkham of Merton met the two brothers a few evenings a week. Soon two or three of John Wesley's pupils joined them and then one of Charles Wesley's—for Charles was now a graduate and college tutor. Two years later, two important recruits were added to the little company—Benjamin Ingham of Queen's and Thomas Broughton of Exeter. The same year there came from Brasenose

John Clayton and two or three of his pupils. About the same time came James Hervey. George Whitefield was not found among them until 1735. That was the year the Wesleys left Oxford, but the Holy Club (as it was nicknamed—'our little company', the members preferred to call it) survived for two or three years longer. With varying fortunes and a changing membership, it had a life of about nine years.

These earnest young men were a band of brothers. At that age discussion and debate is the breath of life. Many of them came from country vicarages and the Church of England was their mother and mistress. The leader said of them, 'They were all zealous members of the Church of England; not only tenacious of all her doctrines, so far as they knew them, but of all her discipline to the minutest circumstance'. This fact by itself should correct a common impression that the clergy were at that time generally corrupt, indifferent, or immoral. All over the country were rectories and vicarages where the Bible and the Prayer Book and the *Whole Duty of Man* were the rule of life. A decent and respectable Christianity prevailed. Many parish churches could have put up similar tablets to their eighteenth-century incumbents to that which describes a Gloucestershire vicar as 'Esteemed for Amenity, admired for Erudition and Benevolence, universally beloved'. The Church was also strong in debate, as the controversy with the Deists had shown. She lacked neither great thinkers nor great men. An imposing list of famous names can be produced from the Anglican clergy of the eighteenth century, from the bishops Butler and Berkeley to Laurence Sterne. That drunken and worthless and immoral clergy existed cannot be denied. If Baxter had been sent round with a new company of Triers to remove the unconverted clergy from their livings, doubtless the list of vacancies would have been appalling. Even where the *Whole Duty of Man* was esteemed *The Reformed Pastor* was now unknown. Even Jeremy Taylor's *Holy Living* was becoming out of date, for it was quite a discovery to John Wesley when Sally Kirkham introduced him to it. Indeed, they felt that the seventeenth century was better forgotten. It had been an age of fierce enthusiasms and bitter conflict. It saw the terrible wars of religion. It left nations and churches exhausted. England began to recover poise and civilized, peaceful life again. The Church had got rid of its enthusiasts. Three great purges had removed

Puritans and Nonconformists and Non-Jurors and there was neither strength nor desire for further adventures. A great lassitude settled on the Anglican Church. There was a new spirit of tolerant moderation, with a dislike for all enthusiasts. Non-conformity was dying out, but the Church was dying too. Its moribund condition was not so obvious as that of the Dissenters, for its thousands of livings must be filled, glebes must be farmed, tithes collected, salaries enjoyed. Christenings and funerals and weddings must go forward as usual; confirmations would still be held, but as rare and occasional crowded observances. Sunday services would drone on, but spiritual life was absent. The institution was strong and seemed a permanent social necessity. It might even be picturesque in the pages of Addison and the person of Sir Roger de Coverley. It seemed improbable that the parish church could ever cease to be the hub of village life. Church and State were the foundations of good society. Parson and squire were to rule the countryside for many years to come. Still, vital religion as the Reformers knew it, as the Puritans knew it, as George Herbert and the Ferrars knew it, even as Jeremy Taylor, Ken, and the Cambridge Platonists knew it, was hard to come by. Up and down the country in scattered groups religious societies, established since the days of Charles II, kept alive the glow of Christian fellowship. Even these were rare.

'Zealous members of the Church of England' coming to Oxford at that time were not likely to find their zeal quickened there. It would be easy to collect extracts from eighteenth-century writings to prove the prevalence of low standards of work, morality, and religion in the University. A just and balanced picture may not so readily be painted. Oxford probably reflected the worldliness of good society, with the added frivolity that accompanies the 'diversions' of youth. Certainly the Holy Club was most unpopular. Its numbers were never great, but its seriousness deepened. The main concern at first was a better standard of work. General studies gave way apparently in the group meetings to Biblical and theological studies. Serious self-examination and a new attempt at a better ordering of life followed. Stoical self-discipline began to play its part. The influence of the leader, who was a 'methodist' from birth, began to show itself. The value of every hour must be extracted. The real aim of life must be discovered and searching questions about the love of God and the love of man must be answered. So they entered the innermost room in the temple of religion. Almost from the beginning they had made their weekly communion at Christ Church. Private prayers lasted for an hour morning and evening. Throughout the day they indulged in ejaculatory prayer for humility, faith, hope, and love. They were diligent in persuading neighbours and friends to attend the regular means of grace. Their service of God led to the service of man. Regular visits were paid to the prisoners in the Castle and the inmates of the parish workhouse; charitable care was given to the bodies as well as the souls of the unfortunate people to be found there. Before even these charitable duties could be undertaken, permission must be obtained from 'the minister of the parish'; also the approval of the bishop had to be secured. So scrupulous were they in matters of ecclesiastical decorum. Whether the leader had to receive episcopal authority to give away in alms all his income above £28 per annum does not appear.

When William Morgan died in August, 1732, it was said that the Holy Club had killed him by their austerities. John Wesley wrote at length to Morgan's father, telling him what the aims and practices of the Club were. He denied all extravagances and excesses and was so persuasive that the father of the dead boy declared that he almost wished he were one of the company himself. He did send another son to be under Charles Wesley's oversight. The younger brother turned out to be of very different temper from William Morgan, and Charles Wesley thought that he would find better guidance from his brother John than from himself. The young man was inclined to go back home to Dublin, but his plans were changed when John Wesley wrote to his father telling him how he hoped to incite his pupil to live a sober, virtuous, and religious life. In the same letter he said: 'Nay, but let me first tell you what religion is. I take religion to be, not the bare saying over so many prayers, morning or evening, in public or in private; nor anything superadded now and then to a careless or worldly life; but a constant ruling habit of the soul; a renewal of our minds in the image of God; a recovery of the Divine likeness; a still increasing conformity of heart and life to the pattern of our most Holy Redeemer.' These words were written in January, 1734. They represent a view of religion as the life of God in the soul of man. The members of the Holy Club have often been

B

represented as High Church Ritualists. So indeed they were. Perhaps John Clayton strengthened that side of their fellowship. He certainly introduced them to the regular practice of fasting and remained himself the Jacobite and High Churchman all his days. Every Wednesday and Friday they fasted, taking no food until three o'clock in the afternoon. They spoke of Holy Communion as a sacrifice, taught a doctrine of the Real Presence, mixed water with the sacramental wine, kept all saint's days and holy days, held the doctrine of apostolic succession, and believed that none but those episcopally ordained should administer the sacraments.

This strictness of regard for Church order and severity in ascetic practices won little reverence in the University. These views were just as unpopular in Oxford as they proved to be in Georgia when John Wesley did his best to transplant them in American soil. It must be confessed that a careful reading of the first volume of his letters leaves one with the impression that there were elements of the religious prig about John Wesley at that time. Yet neither he nor his brother Charles could have been lacking in attractive qualities. The curious set of letters between them and the Granville and Kirkham sisters, written under classical pseudonyms, shows how much the brothers were esteemed by well-bred young women. The romantic and yet serious correspondence trembles on the verge of love throughout. Such delicious tremors stimulate fears in the mind that longs to put the love of God above all human interests. Delightful conversations with these ladies in the Cotswolds needed the correction of a steady course of reading in the Church fathers and the writings of the Non-Jurors when the security of Oxford was reached again. The *Serious Call* of William Law must not be neglected. Birrell is quite wrong in saying that Wesley 'lacked charm'. The grace and fascination of a winning personality shines out most clearly in the *old* Wesley, especially when he is in the company of children and women. There is, however, iron in that personality, too; rigid discipline and method. The soldierly qualities make for leadership and sometimes provoke resentment and reaction. In the Holy Club this leadership is unchallenged. This is clear from all the references to John Wesley found in extant letters of Hervey, Gambold, Ingham, and Whitefield dating from that time. John Gambold entered Christ Church at the same time as Charles Wesley, but lived four years in the same college with him without really knowing him.

He was driven to make his acquaintance when a friend entertained him with an amusing account of the preciseness and pious extravagance of the 'whimsical Mr. Wesley'. This was so intriguing to an earnest young man seeking the way to a better life, that he suspected Charles Wesley might be a good Christian and went immediately to find him and open his heart to him. Charles was sure that his brother John could help him better. 'I never observed', says Gambold, 'any person have a more real deference for another than he constantly had for his brother. Indeed he followed his brother entirely. Could I describe one of them I should describe both and therefore I shall say no more of Charles, but that he was a man made for friendship; who, by his cheerfulness and vivacity would refresh his friend's heart; with attentive consideration would enter into and settle all his concerns; so far as he was able, would do anything for him, great or small; and by a habit of openness and freedom, leave no room for misunderstanding.' This is a lifelike picture. It is Andrew and Peter over again. 'He first findeth his own brother Peter.'

If 'Mr. John Wesley was always the chief manager', it was not only because of the strength of his mind and character. He saw the goal clearly and pursued his way towards it relentlessly. His energy and determination never faltered. No detail was too small for his consideration. 'Moreover,' continues Gambold, 'he had, I think, something of authority in his countenance; though, as he did not want address, he could soften his manner and point it as occasion required. Yet he never assumed anything to himself above his companions.' For some, the pace set was too severe. Young Richard Morgan looked on 'the little company' with very critical eyes and wrote to his father a somewhat satirical account of the activities of these religious devotees. Yet even he was conquered by their zeal in the end. It seems that the friendly and sociable intercourse of James Hervey was more effective in dispersing his prejudices than the earnest directness of his somewhat alarming tutor. John Wesley was inclined to direct all his pupils' reading towards manuals of devotion, while his own reading covered a wider field. To a young undergraduate fond of dogs and diversions, this zeal for religion seemed excessive, as it certainly did to most outsiders. From the distance of London, *Fogg's Journal* regarded the aims of 'the little company' 'as poverty, hypocrisy, enthusiasm, madness, and superstitious scruples'.

Immediately after this violent attack, on January 1, 1733, John Wesley preached his first sermon before the University. He did not make a direct reply, but with his accustomed clarity explained what the religion of the heart truly was. It is clear that he regarded perfection of character as the goal of the Christian life then, as he did to the end of his days. There is no suggestion of the mere ritualist in this sermon. All begins with the humble consciousness of man's frail and corrupt nature. This humility is learned in the school of Christ, who also leads us to faith in a God able to overturn the mountains of sin. Hope and love follow in the footsteps of faith, and the perfect life overflows in its love for God and man. The influence of Jeremy Taylor and William Law is seen throughout. Fifteen years later, when the sermon was republished, Wesley added a paragraph strengthening his definition of faith. It then became much more personal and direct; 'a direct evidence or conviction of His love, His free unmerited love to me a sinner'. Such was the difference made by the Aldersgate Street experience. Yet we cannot say that in his long life he improved on his Oxford ideals. Indeed, he could rise no higher; already he and his friends were bending mind and heart and will, all their time and talents, to do the perfect will of God. Like other men, they had their special problems and weaknesses, but the Holy Club was a little school of perfection. For the time being they were of one heart and mind, a band of brothers. Days would come when they would be widely separated. Several of them would be greatly influenced by the Moravians. Some would settle down to the conventional life of the parish priest, either on the high Church or the Evangelical side of the fence. Some would break away from that ordered and regular life into the strange adventure of the Methodist movement. Even these wandering evangelists would differ in theological outlook. One would fall away into a sad Antinomianism and another into scepticism. For the present, in the springtide of life, they were united in the quest for the will of God. It seemed impossible that such a fellowship should ever be broken. So great also was the love for their common mother, the *Ecclesia Anglicana*, that any waning of that loyalty seemed still more impossible. But life is stranger than fiction, and the campaign of this little company against evil was destined to be a war of surprises.

Chapter III

THE PIONEER

THE English story begins at a breakfast table in Oxford in the year 1735. The host is Charles Wesley and the guest is George White-field. It is their first meeting and the beginning of a friendship that lasted till Whitefield's death, thirty-five years later. Charles Wesley was a bright, handsome little man already student (i.e. fellow) of his college; a man therefore of some consequence at Christ Church and the founder of the Holy Club. His guest was six years younger than himself, an undergraduate of twenty years of age who looked up to Charles Wesley and his associates with adoring admiration. He was charmed to be admitted into that select fellowship and very conscious of his own limitations in knowledge and social standing. He had come up to the University with imperfect preparation, for he had spent a year and a half as tapster in his mother's public house at Gloucester. Also, as servitor at Pembroke College, he held the lowest grade of membership in the University. It was a great honour to be invited to breakfast with Charles Wesley, and he never forgot that morning. Later, when he met the elder and more impressive brother, John Wesley, who was 'more experienced in the spiritual life, God gave me', said Whitefield, 'a teachable temper'. Forty years afterwards Charles wrote of this meeting his impressions of the shyness and modesty of Whitefield:

> An Israelite, without disguise or art,
> I saw, I loved, and clasped him to my heart.
> A stranger as my bosom friend caressed
> And unawares received an angel-guest.

The fame of John Wesley has overshadowed Whitefield to some extent, but it should not be forgotten that if Whitefield was the last to join the Holy Club, he was the first to lead the popular movement of religious awakening in England. He rejoiced in the full assurance of faith three years before the Wesleys entered into the same joyful experience. He was the pioneer of open-air preaching in England. He first gained the ear of the multitudes for the gospel of redeeming love. As he began in 1736 so he continued all his days until he fell in harness at Newburyport, Mass., on September 30, 1770. In the long history of preaching, there cannot be a more remarkable record than that of George Whitefield. Sir James Stephen estimates that his 'homiletical labours' every week were about forty times those of the average preacher in England a hundred years ago. 'If the time spent in travelling from place to place, and some brief intervals of repose and preparation be subtracted, his whole life may be said to have been consumed in the delivery of one continuous and scarcely interrupted sermon.' There was no change in the message and no waning zeal in the whole of that period. His last sermon was of two hours' duration, when he preached from the text, 'Examine yourselves whether you be in the faith', to the last drop of his strength. So he always preached to thousands and sometimes tens of thousands of people, reaching the most distant auditor in the fields without any aid to his marvellous voice. It was Garrick who said that Whitefield could make men weep and tremble by his varied pronunciation of the word 'Mesopotamia'; and again: 'I would give a hundred guineas if I could only say "Oh!" like Mr. Whitefield.' Lord Bolingbroke said, 'Mr. Whitefield is the most extraordinary man in our times. He has the most commanding eloquence I ever heard in any person'. Lord Chesterfield wrote to the Countess of Huntingdon: 'Mr. Whitefield's eloquence is unrivalled.' These are powerful testimonies from men who were listening to a great artist without commenting on his message. Benjamin Franklin, too, had no sympathy with Whitefield's views, though he liked the man. He spoke of the extraordinary influence of his oratory on the people of Philadelphia, in spite of the fact that he abused them by assuring them that in the state of Nature they were half beasts and half devils. 'From being thoughtless and indifferent about religion, it seemed as if all the world were growing religious.' He was as much at home and as influential in America as in England, Scotland, or Wales. Thirteen times he crossed the Atlantic, and spent nearly eleven years of his life in the American colonies. When he died, Toplady said very truly that he was 'the apostle of the English empire'.

Martin Benson of Gloucester, the best-loved bishop of the English Church, ordained Whitefield deacon at the unusually early age of twenty-one. Three years later he ordained him priest, but he was much troubled by Whitefield's enthusiasm, and told the Countess of Huntingdon that he 'bitterly lamented' ever having ordained him. 'Mark my words,' said the Countess, 'when you come upon your dying bed, that will be one of the few ordinations you will reflect upon with complacence.' Although the atmosphere of the Holy Club was distinctly High Church, churchmanship was never a strong point with Whitefield. Indeed, one of our Church historians says, 'he became practically a dissenting minister instead of a parish priest'. Doubtless he preferred to preach in a parish church and, like Wesley, affected the use of cassock and bands in public, but he was equally at home in a Presbyterian assembly or a dissenting conventicle. He always professed his love for the Liturgy of the Book of Common Prayer and used the morning and evening offices in his own congregations, but he was equally ready to make use of extempore prayer. His last sermon in England was at a dissenting chapel and on the previous day he had preached at a Dissenter's ordination service. Much of the reading of the Wesleys in the Holy Club days was in early Church history and the literature of the Non-Jurors, but Whitefield's awakening began with the study of a Presbyterian book, and his meagre reading in later years was chiefly in the tomes of the Puritan divines.

When John and Charles Wesley sailed for Georgia in October, 1735, Whitefield had not yet finished his career as an Oxford undergraduate. That ended the year following, and he dreamed of spending 'some years' in the University. Charles Wesley returned to England with a letter from his brother to Whitefield in which it was stated that the harvest in Georgia was great, but the labourers were few. The letter ended with a characteristic challenge: 'What if thou art the man, Mr. Whitefield?' This kindled at once his missionary fervour. He would go to Georgia; but he was delayed for more than a year. The academic shades were not for him. As the members of the Holy Club had been scattered far and wide, 'the interest of Methodism' in Oxford, he said, 'had visibly declined'. He began to gather a new fellowship together, but was soon called to serve the Church as a deacon in the country and in London. 1737, the year of waiting, was the year that discovered his amazing gifts as a preacher. The churches in Bristol and London were open to him and the weekly lectures gave him opportunities that led to the perpetual round of preaching which became his life. Many of these lectureships were associated with religious societies at parish churches. His second publication was a sermon preached before religious societies. In a prophetic word, he said, 'if the advantages of religious society are so many and so great, then it is the duty of every Christian to establish and promote Societies of this nature. And I believe we may venture to affirm that if ever the spirit of true Christianity is revived in the world, it must be brought about by some such means as this'. His first published sermon had been 'On the necessity of the New Birth'. In these two proclamations the secret of the success of the Revival lay. It was Wesley who made the most of the value of the first, while both of them kept the second message central at all times. What a year of popularity it was for the young preacher of twenty-two. Opposition had not yet begun to drive him from the churches. The crowds gathered and approved and emptied their pockets in the collection plate in support of his stirring appeals for Georgia.

The contrast between Whitefield's popularity in 1737 and his difficulties in 1739, when he came back from America, is striking. It has been suggested that the publication of the young evangelist's *Journal* had raised a strong prejudice against him. It is certainly a naïvely egoistic document and its phraseology could have little appeal to lovers of decorum, who dreaded enthusiasm and the return of the Puritan rule of the 'saints' in the Church more than they dreaded the Devil himself. Certainly the Bishops of London and Bristol, who had looked upon Whitefield as a promising and pious young man, began to think that his activities should be restrained. Much had been happening in different parts of the country to show that gunpowder was lying about. It was necessary for bishops to exceed even their normal caution if explosions were to be avoided. When Whitefield found the Bristol churches closed to him, he was driven to preach in the open air to the colliers at Kingswood. He persuaded the Wesleys to follow in his steps. Already they had awakened criticism by their claim that new illumination had come to them. Then Whitefield learned of the awakening in Wales and, when he met Howell Harris at Cardiff, he found one who had been in the field before him. 'For these three years,' said Whitefield, 'as he told me with his own mouth, he has discoursed almost twice every day for three or four hours together; not authoritatively as a minister, but as a private person, exhorting his Christian brethren. He has been in seven counties .... and is styled by bigots a Dissenter. He discourses generally in a field, from a wall, a table, or anything else, but at other times in a home. He has established near sixty societies in South Wales, and still his sphere of action is enlarged daily.' Nearly all the essential characteristics are thus already present. Hundreds of Welsh witnesses were ready to affirm 'the necessity of the New Birth'. The chief irregularities are there, too, for we find here both lay preaching and preaching outside consecrated buildings. Most significant of all is the formation of societies of converted men and women.

Chapter IV

FELLOWSHIP

Dean Hook, in his *Church Dictionary*, defined Fellowship as 'an establishment in one of the colleges of a university, or in one of the few colleges not belonging to universities, with a share in its revenue'. This definition has been used to prove that, in the Dean's day, the very idea of Christian fellowship had died out in the Church of England. This may not be quite fair, as the Dean would have been quite capable of giving another definition for the κοινωνία mentioned in Acts ii. 42. There is, however, enough truth in the criticism to make it worth repeating. Fellowship, which was one of the four elements in the Pentecostal Church, was but little in evidence in the eighteenth and early nineteenth centuries. It is impossible to say exactly what it meant in those earliest days at Jerusalem. It seems to have been closely associated with 'the breaking of the loaf'. We are, however, not quite sure whether 'the breaking of the loaf' refers to the Eucharist or a common meal. Even if it were a meal shared in common by the early Christians in some private house, it was not an ordinary meal. It was a significant ritual observance. Sharing the gifts and grace of God in common seems to be the meaning of the symbolism of the common meal. Of course, in one sense all public worship is fellowship; but the fellowship of the early Christians must have been more intimate and personal than worship in the great congregation. The strong feeling of the family circle was realized there, especially in days of persecution. They formed indeed—

> a family of faith and love
> Combined to seek the things above,
> To spread the common Saviour's praise.

They were ready to share their possessions, and true fellowship meant this as much as sharing their prayers and meeting together in the Temple worship and joining at the love-feast or the Lord's Table. At all times, when the Christian religion has been alive it has discovered some form of intimate fellowship binding little companies of believers more closely together.

In the medieval Church, groups such as the Friends of God and the Brethren of the Common Life were more alive to the need 'to seek the things above' than 'to spread the common Saviour's praise'. But there were fellowships and orders in which the fire of evangelical ardour burned. The Spiritual Franciscans cherished both the ideals of sharing together the quest for God and the campaign for the Kingdom of the Redeemer. Religious guilds flourished on a basis of fellowship, though the Church looked on such fellowships as those of the Beghards with hesitating approval. Manning, in his Anglican days, said, 'there is nothing schismatical in a separation which both preserves all religious unity and makes those that live apart characteristically humble and charitable'. To the ecclesiastical mind, the danger of such fraternity was that they could exist without priestly direction and control. The life of the soul could be nourished among them. They showed a tendency to sectarianism, clearly visible among the Waldensians and the Puritans. Baxter's weekly Thursday 'experience meeting' at Kidderminster could hardly be an isolated example in days of religious intensity. It was inevitable that 'those that feared the Lord' should 'speak often one with another'. We are not surprised therefore at the persistence of such fellowships throughout the centuries.

After the Puritans were overwhelmed and the days of the Merry Monarch came—'days' (according to Macaulay) 'never to be remembered without a blush'—religious fellowships were not likely to be popular. Yet it was in the reign of Charles II and within the borders of the Established Church that they sprang up again. About the year 1678, through the influence of Dr. Anthony Horneck and Mr. Smithies, a number of young men in London, who were seeking to lead a holy life, began to meet together once a week in order that they might 'apply themselves to good discourse and to things wherein they might edify one another'. Horneck was a Prebendary of Westminster and Preacher at the Savoy. His societies consisted of baptized and confirmed members of the Church of England only. They were led by clergy and no prayers could be used in their meetings but those to be found in the Prayer Book. In their discussions they were to avoid politics and questions of ecclesiastical government. 'Practical divinity' was their theme. The Christian life of love, almsgiving, and service was their aim. Self-examination with directions from 'the minister' their method. These societies evidently grew in numbers, not only in London and Westminster, but in other parts of the country. They seem to have been most flourishing in the days of Queen Anne. They helped the formation of such influential organizations as the Society for Promoting Christian Knowledge, the Society for the Propagation of the Gospel, and the Society for the Reformation of Manners. Their association with the last-named society made them unpopular. With the best of intentions, in the absence of an efficient police force, members of the Religious Societies acted as informers against vice and drunkenness. The lot of the man who acts as censor of the morals of his neighbours is never a particularly happy one. The Religious Societies seem to have been too aggressive in the war against notorious evils. When the Hanoverian kings came in, all 'secret' societies were under suspicion; there were too many Jacobites about. A period of decline set in, but here and there these fellowships maintained a precarious existence. In his early days Samuel Wesley was interested in them, and we shall find how important a part they played in the career of his sons.

The fullest account of them is given in a book by Dr. Josiah Woodward in the 1712 edition. Woodward was 'the minister of Poplar' and the son and nephew of Nonconformists who had been ejected from their livings in 1662. His background, therefore, must have been similar to that of Samuel Wesley. There may be some significance in the enthusiasm of these descendants of the Puritans for these fellowships. In 1712 the Religious Societies were still confined to members of the Church of England, but their scope had broadened since the days of Charles II. All members were to 'frequent the Liturgy', but they were to be careful 'to express due Christian charity, candour and moderation towards all such Dissenters as are of good conversation'. Their aim was still to promote real holiness of heart and life. They were to avoid controversial subjects, though 'the bleeding divisions in Church and State' might often be considered by them. Their rules now aimed at the suppression of vicious habits in others as well as in themselves. Study of the Bible and of books of devotion was enjoined on all; also monthly attendance at the Lord's Supper and monthly fasts. Charity, especially the religious educa-tion of poor children, was one of their chief interests. Throughout their rule runs the earnest desire to remove all 'scandal and reproach from our holy religion' by learning the secret of the good life and achieving it in daily practice. It was expedient, but it had evidently been found difficult, to find parish clergy who could give a regular attendance at these weekly meetings. Provision was therefore made for laymen to act as directors of the gatherings in the absence of the 'minister'. The director was generally one of the stewards who had been chosen to administer the funds of the society. A rather long order of service based on the Prayer Book was arranged for his use, though he could shorten it if necessary. He was also given directions as to the subjects for discussion; the term 'conference' was preferred to 'discussion' in describing these conversations. Forty possible subjects were mentioned and all of them concerned the duties of the inward and outward life of a Christian. Singing was evidently popular in these gatherings, and doubtless Sternhold and Hopkins or Tate and Brady provided the hymns.

It was still expedient that each society should choose 'an orthodox and pious minister' as its director, but evidently this did not always happen. In some clerical circles the societies must have been regarded with suspicion. In spite of their close association with the Church, they might even wear the appearance of conventicles. At any rate, the possibility of schism and dissension was always there if free discussion were encouraged. What happened when the minister was not present? They might have ordered prayers and ordered subjects for conference, but who could resolve their difficulties? The Bible was their rule of faith and practice, but the Bible has been the source from which the wildest theories have been extracted. All the mystical fanatics, the Millenarians and the Fifth Monarchy men, the Diggers and Seekers and Ranters had searched the Scriptures for their prognostications. If they were told that some sound expositor, such as Hammond, was the arbiter, they would doubt whether the members could understand Hammond. Moreover, they invaded the province of the clergy when they visited the sick, catechized children, and distributed alms. It had always been with difficulty that the layman had won for himself the privilege of active Christian service. The time was coming when many restraints would be broken down.

Overton claims that the societies were under clerical control. It is true that the organization and rules of these fellowships kept them very close to the Church of England. It was assumed that normally the leadership was in the hands of the clergy; laymen only came forward when the clergy failed. As the interest of parish priests in personal religion declined, the godly layman took his place. He doubtless accepted the limitations which controlled him willingly enough. No devoted churchman of those days was in danger of breaking out into extempore prayer when the Prayer Book was in his hands. He would welcome the subjects laid down for meditation and conference. He would arrange, wherever possible, special services at his parish church conducted by the clergy. He would also, along with the other members, make his regular Communion. He would serve the causes of the charity schools, of church libraries, of the propagation of Christian knowledge, of the supply of clergy to serve the colonies, of general almsgiving and charity. It was only in the Society for the Reformation of Manners that he co-operated with the Dissenters. All the membership in his Religious Society was Anglican. The only reason why he took a prominent part there was because of the increasing difficulty of finding clergy who were interested in religion as 'the life of God in the soul of man'. There was the whole secret of the gradual movement of the societies outside the organization of the Church. The basis of membership would soon change. First of all, the Germans came in, claiming intercommunion with the Church of England and therefore membership in the Religious Societies. The Moravian leaven would speedily work a complete metamorphosis. Then would come the Evangelical Revival and the growth of many societies all over the land, chiefly under the direction of the Wesleys. Only in rare cases would the parish clergy have any association with these new societies. An Ecclesiola within the Ecclesia was growing up. Fellowship of this kind was the natural expression of the quickening of religious life.

It is impossible to say how many of the older type of religious societies existed in 1738. Once there had been forty of them in the Metropolitan area and several seem to have survived. We read of a few of them in Wesley's *Journal* for that year and also of an annual sermon preached to the societies at the Church of St. Mary-le-Bow. The preacher was, however, out of tune with his congregation—at least with that member of it whose impressions survive. He had to fall back on the doggerel of Sternhold and Hopkins to derive any spiritual sustenance from the service. This is a parable of the failure of the Church of England at the moment of its greatest opportunity. 'The children were come to the birth and there was no strength to bring them forth.' With imagination and leadership, the Established Church might then have come into its Kingdom and absorbed this new movement towards fellowship into its own organization. The opportunity lay there before the gaze of the whole panel of bishops, not for a few months, but for two generations, and it was not accepted. Seldom can so tragic a lack of vision have been recorded in Christian history.

Chapter V

THE GERMAN CONTRIBUTION

THE importance of the Moravian influence on the Revival of Religion has certainly not been exaggerated. Their most celebrated bishop, Comenius, is best known as an educational reformer. There is indeed no greater name in the story of modern education, yet it may be argued that his services to his own Church were greater still. In dark days of persecution and war, he kept alive the 'hidden seed' of the broad and simple faith of the Bohemian Brethren. He was an exile in Poland, but his catechism entitled 'The Old Catholic Christian Religion of Short Questions and Answers' circulated among those worshipping in secret in Bohemia and Moravia. He himself had been born in Moravia, and, after a theological training in Germany, had become minister of the Brethren's congregation at Fulneck and teacher of their school. He and his wife and children were driven out of their native country when their little town was sacked by the Austrian soldiery; his wife and one of his children died in the flight. These were the early days of the terrible Thirty Years' War that left Germany a desert. The country we now call Czechoslovakia had suffered sadly before ever the new war began. It was not only the scene of racial hatreds between German and Czech; from the days of Hus, a century before Luther's Reformation, the corruptions and superstitions of the medieval Church had been challenged there. Out of the turmoil that followed the execution of Hus arose a communion of earnest Christians whose main aim was to recover the simplicity and faith of the early Church. For a time they accepted the ministry of their own native Utraquist clergy, though they renounced the Papacy. The Utraquist compromise had been won from Rome at the cost of war. The Bohemian Church was allowed to administer both elements of bread and wine to lay communicants, a unique privilege for which they emblazoned the sacred Communion cup on their banners. This compromise was not enough for the Brethren. In 1467 they established an ordained ministry of their own, receiving the ordination from a Waldensian bishop. So they claimed a succession in faithful devotion to Christ and His teaching back to the

Apostles themselves. They had days of prosperity and even more days of adversity. Their hearts were lifted up by the German Reformation, and at one time it seemed as if all Czechoslovakia might be Protestant. Then came the reaction; exile, persecution, and declension. By the end of the seventeenth century the 'hidden seed' was but feebly surviving. Comenius was dead, but he had kept the Bohemian fellowship alive through its darkest days. The succession of its bishops had continued and the validity of their episcopacy was acknowledged by Archbishop Wake in 1715.

The Bohemian Brethren came to life again in the eighteenth century as the Moravian Church. The chief instrument in this revival was a Saxon Lutheran noble. Nicholas Lewis, Count of Zinzendorf, was born in 1700 and brought up in the Pietist centres of Saxony. Spener, Francke, Gerhardt—the Pietist leaders —were reverenced in his home, and from earliest childhood Zinzendorf absorbed their teaching. His precocious piety was not checked by a university career at Wittenberg. He remained as devoted to the writings of Spener as to those of Luther. The Moravian revival began when Zinzendorf in 1722 invited these harassed and persecuted people to settle on his estate at Berthels-dorf, which was in Saxony, just over the Bohemian border. Their colony prospered and was given the name Herrnhut. Zinzendorf's interest in it deepened and he found that the new community shared many of his Pietist views. He became a member of the Brethren's Church himself and eventually one of their bishops. Before becoming a Moravian bishop he had been ordained a Lutheran minister and never resolved this inconsistency. He seems to have held that the Moravians formed a Church within the Lutheran Church just as the Pietists were said to do. This was an opinion which he shared with no one else; but many of Zinzendorf's views were so much his own that they never passed into circulation. The drawing-room meetings and fellowships of devotion of the Pietists had been called *Ecclesiolae in Ecclesia*. In spite of his high rank, Zinzendorf was regarded with suspicion by his own Government and was exiled from the country. The Herrnhut colony was allowed to remain as a toler-ated, industrial community. It became, however, a hiving swarm, which in a remarkably short space of time sent wandering swarms to England, to Georgia, to Greenland, to Ceylon, to West and

C

South Africa, and to the remotest places on earth. It was surely in the Providence of God that in days of world movement this simple form of missionary Christianity appeared. The Moravians had known persecution and poverty and, although they preserved a high sense of churchmanship, they had to reduce the paraphernalia of ritual and order to a minimum. They proved themselves to be admirable colonists and serious labour went hand in hand with a serious religion. At the close of the day they would kneel in prayer together and commend each other to the grace and goodness of their Eternal Father. The greater their difficulties, the closer they were knit together in God's family circle. If a ministering priest were available, so much the better; if not, they must become ministers to one another or learn to develop a separated ministry. The simpler the organization and the closer its resemblance to 'primitive Christianity' the better.

This is where the Moravians came in. From the early days of the Waldensian influence they had loved simplicity. As a Church 'under the Cross', they had been nourished in it. They turned back to the Gospels and to the Sermon on the Mount continually. They taught all their children to read and write, in order that they might know the New Testament. They excelled others not so much by their doctrine as in their lives. They became known as 'Brethren of the Law of Christ'. They had a separated ministry, even an episcopacy, but made it a rule that their clergy should learn a trade. They preferred that they should remain unmarried. That requirement was really secondary, but it was of primary consequence that all should know the Bible and have a living faith in Christ. One of their chief endeavours was to revive the practices of the Early Church. This is the explanation of their 'choirs' of single and married, widows and widowers; of the love-feast and the use of the lot in making great decisions for individuals and for the community. This use of the lot seems to have been common among the Pietists and was much in evidence among the revived Moravians at Herrnhut. Although for a time they passed as orthodox members of the Lutheran Church at Herrnhut, they still preserved most of the old practices of the Bohemian Brethren there. Orthodox they certainly were, if the acceptance of the Apostles' Creed and the central doctrines of Christianity constitutes orthodoxy. In their preaching they stressed the presence of their ascended Lord in their midst and realized the truth of their belief in their hearts. If they talked less of Justification by Faith than the Lutherans did, they made faith in the Saviour fundamental. 'What is Faith in Christ?' they asked in their old 1522 Catechism. 'It is to listen to His word, to know Him, to honour Him, to love Him, and to join the company of His followers.' Faith and works are both there, together with hope and charity.

What did the Moravians contribute to the Oxford Methodists? First of all, a deeper sense of Christian fellowship. They had already begun to see the value of fellowship in the Holy Club. They knew of its existence in the Religious Societies. They even debated whether they should turn the Holy Club itself into a Religious Society, but decided that such a change was not necessary.[1] It is significant that five of the Oxford group joined the Moravian brethren and one of them, John Gambold, became a Moravian bishop. When he formally resigned his living at Stanton Harcourt in 1742 to become a Moravian, it was fellowship with other newly awakened souls he most of all desired. Wesley had just provided this for the Methodists by dividing his societies into classes. Such intimate fellowship could only be found among the Moravians and Wesley's people. In his farewell address to his parishioners, Gambold said he had no quarrel with the forms of the worship of God in the Church of England. 'I can find no fault with any passage or clause in the Common Prayer Book. Nor can I, in justice, be considered in the same light with such persons as slight and forsake one party of Christians to go over to another without sufficient cause. But that which has determined the choice which I have made, was the earnest desire I found in myself of that improvement in the knowledge of the Gospel and in the experience of the grace of Jesus Christ which I stood in need of. The blessings purchased by the blood of the Shepherd of our souls, I longed to enjoy in *fellowship* with a little flock of His sheep, who daily feed on the merits of His passion, and whose great concern is to build up one another in their most holy faith, and to propagate the truth, as it is in Jesus, for the good of others.'

At an earlier date, just before his ordination, James Hervey had written to a student at Doddridge's Academy an interesting

[1] See *John Wesley, Evangelist*, R. Green, p. 104.

letter on the value of such fellowship. The young Dissenter wished to found at Northampton a society similar to that of the Holy Club at Oxford. Hervey encouraged him to go forward. He showed how in fellowship Christians may develop in wisdom by pooling their experience; they may also learn their faults and limitations from the sincerity of their friends; they may inspire one another with constancy and courage, and they may kindle each other into 'holy fervour'. 'How often', he says, 'have I gone into the company of my dear friends, listless and spiritless; yet, when I came home, I have found myself quite another person; vigorous and active, sanguine and zealously affected in good matters!' Charles Wesley was to get the people to sing about this truth:

> Two are better far than one
>   For counsel or for fight;
> How can one be warm alone,
>   Or serve his God aright?
> Join we then our hearts and hands;
>   Each to love provoke his friend;
> Run the way of His commands,
>   And keep it to the end.

In the second place, the Moravians led the Holy Club back to the Church of the Apostolic age. From devotional reading and the study of the Greek Testament, the Holy Club had been led on to Church history, liturgiology and Canon Law. John Clayton strengthened this tendency when he joined them. At his home in Manchester he was greatly influenced by Dr. Deacon, who had now become the leader of the Non-Jurors when so many of the original company of Non-Jurors had passed away. Clayton remained a strict High Churchman throughout his life and disapproved of the Evangelical Revival, though he never became a Non-Juror himself. He advised John Wesley on his reading in the Fathers and in the worship and discipline of the 'primitive Christians'. Wesley's first publication was in collaboration with Clayton and appeared in 1733, *A Collection of Forms of Prayer*. On the voyage to Georgia, Wesley was still deep in his ecclesiastical studies. Of the twenty books he read on board ship, five were by Non-Jurors, three by Roman Catholics, and others tended to the views which were later to be known as Anglo-Catholic. The only books that did not show this High Church tendency were the *Theologia Germanica*, Francke's *Nicodemus*, and his *Pietas Hallensis*. Here comes in the German influence towards mysticism and Pietism. His study of William Law prepared the way for one, and the presence of some Moravians on board provided a living link with the other. We know how impressed he was by the cheerful and steady behaviour of the Moravians in the great storm. He began to learn German to be able to talk with them. He also joined in their services and taught their Bishop Nitschmann English. What was still more important, he was introduced to the Moravian *Gesang-buch* and began to translate some of the great German hymns. There can be little doubt that he learned some of their tunes at the same time.

There must have been something very fascinating about these simple, pious foreigners. Stumbling through the clumsy German sentences to the discovery of their devotion to their common Saviour, Wesley cannot have failed to find his heart 'strangely warmed' by this new and unexpected form of churchmanship. He was to meet them frequently in Georgia and to react in varying ways to their presence. At one time he is learning from Spangenberg the meaning of the assurance of salvation; at another he is refusing the sacrament of the Lord's Supper to John Martin Bolzius because he had not been baptized by an episcopally ordained priest. It was Spangenberg also who told him about Zinzendorf and the story of Herrnhut. For a time he lived with the Moravians at Savannah and was able to notice their conduct from morning to night. 'They were always employed, always cheerful themselves and in good humour with one another; they had put away all anger, and strife, and wrath, and bitterness, and clamour, and evil-speaking; they walked worthy of the vocation wherewith they were called and adorned the Gospel of our Lord in all things.' Three years later he was to confirm these early impressions when he visited Herrnhut.

Meanwhile Spangenberg in particular seems to have influenced Wesley by his frequent conversations with him. He was the son of a Lutheran clergyman; educated at Jena he had been professor at Halle for a time. A learned man, he professed to renounce worldly learning when he became a Moravian minister. He startled Wesley by denying the doctrine of apostolic succession, though he sought ordination himself from the Bishop of London. He led the little group of Germans in Georgia until Nitschmann came out as a bishop. When Spangenberg and Nitschmann left the colony, Anton Neifert was made bishop, and Wesley had the privilege of being present at the ordination. It followed several hours of conference and prayer. Wesley was deeply moved by the service. 'The great simplicity as well as solemnity of the whole', he wrote in his *Journal*, 'almost made me forget the seventeen hundred years between, and imagine myself in one of those assemblies where form and state were not, but Paul the tent-maker or Peter the fisherman presided, yet with the demonstration of the Spirit and of power.' This took place before Wesley really began his ministry at Savannah, and it seems to have made a lifelong impression. Somehow or other, these humble people had got nearer to the secret of the Christian life than he had at Oxford, or than he was to do in his diligent and careful ritual in Georgia. His comparative failure with his English flock threw him more and more on the friendship of the Germans. Indeed, the Religious Society he formed at Savannah seems to have consisted chiefly of Moravians. He was fusing the Oxford and Moravian ideals of an intimate fellowship together and discovering the secret of the Methodist class meeting. Presently we find him joining in Communion with the Moravians. It is quite possible that he had heard from James Hutton in London that Archbishop Potter (who had ordained Wesley, Ingham, Gambold, and other members of the Holy Club) considered the objections to the Moravian episcopal succession 'trivial'. Zinzendorf was at that time seeking recognition of Moravian orders from the Anglican Church. Wesley was still so strict a churchman that he could not have joined in Communion with irregularly ordained clergy and could not administer Communion to a Dissenter. Yet he had caught a glimpse of a greater Church than that limited to the obedience of Rome or Canterbury. The Moravians had not only taught Wesley some new methods in Church worship and fellowship, they had driven him back to the Apostolic Church. Spangenberg had denied that the apostolic succession could be traced through a long chain of bishops duly ordained, but he was quite sure that he could go back to the Early Church at Jerusalem or Antioch or Corinth and meet the Apostles and find Jesus in the midst. Wesley might be dreaming of some Christian family living in Georgia as the Ferrars lived at Little Gidding, but he dreamed still more of the revival of 'Primitive Christianity'.

This was a dream that would never more leave him. To live as the first Apostles lived in the presence of their Divine Master, to serve as He served and, if necessary, to die as He died became the master passion of his life. But first of all he must know that Master more intimately.

The third contribution the Moravians made to the Evangelical Revival, and perhaps the greatest of all, was their confident belief that it was possible to know one's sins were forgiven and to know Christ as a personal Saviour. The assurance of faith, they said, should accompany conversion. It might come instantaneously, as conversion itself frequently did. It might grow in strength as the Lord opened the heart of the timid, hesitating believer. 'Do you know Jesus Christ?' said Spangenberg to Wesley. 'I know He is the Saviour of the world,' said Wesley. 'True,' said Spangenberg. 'But do you know that He has saved you?' 'I hope He has died to save me,' was the reply. 'I fear they were vain words', he added when he wrote this conversation down. This probing inquiry was to be resumed in England, not by Spangenberg, but by a young man, Peter Böhler, whom Spangenberg himself had led into the light. Böhler happened to arrive in London from Germany five days before Wesley landed from Georgia. They met at the house of a Dutch merchant and Moravianism linked them together at once. Together they travelled to Oxford. 'He knew that he did not properly believe in the Saviour', said Böhler in a letter to Zinzendorf. In spite of this, Böhler advised him to preach the Gospel to others when Wesley was inclined to give up preaching altogether. 'But what can I preach?' he asked. 'Preach faith until you have it, and then, because you have it, you will preach faith.' Böhler talked of his own sudden conversion and forced Wesley to believe from eighteenth-century evidence, as well as from the New Testament, that his position was sound. These affirmations from such men as Spangenberg and Böhler worked powerfully in Wesley's honest and logical mind. Convinced that they were right, he marched straight forward to his own transforming experience in the little room in Aldersgate Street.

Step by step, Wesley was driven from the medieval view of salvation to what can best be described as a Protestant view. In 1725 he had decided to dedicate his life to God and proceeded to do so with complete devotion. In asceticism, in conscientious application to duty, in self-denying labours, he climbed up the *Scala Santa* on his way to heaven. The result had been the great disappointment of Georgia. Spangenberg and Böhler came from the schools of German Protestantism, and their doctrine of justification by faith was one with that of Luther and Calvin. It was, indeed, one with the formularies and homilies of the Church of England. It had never come to life in High Church circles and the reality of its personal application came as a new discovery to both John and Charles Wesley. So did the emphasis both of the New Testament and of recent religious awakings or instantaneous conversions. When the brothers could say, 'I believe', with full conviction of heart in the same wonderful week they, too, stepped immediately on to a new plane of feeling and action. Father Piette, in his delightful study of the Methodist Revival, does his best to show that Luther's doctrine was very different from that accepted by Wesley in his arguments with Peter Böhler and experienced in the Society meeting at Aldersgate Street. He would prefer to speak of the realization of the love of God rather than of justification by faith. 'Wesley's asceticisms, good in themselves,' he says, 'were all in vain unless inspired by the love of God. He had depended too much on rule, mortifications, and examination of conscience.' He is making a distinction without any real difference here. As a loyal Roman Catholic, he is bound to disapprove of the Lutheran doctrine of faith without works, but he quite fails to bring conviction by his arguments. Dr. George Cell is quite correct in his demonstration that Luther, Calvin, and Wesley were at one in their acceptance of the central doctrine of the Reformation. They all went back to Paul's doctrine and Paul's experience; 'not by works of righteousness which we did ourselves, but according to his mercy he saved us'. The stiff High Church way of salvation had melted into the way of Wittenberg, of Herrnhut, of Aldersgate.

The *Journals* of John and Charles Wesley reflect the widely differing temperaments of the two brothers, and that of John is much more detailed in its references to the Moravian influence; but that influence was clearly as powerful with the younger brother. It was even more powerful with such men as Ingham and Gambold, who belonged to the Holy Club, and Hutton and Charles Delamotte, who did not. These four members of an intimate circle of friends remained in the fellowship of the

Moravians to the end. Ingham and Delamotte had been on the *Simmonds* with the Wesleys on the voyage to Georgia. They, too, must have observed the humility of the Moravians, who 'performed those servile offices for the other passengers which none of the English would undertake; for which they desired and would receive no pay saying, "It was good for their proud hearts, and their loving Saviour had done more for them". But every day had given them an opportunity which no injury could move. If they were pushed, struck or thrown down, they rose and went away; but no complaint was found in their mouth'. Then came the storm and the demonstration of their steady courage. Curnock, in his note on this incident in Wesley's *Journal*, says: 'The storm was one of the crucial facts of early Methodism. It may have been said to have made Ingham a Moravian, and no doubt influenced Delamotte in the same direction.' It has been said that the Methodist authorities have exaggerated the Moravian influence as a creative factor in the revival of religion. It appears from a careful examination of these formative years that this influence has really been *under*estimated.

Chapter VI

IRREGULARITIES

AFTER all that has been written about the Evangelical Revival, there remains an element of mystery in the phenomenon that separation from the Church of England by so large a body as the Methodists should result from the activities of certain members of the Holy Club. Discipline and order were the keynotes of that Oxford fellowship. Loyalty to the Church characterized them all. After the straitest sect of their religion, they were perfect Pharisees. Of none was this more true than of the leader, John Wesley. With him respect for tradition and properly constituted authority was second nature. How, then, did it come about that this perfectly trained churchman was guilty of so many irregularities in ecclesiastical eyes? His first irregularities were due to excessive regard for tradition. Not only in Georgia was this true, but when he returned to England he was reproved by the Bishop of London for having re-baptized an adult person because he considered that baptism by a Dissenter was not valid. Charles Wesley waited on the bishop to inform him 'that a woman, not satisfied with having been baptized by a Dissenter, wished him to baptize her and he intended to comply with her request'. 'The bishop', said Charles Wesley, 'immediately took fire, and interrupted me, saying, "I wholly disapprove of it; it is irregular".' Here the brothers were inclined to be more episcopal than the bishops themselves. We can understand the annoyance of a man like Edmund Gibson at this excess of zeal, though he seems to have been kindly disposed to the Wesleys at that time. The archbishop also gave them good advice, urging them 'to keep to the doctrines of the Church, to avoid all exceptionable phrases, and to preach and enforce only the essentials of religion; other things time and the providence of God only can cure'.

Had the irregularities risen only from High Church zeal nothing further would have been heard of them. It was when they began to move in the opposite direction that real hostility was aroused. John Wesley pressed Gibson to say whether the Religious Societies were conventicles. As the bishop had himself established a Religious Society in his own parish when he had been Rector of

Lambeth, he was not inclined to commit himself on this subject. 'No, I think not,' he said. 'However, you can read the Acts and laws as well as I. I determine nothing.' Presumably all depended on the rules of the particular society and the manner in which it was conducted. This was to become a point of great consequence at a later date. A great subject of disagreement arose over the authority that Charles claimed to baptize 'in any part of the known world'. Could any minister of the Established Church exercise parochial duty without the authorization of a bishop? Presently we shall find John Wesley writing to Hervey on the subject and using an expression that was to become famous: 'I look upon all the world as my parish.' Why did neither of the Wesleys, nor Whitefield, nor Ingham accept any parochial responsibility? Why did John Gambold resign his living? Charles Wesley was for a time curate to his friend Stonehouse at Islington, though the appointment was not confirmed by the bishop. Indeed, when the churchwardens wished to get rid of Charles, the bishop supported them and Charles Wesley's brief curacy came to an inglorious end. While he was still at Oxford John Wesley had refused to allow his name to go forward as a possible successor to his father as Rector of Epworth. At that time he preferred the attraction of 'academic shades' or even (for a moment) toyed with the idea of becoming a rural schoolmaster. Later, it was the romantic appeal of a mission to the American Indians that claimed his devotion. Whitefield had some weeks' experience as acting curate at Dummer in Hampshire. Such livings as were held by members of the Holy Club were at tiny villages such as Dummer, Stanton Harcourt, Weston Favel, Thorp Arch, or Wootton-Rivers. Only Clayton, Broughton, and Hutchins received suitable appointments. Clayton was Chaplain and Fellow of the Collegiate Church at Manchester (now the Cathedral) for many years, and broke entirely with his Oxford friends. Broughton was Secretary of the Society for the Promotion of Christian Knowledge for thirty-four years. He was also lecturer at All Hallows, Lombard Street, for many years and afterwards Rector of Wootton (Surrey). It was Henry Venn who persuaded Sir John Evelyn to give Broughton the living of a village known only because of its association with a famous diarist. Hutchins remained in Oxford as Fellow of Lincoln and became Rector of his College in 1755. Until 1781 he remained in that post, the last of the Oxford Methodists at Oxford when his old friends had long been scattered far and wide.

Influence in aristocratic circles or with the bench of bishops was almost a necessity if preferment in the Church was to be secured at that time. There are many interesting sidelights on this question in that strange book, *Memoirs of a Royal Chaplain*, 1729–1763. Influence was certainly not on the side of preachers of exciting doctrines of instantaneous conversion, the assurance of faith, or even justification by faith. It all savoured so much of that 'horrid enthusiasm' that Horace Walpole detested so thoroughly. It might be perfectly orthodox when explained quietly by the fireside in the study, but, when proclaimed with dramatic vigour from the pulpit, it was too reminiscent of the seventeenth-century fanatics and Puritans. Besides, there was not enough emphasis on good works and decent behaviour. All men were condemned as such intolerable sinners, and the way of salvation was by faith and faith alone. The preachers took themselves and their message so seriously that they crowded the churches. Regular churchgoers found their cushions disarranged and a motley mob swarming into their decent pews, which seem to us so much like horse boxes. Religion was actually beginning to invade the sanctities of private life. Very soon the Wesleys and Whitefield (for they were the chief offenders) found themselves excluded from most of the churches of London and Bristol. At St. Margaret's, Westminster, party spirit ran so high that they seemed near to using violence to keep Whitefield out of the pulpit. Dr. Hooker wrote in his *Weekly Register* on February 10, 1739, that the Methodists 'distinguish themselves from others by having *received the faith* with which, and other cant phrases, they are united together like a sect of *Religious Freemasons*. In general, they seem to be practising over the lesson set them by the old *Puritans* before the beginning of the *grand rebellion*'.

At Bristol, the Chancellor of the Diocese threatened to suspend Whitefield and then excommunicate him if he preached there. Whitefield appealed to the bishop, the greatest philosopher the English Church produced in that century. Butler seems to have given him a moderate reply, to which Whitefield answered, 'What evil have I done? I answer, None, save that I visit the Religious Societies, preach to the prisoners in Newgate, and to the poor colliers in Kingswood, who, I am told, are little better than heathens. I am charged with being a Dissenter; though many are brought to the Church by my preaching, no one taken from it'. At a later date Bishop Butler had a conversation in which he thought that Wesley's stress on faith only as the way to justification would lead to 'pure Calvinism'. The interview closed with the bishop saying: 'Mr. Wesley, I will deal plainly with you: I once thought you and Mr. Whitefield well-meaning men, but I cannot think so now, for I have heard more of you—matters of fact, sir. And Mr. Whitefield says in his journal, "There are promises still to be fulfilled in me". Sir, the pretending to extraordinary revelations and gifts of the Holy Ghost is a horrid thing, a very horrid thing.' It sounds like Dr. Johnson talking, and we must regret that Butler could not see that Wesley and Whitefield were still well-meaning men. Yet it is not difficult to understand why the author of *The Analogy of Religion* should have been irritated by Whitefield's crude and precocious journal. Dr. Johnson was at Pembroke College with Whitefield and never had a very high opinion of him, though Boswell is good enough to tell us that Whitefield's character was fully vindicated after his death. It needed no vindication, but good old-fashioned eighteenth-century prejudice comes out in Johnson's remarks about Whitefield's preaching on more than one occasion. 'He would be followed by crowds were he to wear a nightcap in the pulpit, or were he to preach from a tree.' Several years after Whitefield's death, Johnson said, 'Whitefield never drew as much attention as a mountebank does; he did not draw attention by doing better than others, but by doing what was strange. Were Astley to preach a sermon standing upon his head on a horse's back, he would collect a multitude to hear him; but no man would say he had made a better sermon for that. I never treated Whitefield's ministry with contempt; I believe he did good. He had devoted himself to the lower classes of mankind, and among them he was of use. But when familiarity and noise claim the praise due to knowledge, art and elegance, we must beat down such pretensions'. It is more than likely that neither Johnson nor Butler heard Whitefield preach. Their judgements are those of bookworms, not lacking in dogmatism, but quite understandable. Both had their blind spots and both underestimated the powers of the most successful orator of the age.

Whitefield indignantly denied that he was a Dissenter, but he was much more like a dissenting minister all his days than a priest of the Church of England. He had far less regard for Church order than John Wesley, though professing the strictest regard for the Prayer Book. The Wesleys had lifelong prejudices against Dissent, which they moderated with difficulty. Whitefield's early reading was in the pages of Alleine, Baxter, and Janeway. 'I bless God', he said, 'the partition wall of bigotry and sect-religion was soon broken down in my heart.' In later years his sole reading seems to have been the Bible and Puritan literature. As a boy at Gloucester he had often attended the services of the Independents. No doubt he did his best to be loyal to the Church which had given him Orders, but order and tradition were to him secondary matters compared with God's direct call to George Whitefield to preach the Gospel. 'This order undoes us', he wrote to Madan in 1757. 'As affairs now stand, we must be disorderly or useless. O for more labourers.' The most popular orator in England could not keep silent even if all the churches were closed to him. So on February 17, 1739, in Kingswood, near Bristol, where there was no parish church, he began his open-air preaching and kept it up for six weeks in bitter wintry weather to ever-increasing crowds. All the time he was collecting money for his orphan-house in Georgia. As he was about to set sail for America, he called in John Wesley to carry on the good work.

This caused great searchings of heart in London. Charles Wesley was strongly opposed to any such enterprise. The Fetter Lane Society had to be consulted and were themselves divided in judgement. It was settled by opening the Bible at random, to find an oracular response in some passage of Scripture. Charles had a strange foreboding that this adventure would prove fatal to his brother. Perhaps it did prove fatal to a normal career for him in the Established Church. Clearly he went to Bristol in some trepidation, in spite of the fact that the oracles of God were on his side. He was no Whitefield to break away impulsively from the common and beloved ways of regular worship. 'I could scarcely reconcile myself at first to this strange way of preaching in the fields, of which he [Whitefield] set me an example on Sunday; having been all my life (till very lately) so tenacious of every point relating to decency and order, that I should have thought the saving of souls almost a sin, if it had not been done in a church.' There speaks the authentic John Wesley. He had preached in the open-air before now, but that was in Georgia. It seemed so different in England, especially when he had no parochial authority. The struggle was a very hard one, but he 'submitted to be more vile' and began his great campaign for the soul of England on April 2, 1739, at four o'clock in the afternoon by proclaiming 'the glad tidings of salvation' to a crowd of three thousand just outside the walls of the city of Bristol. Whitefield was the pioneer and Wesley followed him. Strange to say, it was the more orderly and logical, the quieter of the two preachers whose utterances were accompanied by the greater excitement among the hearers. It must have been very bewildering to the little correct clergyman, but a power greater than his own swept him forward. Moreover, no one is so great an innovator as the traditionalist who has broken loose. Presently this model of churchmanship will say, 'Church or no church, we must save souls'. Charles was soon following his example in Essex and in London and many others were to do the same. Howell Harris, a layman, had been guilty of this irregularity months before. He considered himself as true a churchman as Whitefield, though like Whitefield he was as ready to co-operate with Dissenters as with Anglicans in the service of the Kingdom of God. The dormant religious fervour of Wales was waking; presently clergy, ministers, and laymen would be working together there for the same high endeavour. His own apology for irregularity is worth quoting: 'As to the lawfulness of Laymen's preaching, in some cases, and at times of necessity,' he says, 'I saw in the Acts of the Apostles the account of Apollos and others, who were scattered at the death of Stephen, having no other Mission than being moved by the Holy Ghost, and love to the immortal souls of their fellow creatures;—I thought a greater time of necessity could hardly be than at present, when the whole country, in a cursory sense, lay in a lukewarm, dead condition— in many Churches, for some months together, there was no sermon; and in other places, an English learned discourse to a Welsh illiterate congregation—and where an intelligible sermon was preached, it was so legal, in the language of the Old Covenant, and advancing man's works, etc., not treating of a Mediator, that should any give heed to it they could easily perceive that they were far from being led thereby to Christ, the only new and living way to God. Seeing this, and feeling the love of God in my heart, I saw an absolute necessity of going about to propagate the Gospel of my dear Master and Redeemer.'[1]

This brings us to the second great innovation of the Evangelical Revival: the employment of laymen in the public services of the Church. They had played a great part in the Religious Societies, but their activities were strictly limited by the rules of the Societies. If, in the absence of the 'parish minister', they led the society meeting, their prayers were to be taken from the Book of Common Prayer and the subjects of their meditations and discussions were laid down. It was a new thing in the eighteenth century for laymen to preach. It had been done a century before by the soldiers in Cromwell's army, but the mere mention of those dangerous irregularities made a good Anglican shudder. Practices of this kind in the last century, according to the bishop of London, had a great share 'in bringing in those religions confusions, which brought a reproach upon Christianity in general, and which, by degrees, worked the body of the people into a national madness and frenzy in matters of religion'. Here again it was that rigid Tory, John Wesley, who proved himself the greatest innovator. Once again he was working against the grain. He hoped that a sufficient number of ordained clergy would be forthcoming, who, converted themselves, would be the evangelists of town and countryside working through the Religious Societies a new reformation. He soon discovered that the work spread far beyond the compass that he and his brother and their clerical helpers could reach. He was more open-minded and ready to be persuaded out of his prejudices than either Whitefield or his brother Charles. Both of these were for a time opposed to lay preaching; it may be doubted whether Charles ever overcame his prejudice on this subject. Both of these enthusiastic and illogical men could thoroughly approve the mission of Howell Harris and yet argue against lay preaching. With John Wesley it was different. He heard the wonderful story of Harris from his own lips and was convinced that the Welshman was as much called to such a ministry as he was. When Joseph Humphries helped with expositions in the Religious Societies in London, he approved. When the Kingswood colliers persuaded John Cennick to preach to them, he

---

[1] *Life of Howell Harris*, p. 41.

encouraged him and refused to listen to those who would have silenced him.

Thomas Maxfield, one of Wesley's Bristol converts, moved to London and was allowed to lead the Society in the Foundery. Lady Huntingdon heard him and was profoundly impressed by his power in prayer and gift of exposition. From exposition he turned to preaching and became helpful to many. His popularity grew and murmurs arose about this irregularity. John Wesley was called back from Bristol to settle the problem. He came 'home' troubled by a difficult question which threatened to develop a new crisis. His mother solved it for him by saying, 'Take care what you do with respect to that young man, for he is as surely called of God to preach as you are'. The testimony of Selina and Susanna was too powerful to be resisted by one who was already half-convinced. John Wesley never doubted again whether a devout and earnest layman should be allowed to preach or not. He would require tests of capacity and make plans for training, but he had embarked on a wider use of laymen in the direct work of evangelization than the Christian Church had known hitherto. That a momentous step had been taken can be seen from the fact that to-day the Methodist Church in this country uses over 30,000 lay preachers, to say nothing of the great army of Sunday-school teachers and the lay helpers in the Methodism spread abroad through six continents.

Was the erection of buildings for the use of Religious Societies another irregularity? Wesley apparently did not think so, as he had no intention of separating from the Church of England. He had been offered no preferment in the Church and would probably have refused a living if one had been offered. More and more churches were closed to his preaching and the archbishop was even talking of excommunication. Wesley believed that his work lay with the Religious Societies. It was for the growing Societies in Nicholas Street and Baldwin Street in Bristol that he purchased a site in the Horsefair for a 'New Room' in May, 1739. The 'New Room' is now the oldest Methodist chapel in the world. In November of the same year he was led to purchase the ruined Foundery in London to become the home of his Society separated from the Religious Society in Fetter Lane. There is some irony in the fact that one reason for the separation was that the Fetter Lane group was becoming increasingly Moravian and wished to

D

break with the Anglican Church. Wesley objected to this development, but in settling his own followers in the Foundery, he laid down only one condition of membership: 'a desire to flee from the wrath to come, to be saved from their sins'. Calvinist and Arminian, Churchman, and Dissenter were alike welcome. 'We never mount so high', said Cromwell, 'as when we know not whither we are going.' Wesley embarked on this new enterprise with great reluctance. He began by settling property on trustees, but soon found that he had to take over the whole responsibility for these new buildings himself. The Bristol and London rooms were to be the precursors of tens of thousands of churches and schools of which the trusteeship was to pass from the Wesley brothers to local men, who acted on behalf of the Conference.

In these society rooms it was easy for prayers, discussions, and expositions of Scripture to pass into regular services, though the change took place slowly and gradually. While there was no irregularity in providing meeting places for Religious Societies still in theory associated with the Established Church, the appearance of setting tabernacle over against tabernacle could not be avoided. This was emphasized when the Methodists were repelled from Communion at their parish churches, and Methodist ordained clergy of the Church of England were compelled to administer Communion to the members of their societies in their new rooms. There would come a time when the Methodists would ask for Communion from all their preachers and the separation would be complete.

The same phenomenon had reached a more advanced stage in Moravian circles. Zinzendorf might be discussing with the leaders of the Church of England the question of the recognition of Moravian orders and hoping that the *Unitas Fratrum* would become a fellowship within the Church, but his followers had other ideas. Ingham was building up a growing group of societies in Yorkshire and the North of England; these were entirely separated, though he remained in the Church of England himself. Gambold had resigned his living to become a Moravian and Kinchin was inclined to do the same. His early death alone prevented this purpose being fulfilled. The Oxford Methodists were moving in different directions, but the chief reason for their irregularities was that their sleepy mother was quite unable to help them. A Church that turned its back on its most devoted sons, that neglected the doctrines of the New Testament and its own formularies concerning personal salvation, that was concerned with what Wesley called 'outward things' in its view of membership in the body of Christ and even of sanctification, was sure to provoke irregularity.

Since Convocation had ceased to meet, the Church could hardly be said to have any definite policy or even any clear power of direction. Bishops could speak, but they were inclined to contradict one another. None of them had the imagination or vision to know that a great day of opportunity was beginning. They reacted against all enthusiasm and swung back to decent behaviour as the only standard by which the Christian life could be judged. They were afraid of sudden conversions, of this talk of justification by faith without works, and of the life of God in the soul of man. Henry Moore says about the archbishop's intervention: 'It does not appear that the archbishop condemned the doctrines Mr. Wesley preached, but the manner of preaching them. It was irregular, and this was judged a cause sufficient for condemning him. Regularity is undoubtedly necessary in the government both of Church and State. But when a system of rules and orders, *purely human*, is so established for the Church as to be made *perpetual*, whatever the state of the people may be, it must, in many cases, become injurious rather than useful. A minister of Christ may be so circumstanced, that regularity would obstruct rather than promote his usefulness. Irregularity then becomes his duty, the end to be attained being infinitely more important than any prudential rules. If this be not allowed, we hearken to man rather than to God.'[1] Charles Wesley received the archbishop's rebuke boldly, but was very depressed about it all and was in considerable uncertainty for several days, until he realized that his depression arose merely from the fear of man.

It was a later archbishop, who, under the assumed name of John Smith, in the course of a long correspondence with John Wesley, still objected to the 'disorderly preaching at Kennington and Moorfields, assisted elsewhere by the still more irregular preaching of lay brethren'. To which John Wesley replied: 'Whatever may be the fruits of lay-preaching, when you and I are gone to our long home, every serious man has cause to bless God for these he may now see with his eyes; for the saving so many

[1] *Life of Wesley*, Moore, I, p. 471.

souls from death; and hiding a multitude of sins. The instances glare in the face of the sun.' When in 1741 he called out lay preachers wholly devoted to the work of preaching and visitation he was still more emphatic. 'I do assure you', he said, 'this is my chief embarrassment. That I have not gone too far yet, I know, but whether I have gone far enough I am extremely doubtful.— Soul-damning clergymen lay me under more difficulties than soul-saving laymen.'

Chapter VII

THE CRUSADE

WHY did the crowds fill the churches in London and Bristol when Whitefield began to preach? After the churches were closed against them, why did the people still gather in their thousands and tens of thousands on Moorfields and Kennington Common, at Kingswood and on the open spaces at Bristol? It may be that it was mere curiosity at some new phenomenon. Dr. Johnson certainly gave a prejudiced and distorted view when he told Boswell: 'Whitefield never drew as much attention as a mountebank does.' From the mountebank standpoint, Whitefield was a great success; indeed, it is difficult to think of any popular entertainer who ever drew the crowd with such persistency for so long a period. Also his performance fell far short in mountebank interest of preaching on his head on a horse's back. Merely talking to people for an hour on end would normally soon become boring. Yet Whitefield's popularity never waned for a moment until as a dying man he roused himself to make his last proclamation of the 'everlasting gospel' at Newburyport.

Let it be admitted that there was little of learning or variety in Whitefield's preaching; that he had nothing new to say. He was only repeating the words of the New Testament, reaffirming the first principles of the Reformers and the formularies and Homilies of his own Church; but he was proclaiming them to an age that had forgotten them. The same is true of John and Charles Wesley, of Howell Harris, and the great company of preachers that followed them. The novelty of open-air preaching and of lay preaching may account to some extent for the early excitement, but it cannot explain the developing tide that swept through the countries, not only of England and Wales, but of New England and the American colonies and, in a less degree, through Scotland and Ireland throughout the whole of the century. Isaac Taylor may be quoted as a nineteenth-century critic who looked at the movement from the outside as Dr. Johnson did in the previous century. He fastens upon Whitefield as the true type of the evangelist on account of the 'undecayed vitality' in his ministry with its 'oneness of tune' from first to last. Wesley was the states-man who developed in judgement and discretion as his responsi-bilities increased. Whitefield also grew in wisdom, but 'an ever-deepening sense of the richness, freeness, and boundless sufficiency of that Gospel which he preached, held him always to the same path, and made it impossible that he should tread upon a lower level'. In varying degrees this was the characteristic mark of the preacher of what Isaac Taylor calls 'the Methodist era'. 'On this special ground', he says, 'where do we find their equals—that is to say, where within the compass of Christian history, shall we find—not eminent and solitary instances—but a company of men, of untainted orthodoxy, clear of sectarian virulence, indifferent to things indifferent, intent only upon the first Truths;—in labours and sufferings equal to the most zealous, and surpassing perhaps all in simplicity of purpose, as ambassadors for Christ—entreating men everywhere in Christ's stead to be reconciled to God?' That is well said and it has the merit of being true. The only parallel that occurs to mind is found in the early days of the Franciscan movement, when a company of laymen wandered up and down Italy, working with the peasants in the fields, or mingling with the crowds in the towns, awaking by example as much as by their preaching the dormant faith and love of the people. The pent-up enthusiasms of Europe were for a time let loose. It seems, as one historian has said, 'it was bringing the dead Christ from his grave of centuries'. Can less be said of the Methodist revival?

The more the relevant documents are studied the more the wonder grows. Here the Gospel is confronted, not by crowds of mercurial Latin races, but by the dour stubbornness of the North. Wesley found Scotland difficult, but Whitefield did not; some of his greatest triumphs were seen there. Among the tough colonists of the American seaboard he could tell the same story of victory. At a later date Asbury and his companions and successors had a still greater achievement to report. Ireland and Wales and Cornwall might be expected to show signs of Celtic fire, but the miners of Kingswood, the iron-workers of the Black Country, the quarrymen of Portland, the sailors and shipwrights of Plymouth and Newcastle, the soldiers of Cumberland's army, the weavers of Lancashire and Yorkshire, and the dull rustics from the agri-cultural counties provided less likely material. Yet they not only listened in their tens of thousands, they melted before the fire of divine love. Great numbers of them were transformed from persecutors and opponents into disciples and, in many cases, apostles. If we have forgotten the records of the *Lives of the Early Methodist Preachers*, Charles Wesley has preserved the core of that remarkable story in hymns that are still alive.

> Ye mountains and vales, in praises abound,
> Ye hills and ye dales, continue the sound.
> Break forth into singing, ye trees of the wood,
> For Jesus is bringing lost sinners to God.

John Wesley said in his funeral sermon on Whitefield: 'Have we read or heard of any person, who called so many thousands, so many myriads of sinners to repentance? Above all, have we read or heard of any, who has been a blessed instrument in the hands of God of bringing so many sinners from darkness to light, and from the power of Satan unto God?' For thirty years and more, his career seems to be one long appeal to men to return to their Father. Henry Venn declared that it was Whitefield's custom to preach from forty to sixty hours every week. In this unparalleled record of preaching be preached more than 18,000 sermons. As a mere physical achievement this is a very remarkable performance, but as the work of a pioneer in the pathway to Anglo-American understanding it is of supreme importance. 'If the time spent in travelling from place to place, and some brief intervals of repose and preparation be subtracted,' says Sir James Stephen, 'his whole life may be said to have been consumed in the delivery of one continuous or scarcely interrupted sermon. Neither English reserve, nor the theological discrimination of the Scots, nor the callous nerves of the slave-dealers of America, nor the stately self-possession of her aborigines, could resist the enchantment.' But when he goes on to say that never was mortal man gifted with such an incapacity for fatiguing or being fatigued, he was possibly overlooking the equally remarkable record of John Wesley. Wesley was eleven years older than Whitefield, but he carried on his campaign for the soul of England for twenty years after Whitefield's death. He, too, admitted no respite in that warfare. He preached more than twice as many sermons, though not to such vast multitudes. He travelled more miles in his Gospel progress, though not so extensively. He concentrated also on that oversight of souls, which left a permanent memorial in many a place where the passage of Whitefield has been forgotten.

Whitefield formed no societies, but Wesley not only collected his converts into societies, classes, and bands, but, quarter by quarter—indeed, week by week through his leaders—he met them to examine whether they were in the faith. In this careful organization in detail he revealed his superior genius and has left us a record of the steady growth of the societies by which we can test the permanence of the work he did. The number had grown at his death to 57,562 in Great Britain and 48,565 in America. So surely had he laid the foundations that the increase in the eighteen years after his death was even greater than during his lifetime and the numbers rose to 171,590 in Great Britain and 159,500 in America.

In the early days of the Revival, Charles Wesley seems to have been even more effective than his brother. His engaging and impulsive manner contrasted with the steadier, if weightier, style of John. Yet it was under this preaching and not that of either Charles Wesley or Whitefield that John Nelson says: 'My heart began to beat like the pendulum of a clock.' The clear, incisive, and direct words of John Wesley were followed, in the early days of the Revival at least, by strange scenes of excitement. Men and women fell to the ground as though struck by a bludgeon. Groans and cries broke out on all sides. Multitudes were moved to tears. The preacher himself was not disturbed, but considered it quite natural that some 'under strong impressions of grief or fear, from a sense of the wrath of God, should for a season forget all things else, and scarce be able to answer a common question; that some should imagine they see strange sights, or that others should be thrown into great fears. But all these effects vanish away in a moment, whenever the person convinced tastes of the pardoning love of God'. At other times the reactions were so overwhelming that he thought supernatural forces must be at work. It was Satan making a last effort to defend his kingdom. Other preachers disliked these demonstrations intensely and did their best to suppress them. We may well wonder why an English crowd should have behaved in this manner in that very prosaic century. It has been the custom to assert that the preaching centred mainly round the Cross of Christ and was a proclamation of the love of God in Christ and a confession of love to the suffering and triumphant Lord. Doubtless that was frequently the preacher's message. There can also be little doubt that it was proclaimed against an alarming background of judgement and that the fear of hell was a real and powerful element in the half-beliefs of the hearers. It is impossible to read the testimonies of numbers of the early preachers themselves without discovering that they were as much alarmed at the prospect of damnation as John Bunyan was. The very condition of membership in the societies was that they should 'flee from the wrath to come to be saved from their sins'.

Whatever the secondary causes of this great awaking were, there is unity in judgement among the chief instruments as to the primary cause. They knew that they themselves were quite incapable of such mighty achievements. For them it was always 'the work of God'. The expression was so constantly on their lips that it has survived for two hundred years and is now the conventional phrase for the routine work of Methodism. 'The Sunday offertories are for the work of God in this church and circuit.' With Wesley and Whitefield and their associates, however, it was much more than a conventional phrase; it was a vivid reality. Whenever Wesley reviewed the moving story he instinctively said, 'What hath God wrought?' That was his text, not only at the opening of City Road Chapel in 1777, but at other special occasions. In his statement at the age of seventy-three, he said: 'This revival of religion has spread to such a degree, as neither we nor our fathers had known. How *extensive* has it been! There is scarcely a considerable town in the kingdom, where some have not been made witnesses of it. It has spread to every age and sex, to most orders and degrees of men; and even to abundance of those, who, in time past, were accounted monsters of wickedness. Consider the *swiftness* as well as the extent of it. In what age has such a number of sinners been recovered in so short a time from the error of their ways? When has true religion, I will not say, since the Reformation, but since the time of Constantine the Great, made so large a progress in any nation, within so small a space? I believe hardly can ancient or modern history afford a parallel instance. We may likewise observe the *depth* of the work so extensively and swiftly wrought. Multitudes have been thoroughly convinced of sin; and shortly after, so filled with joy and love, that whether they were in the body, or out of the body, they could hardly tell; and, in the power of this love, they have trampled under foot whatever the world accounts either terrible or desirable, having evidenced, in the severest trials, an invariable and tender goodwill to mankind, and all the fruits of holiness. Now so deep a repentance, so strong a faith, so fervent love, and so unblemished holiness wrought in so many persons in so short a time, the world has not seen for many ages.'

Wesley seemed to have as strong a consciousness that he was carried along by the power of God and the direction of the Holy Spirit as St. Paul himself. He saw the story of Ephesus, of Philippi, of Corinth repeating itself on English soil. The facts cannot be doubted and our present-day psychologists have been able to add little by way of explanation to what Wesley himself had to say. At the end of the century, Joseph Benson said about the results of the Revival in Cornwall: 'There is hardly any part of the three kingdoms, where a change has been more visible and general, in the manners of the people. Hurling, their favourite diversion, at which limbs were often broken, and frequently lives lost, is now hardly heard of, and that scandal of humanity, so constantly practised on the coasts of Cornwall, the plundering vessels that struck upon the rocks, and afterwards murdering those who escaped out of the wreck, is now either quite at an end, or the Gentlemen, and not the poor Tinners, are to be blamed. And more has been done, to suppress smuggling, by preaching the gospel in the country, and enforcing the rules of the Society, than either the laws of the country, or the officers of the Excise were ever able to effect. But it is not harmless or outward decency alone which has so succeeded, but the religion of the heart;—and faith working by love, for producing all inward and outward holiness.' Fletcher, in his own characteristic way, had given his view of these wonderful days when he said: 'Leaning on her fair daughters Truth and Love, Religion took a solemn walk through the kingdom, and gave a foretaste of heaven to all that entertained her.'

Fletcher's pleasing picture of the mild and heavenly influences of the Revival, as it spread through the United Kingdom, overlooks in the 'solemn walk' the frenzies of early converts and the wild violence of persecuting mobs. Much has been written about the cruel treatment of the Methodists in town and countryside, but the widespread and long-continued nature of these attacks has been underestimated. It is true that the actual number of martyrs who gave their lives in the cause of preaching the Gospel to this Christian country is small; the number of those who suffered permanent bodily injury cannot be estimated. If we read through the six volumes of the *Lives of the Early Methodist Preachers*, we find that very few of them escaped the tender mercies of the brutal English and Irish crowds. Wales, too, had some prominence in this record, but Scotland received Whitefield with devotion and Wesley with comparative calm. Had they been persecuted, Wesley's preachers might have been more successful in Scotland. We are familiar with the stories of the wild scenes of outrage in the Black Country, in Cornwall, in Bristol, Devizes, Colne, Sheffield, Nottingham, Cork, and on Tyneside. These scenes in different ways were repeated in smaller towns and in obscure villages throughout the country. In too many cases bigoted and ignorant clergy had stirred up a still more bigoted and ignorant crowd. The best-known of these stories come from the *Journals* of John and Charles Wesley. There is a moving picture of the meeting of the brothers in Nottingham after John had barely escaped with his life from the mob at Wednesbury. Charles stared at him with astonishment and wrote in his *Journal*: 'My brother came delivered out of the mouth of the lion. He *looked* like a soldier of Christ; his clothes were torn to tatters. But his work is not finished or he had now been with the souls under the altar.'

Whitefield had less experience of actual violence; though, when John Cennick joined him, he reported of the Swindon mob: 'Without respect to age or sex, they knocked down all who stood in their way, so that some had blood streaming down their faces, and others were taken up almost beaten and trampled to death. Many of our dear friends were cut or bruised sadly; and I got many severe blows myself.' Whitefield wrote about these Wiltshire mobs to the Bishop of Salisbury, saying that Cennick was a member of the Church of England, 'but he is sadly opposed by the clergy in Wiltshire'. To keep people in the Church, Methodists were denied parish relief.

John Nelson's trials after his enemies got him pressed for a soldier are well known, but the later attempt (which came near murder) 'to tread the Holy Spirit out of me' is less familiar. Sometimes there is a cool good humour in the preachers' accounts of their adventures, as when Thomas Olivers says of his experiences at Yarmouth: 'My fellow traveller gallopped out of the town as fast as he was able; but I watched the motions of the sticks and stones which were likely to hit me, so as to preserve a regular retreat. When I overtook my companion, we were thankful that we escaped with our lives; as were our friends at Norwich on seeing us return.' Olivers was fortunate in his horse. He bought it for five pounds and it itinerated with him for twenty-five years, so that he claims to have travelled comfortably on him 'not less than 100,000 miles in preaching the Gospel'. An Austin-Seven could hardly have done better, and the expense was less.

The records of these attacks in one after another of these forty-one biographies are so monotonous that they are best summed up in the terse sentences of Peter Jaco: 'Very frequently we had also violent oppositions. At Warrington I was struck so violently on the breast, that the blood gushed out through my mouth, nose and ears. At Grampound I was pressed for a soldier; kept under a strong guard for several days without meat or drink, but what I was obliged to procure at a large expense; and threatened to have my feet tied under the horse's belly while I was carried eight miles before the commissioners, and though I was honourably acquitted by them, yet it cost me a pretty large sum of money, as well as much trouble.' Thomas Beard was not so fortunate, for he died under his afflictions in the Army. A peaceable man, he had been torn away from his trade and wife and children, as Wesley said, 'for no other crime than that of calling sinners to repentance'. Nelson and Beard were not willing to bear arms, but there were in the Army large numbers of Methodist soldiers, who carried the Gospel round the world. The most vivid pictures we have of the Fontenoy campaign came from the records of John Haime and Sampson Staniforth. The former claimed that he had three armies to fight against: 'The French army, the wicked English army, and an army of devils.' He formed strong societies in the army and lived to preach the Gospel for forty years at home. At Gibraltar, in Canada, the American colonies, the West Indies, and West Africa, Methodist soldiers became ambassadors for Christ. They also had a difficult battle to fight for freedom of speech. The whole story of persecution and opposition turned out for the furtherance of the Gospel.

The story continued well on into the nineteenth century in the petty tyranny of squire and parson. It was, however, in the earliest days that misunderstanding and misrepresentation were at their worst and the most dramatic and alarming records are to be found. Bitter attacks from the pulpit and the Press served as advertisements. In the quiet countryside, where nothing happened from January to December, the coming of the open-air preachers was an event. Whether out of mere curiosity or with good or malicious purpose, the crowds gathered, the witness was given, and societies were formed. The same story was being told in the Colonies, but in the absence of a strongly entrenched Established Church there is less record of persecution. Surely it was in the providence of God that this movement occurred in the great colonizing days of England. When the British people were being scattered abroad through five continents, a warm-hearted and simple belief in the fundamentals of Christianity went with them. Frequently men and women were found there who had the love of Christ shed abroad in their hearts. They believed that the way of life was to love God with all their heart and mind and soul and strength and their neighbour as themselves. They came to many a post on the frontiers of civilization where there were no church buildings, no bishops, no priests, and no deacons. When the Lord's Day came, they might be destitute of the loved and wonted solemnities of the parish church at home, but they could at least read the New Testament together, they could join in prayer together, and sing the familiar songs of Zion, though in a strange land. They might even be able to discover some one to prophesy in the name of the Lord. As they joined in that loving fellowship, they became a part of the great catholic Church of Christ. They were back with Peter the fisherman and Paul the tent-maker. They realized anew the truth of the words of that second-century Father: 'Where Christ is there is the Church.'

Chapter VIII

DIVISIONS

EVERY vigorous reform movement is in danger of breaking up into groups and sub-divisions. This is the penalty of the surge of new life within its borders; it is the outcome of free discussion. Even in England, the home of compromise and toleration, this has been true. In politics, parties of the right hang together much more readily than those of the left. After the Civil War, Parliament and Army failed to find agreement, and Cromwell's task was the heavier on that account. Whig and Radical kept an uneasy fellowship until the Liberal Party emerged, only to be rent by Liberal-Unionist and Labour divisions. Labour itself had to confront Communist and I.L.P. extremists. We may deplore the divisive spirit in the Church, but facts compel us to admit that the danger of sharp differences has always been present when thought and feeling were stirred. St. Paul had not only his long struggle with the Judaizers over great principles, but he had to exhort Euodia and Syntyche and many others to 'keep the unity of the Spirit in the bond of peace'.

The fine fellowships in faith, hope, and charity with which the Revival in England began, soon showed signs of strain. We have seen how large a part the Moravians played in the opening scene of the great religious drama; they also provided the first reasons for division. Peter Böhler's chief contribution was not the influence he had on John Wesley, but the help he gave to the Religious Society which met at the house of James Hutton. He drew up the rules for it just before he left for America in May, 1738, though it was still in association with the Church of England. The members were to meet once a week to confess their faults to each other and to pray for one another; they divided the Society into bands with a leader at the head of each band; they declared that 'every one, without distinction, submit to the determination of the Brethren'. The Society increased in numbers until the room in Hutton's house was too small. It was Hutton who hired the Great Meeting House, which became their new home in Fetter Lane. Charles Wesley and James Hutton were the leading spirits here. For nearly two years, this Society was the headquarters of the growing Revival.

John Wesley, after his Aldersgate Street experience, visited the Moravian Mecca at Herrnhut in the summer of 1738. He was so delighted with what he saw that he wrote in his *Journal* (August 12, 1738): 'I would gladly have spent my life here; but my Master, calling me to labour in another part of His vineyard, I was constrained to take my leave of this happy place. . . . Oh, when shall *this* Christianity cover the earth as the waters cover the sea.' It was in this spirit that he returned to England and found great joy in the simple fellowship of the newly constituted Society. Very soon, however, what had appeared so good at Herrnhut seemed much less attractive at Fetter Lane. He met there, not only his brother and James Hutton and Benjamin Ingham, who had travelled with him both to Georgia and Germany, but artisans like Bray the brazier and an increasing number of Germans who were giving the Society a definite Moravian character. This influence was not predominant at the beginning of 1739, as we learn from Wesley's description of the love-feast held at Fetter Lane to usher in the New Year. There were seven clergymen of the Church of England present, with 'sixty of our brethren', but there is no mention of any Moravian minister. All seven belonged to the Oxford Holy Club, the Wesleys, Whitefield, Ingham, Westley Hall, Kinchin, and Hutchins. It was a memorable restoration of early Christian custom as revived by the Moravians. After a night spent in prayer and thanksgiving, Wesley says: 'About three in the morning as we were continuing instant in prayer, the power of God came mightily upon us, inasmuch that many cried out for exceeding joy, and many fell to the ground.'

This was early in the morning of Monday, January 1, 1739. On Friday of the same week, we find the same group of seven in conference at Islington from 8.30 in the morning till 3 in the afternoon. We know that there was singing and prayer as well as conversation, but the only light on the subjects considered comes from Charles Wesley's *Journal*, in which he tells us that they all 'set upon him' to settle at Oxford, but he remained unwilling without further divine guidance. What stands out clearly is the consciousness that some new and striking manifestation of God's power was shortly to be seen. They seem to have had no plans, except to preach in whatever churches were open to them and to develop the London Societies; Kinchin was working in the Society at Oxford.

In a few weeks Whitefield opened a campaign in Bristol which was to change the whole course of the movement. The open-air preaching alarmed some of the company. James Hervey, from a remote part of Devonshire, pointed out the dangers of irregularity, and it was in his reply to this letter that John Wesley claimed the world as his parish. In the same letter he says: 'As to your advice that I should settle in college, I have no business there, having no office and no pupils. And whether the other branch of your proposal be expedient for me, viz. "To accept of a cure of souls", it will be time enough to consider it when one is offered to me.' 'God in Scripture commands me, according to my power, to instruct the ignorant, reform the wicked, confirm the virtuous. Man forbids me to do this in another's parish: that is, in effect, not to do it at all; seeing I have now no parish of my own, nor probably ever shall.' The problem of the ineffectiveness of the parochial system as it was then working in England, still more in the American colonies, was with him to the end. He, along with his brother, Ingham, and George Whitefield, had definitely embarked on another plan of service for the Kingdom of God. It was a time of great searching of heart for the Holy Club. Kinchin and Gambold were thinking of renouncing their orders.

In the midst of these excitements, John Wesley was called back to London in June, 1739, because of the great confusion that prevailed at Fetter Lane. His guidance was sadly needed there and he soon helped to clear away the difficulties and misunderstandings that had arisen. Back he went to Bristol, which seemed for the time being the more important centre. When he returned to London in the late autumn he was confronted by a very difficult situation. In October, 1739, there arrived in London from Germany on his way to America a young man named Philip Henry Molther. He had spent some months as tutor in Zinzendorf's family and had only been a member of the Brethren's Church for about a year. He had all the confidence and dogmatism of a young convert and shocked Wesley by his dangerous teaching. He was the apostle of stillness and his favourite text was, 'Be still, and know that I am God'. It was useless, he said, to strive to obtain saving grace by using the ordinances of religion. Public worship, Holy Communion, fasting, and prayer were to be laid aside until God should vouchsafe to reveal Himself to the waiting soul. Wesley believed that we find our way into the fellowship of the redeemed by the study of the Bible, by using the ordinary means of grace, by waiting upon God in prayer. Molther taught the very opposite. He considered that we are not fit to join in public worship, nor to communicate, nor to pray in private, nor even to read the Holy Scriptures until God has spoken peace to our soul. There could be no reconciliation between such quietism and John Wesley's High Church principles, for though Wesley had discovered a new meaning and experience in the Gospel, he was a High Churchman still. Molther's popularity won for him a strong following. 'I think', says Wesley in his *Journal* for November 10, 1739, 'I did not meet with one woman of the [Fetter Lane] Society, who had not been upon the point of casting away her confidence in God.'

In the midst of these afflictions, he heard of the death of his eldest brother, Samuel, and posted away to Tiverton to comfort his sister-in-law. Nothing, however, was permitted to check his apostolic ministry. All his journeyings were used for the advancement of the Gospel. At the end of the year we find him discussing with Molther the dangerous elements in his teaching, but quite unable to make an impression. This weakness in the Fetter Lane Society increased as the Moravian numbers grew. In April, 1740, both the Wesleys had a two-hour conversation with Molther. He still held to his strange views about the necessity for stillness and abstention from the means of grace, except for those who were pure in heart and were moved to communicate at the Lord's Table or to attend the public acts of worship. What is more extraordinary is that, for a time, Westley Hall and Gambold and even Charles Wesley were inclined to become quietists. It was not until June, 1740, that John Wesley began to carry out, what he had long seen to be necessary, an attack on this 'grand delusion'. It was really the beginning of a battle against Antinomianism that Wesley kept up throughout the rest of his ministry. The extremists, who over-emphasized the doctrine of salvation by faith only, held that weak faith was no faith at all; there were no degrees in faith. Neither prayer, nor reading the Scriptures, nor worship, nor Holy Communion could produce faith; nothing but a completely passive attitude was needed. The only commandment laid on man by the Almighty was to believe. After vigorous New-Testament expositions to refute these errors, on July 16 Wesley appealed directly to the Society and found a clearly

E

marked division there. On the following Sunday evening, he attended the Fetter Lane love-feast and read out a statement of the teaching which he considered to be contrary to the Word of God, and called on those who agreed with him to follow him. Eighteen or nineteen did so, and the separation of the Methodists from the Moravians began. 'Why was not this done six months ago?' asked Charles Wesley. 'How fatal was our delay and moderation.'

It is still uncertain how far the terms Methodist and Moravian were used for the two parties, but there is no doubt that the Fetter Lane group had now become a Moravian Society, while the group that followed Wesley to the Foundery were known as Methodists. It was a sad business, yet it freed Wesley for a much more effective scheme for evangelizing England. Parting from such old friends as James Hutton, Ingham, William Delamotte, and Gambold cut very deeply, but for Wesley truth was above all. The Moravians claim that this lapse into stillness was only temporary and that Molther alone was responsible for it. Wesley, however, retained his suspicions that the Moravians followed the teaching of Luther too closely; they despised the Law, the Commandments, good works, and self-denial. The situation was not improved by the well-meant intervention of Count Zinzendorf. Zinzendorf was labouring for the recognition of the Moravians by the Church of England. His great dream was that they should be in communion with the Lutheran Church in Germany and the Anglican Church in England; the Orders of their ministers should be acknowledged equally by Lutheran and Anglican. He had no more desire to see a Moravian Church than Wesley had to see a Methodist Church.

A year later, on September 3, 1741, the two leaders met in the interests of peace in Gray's Inn Gardens. The conversation in Latin between these two remarkable men is given in full in Wesley's *Journal*. It was difficult for the mystical, imaginative German to come to terms with the logical, practical Englishman. Zinzendorf quarrelled with Wesley's doctrine of Christian perfection. He could not understand Wesley's fear of loose morality and his insistence on the highest ideal possible for the Christian character as the necessary concomitant of the doctrine of justification by faith. The Count continued to talk of the imputed righteousness of Christ, while Wesley was anxious to see a real righteousness in those who professed to be Christians. Both believed that the Christian life began in an act of faith in the divine Saviour, but they differed as to the meaning of progress in the divine life. 'We spurn all self-denial', said Zinzendorf; 'We trample it under foot. Being believers, we do whatsoever we will, and nothing more. We ridicule all mortification. No purification precedes perfect love.' Zinzendorf only succeeded in driving the Moravians and the Methodists farther apart, when he had hoped to bring them together. Wesley disliked their sentimental, odd phraseology and their undue deference to the Count, 'calling him Rabbi'. It was an unfortunate division, but the conversation helps us to understand why the Methodists were more likely to serve the people of England than the Moravians.

Gambold was the only one of the Oxford Methodists who remained a Moravian all his days, but it was Ingham who was of the greatest service to them. His Societies in Yorkshire and elsewhere were handed over to the Moravian Church, though he himself never left the Church of England. He believed that the Moravians were 'more like the Primitive Christians than any other Church now in the world, for they retain both the faith, practice, and discipline delivered by the Apostles'. He repudiated the belief that the Moravians neglected the means of grace, and was charmed by their meekness and simplicity. He had married Lady Margaret Hastings, the sister-in-law of the Countess of Huntingdon, and lived at Aberford in Yorkshire. As he was a priest without a cure of souls, like Whitefield and the Wesleys, he became a touring evangelist. He shared Wesley's view that such work was ineffective unless Societies were established wherever possible. He was actually the first to adopt this plan systematically, for in the early part of 1739 he was most successful in his Yorkshire activities. The Church authorities were so alarmed that, on June 6 of that year, he was inhibited from preaching in any of the churches in the Diocese of York. He then took to open-air preaching, as Wesley had done in Bristol and London. Very soon he had formed forty Religious Societies in different parts of Yorkshire. Wesley corresponded with him in February, 1740, about the problem of divine guidance and the meaning of the witness of the Spirit to those who had been forgiven. It was on this point that the Moravians and the Methodists were then at variance, and Ingham leaned to the Moravian 'poor sinnership' view rather than to the Methodist doctrine of Christian assurance. Led by the Spirit, the Methodist believed that he could march confidently forward in the power of Christ to the goal of perfect love.

It is now that John Nelson appears on the scene. The Yorkshire stonemason had been converted by the preaching of John Wesley in London and remained his devoted follower all his days. He had come across the Moravians at the time of Molther's proclamation of the gospel of stillness and had heard from them that 'Mr. Wesley was only a John Baptist to go before and prepare them for the Brethren to build up'. Wesley, they told him, was but a blind servant of the Law. This roused his indignation, and he returned to his home in Yorkshire with some prejudice against the 'poor sinners', as he called them. It seemed to him, as he listened and compared their preaching with that of his hero, that 'they had not stayed long enough in the large room at Jerusalem'. When he met Ingham himself, they had a long talk together, and · Ingham told him that 'he pitied poor Mr. Wesley, for he was ignorant of his own state; and he spoke as if he believed Mr. Wesley to be an unconverted man; at which words my corrupt nature began to stir. But it came to my mind: "The wrath of man worketh not the righteousness of God." ' At the same time it was most unlikely that Nelson would listen to Ingham when he was told not to preach, lest he should awaken persecution. He was the more surprised when he heard Ingham preaching the very doctrines which he would not allow Nelson to utter aloud.

Nelson fully approved Peter Böhler when he came to Yorkshire; they seemed made to be friends. He soon found that both Böhler and Töltschig were quite changed after a visit to the London headquarters. It may have been Zinzendorf who changed them, as it was certainly Zinzendorf's influence that changed the whole policy of evangelization in Yorkshire after Ingham's Societies had been handed over to the Moravians in May, 1742. Nelson, too, had begun to gather his converts into Societies, and watched over them with a godly jealousy. He was now so suspicious of the Moravians that he said he would rather die than live to see his children 'devoured by these bears out of the German wood'. The Moravians certainly talked a great deal of nonsense at this time, both about their own inspiration and the familiar terms in which Count Zinzendorf stood with 'the Lamb'. In response to a further appeal from Ingham that Nelson should be silent, he

agreed on one proviso. ' "What is that?" said Ingham. I answered: "If you can persuade the devil to be silent for a month." '
Honest Yorkshire common sense in Nelson longed for the practical mind of Wesley, and Nelson was delighted when Wesley called to see him at Birstall in May, 1742, on his way north to Newcastle.

Nelson had longed for and even dreamed of this visit. 'He sat down by my fire-side', he wrote, 'in the very posture I had dreamed about four months before, and spoke the same words I dreamed he spoke'. He must have told Wesley of all his difficulties with Ingham, and when he came to tell how Ingham had said that the Church of England was no Church, 'we [the Moravians] are the Church', and that Wesley and Nelson could not be admitted to that true fold until Wesley publicly declared that he had preached false doctrine, it was clearer than ever that Moravians and Methodists must henceforth go separate ways. Nelson was as firmly attached to the Church of England—in spite of his lay preaching—as Wesley himself. At the very moment when Wesley was sitting by Nelson's fire, Ingham was handing his Societies over by a written agreement to the Moravians. He passed through Birstall while Wesley was there and did not call to see him, though it was not so long before that he had exalted Wesley above every man he had ever known. He was in a peculiar position as a priest of the Church of England who believed that that Church was no true Church, as working for the Moravians and yet not a Moravian himself.

When Zinzendorf took charge of the work in Yorkshire, all was changed. He was not in favour of this aggressive evangelism, and centred all the Yorkshire Moravian activities in the Fulneck Settlement, near Pudsey. There is something very attractive about these Moravian settlements. They were copies of Herrnhut on a smaller scale. Some of the communal ideals of the Early Church and some of the monastic ideals of the Medieval Church found expression there. Yet, as their historian says, 'it was not the road to Church extension but to Church extinction'.[1] Wesley's decision to part company with the Moravians was clearly right if his own work was to go forward untrammelled. Perhaps he was a little unfair in some of the expressions he used, but quietism and the tendency to Antinomianism and Sectarianism were real dangers at that time. Wesley saw clearly enough the path God

[1] *History of the Moravian Church*, J. E. Hutton, p. 314.

was marking out for him, and was ready to follow it even at the cost of losing old friends and saying good-bye to many pleasant memories of Oxford, Georgia, Germany, and elsewhere.

In 1745 he published a statement about this difference with the Moravians, and a few years later Ingham himself found it impossible to continue to work with Count Zinzendorf. He resumed his work as a circuit evangelist, though he had long given up open-air preaching. Some Inghamite Societies still survive in the North of England. At the Methodist Conference of 1753 the question was asked whether it was possible to unite with Mr. Ingham, and the answer was given: 'We may now behave to him with all tenderness and love, and unite with him when he returns to the old Methodist doctrine.' Two years later Ingham himself was present with Wesley at the yearly Conference of the preachers at Leeds. As that Conference decided that whether it was lawful to separate from the Church of England or not, it was not expedient, it must have settled the question of reunion between Wesley's Societies and those of Ingham. The Inghamites were already separated, for they had separate sacramental services of their own. Shortly afterwards Ingham became the bishop of his flock and ordained ministers for the work.

Lady Huntingdon and Whitefield did their best at this time to bring these different groups together, and Charles Wesley favoured the attempt. He believed that Ingham was now wholly free from the weaknesses of Moravianism, but John Wesley saw other difficulties and the opportunity for reunion passed.

Once more the elder brother proved right, for Ingham was soon attracted by Sandemanianism and his Societies were divided and weakened. Throughout Yorkshire it was the Methodist Societies that flourished. There was some inherent weakness and instability in Benjamin Ingham, though he always continued to be a true evangelist. His son, for a time at least, joined Wesley's Societies and helped as a local preacher; so the Wesley influence remained in the family for sixty years. The other Oxford Methodist who was most closely associated with the Moravians, John Gambold, became one of their bishops and remained a Moravian till his death in 1771. There is a sad note in Wesley's *Journal* about him under the date, November 5, 1763: 'I spent some time with my old friend, John Gambold. Who but Count Zinzendorf could have separated such friends as we were. Shall we never unite again?' And a month later: 'Dec. 16. I spent an agreeable hour and not unprofitable, with my old friend, John Gambold. O, how gladly could I join heart and hand again! But alas! thy heart is not as my heart!'

The second division in the ranks of the evangelical leaders was caused by differences of opinion over Calvinism. Fortunately, it did not lead to the severance of old friendships, for Whitefield died before the full fury of the Calvinistic attack on Wesley broke out. None the less, the triumphant forward march of the Revival was hindered by a new cleavage in the ranks. Wesley had been brought up with the Arminian theological outlook that was common among seventeenth-century High Churchmen. White-field's leanings to Calvinism were strengthened by his visits to America. As early as June, 1739, he wrote to John Wesley: 'I hear, honoured sir, that you are about to print a sermon against predestination. It shocks me to think of it.' Already Ralph Erskine had influenced his reading in favour of the doctrines of the decrees, but when he went to America in the autumn of 1739 he associated chiefly with Presbyterians of the same outlook as Erskine. He even read the difficult work of Jonathan Edwards on the freedom of the will, though he admitted: 'I never read a line that Calvin wrote.' He was more at home with the writings of the English Puritans, where he found much of 'the sweet doctrine of election'.

The idea of a quarrel with the Wesleys on this subject filled him with horror, and he wrote to John: 'I had rather you saw me dead at your feet than openly opposing you.' Charles Wesley wrote satirical poems on the 'horrible decree' and John Wesley preached and printed his vigorous sermon on Free Grace; strong language was used against those who would limit the scope of God's universal redemption, but it was not so strong as that of those who 'called for damnation on their own souls if Christ died for all, and if God was willing that all should be saved'. Whitefield did not use language of this kind, and his warm-hearted, affectionate nature, while saddened by the fact that the threefold cord of unity with the Wesley brothers was broken, would never allow friendship to suffer shipwreck. When he died, it was John Wesley who preached the funeral sermon and paid a fine tribute to Whitefield's memory. Howell Harris, too, another Calvinist, maintained his friendship with the Wesleys. In discussion with them, he was always moderate and reasonable, and could well have worked with them but for other influences.

The cleavage was brought about neither by Whitefield nor by Howell Harris, but by John Cennick. Cennick was one of the first of Wesley's lay preachers and was employed by him in the school at Kingswood. He is remembered to-day as the author of the grace, 'Be present at our table, Lord', and was at first a believer in universal redemption. Having changed his views, he opposed both John and Charles Wesley in public and wrote to Whitefield, begging him to return from America without delay and settle the controversies that had arisen in Bristol. Whitefield had read Wesley's sermon on Free Grace, and in December, 1740, before he sailed for England, he wrote a reply to it. He wrote to the Wesleys on February 1, 1741: 'Why did you print that sermon against predestination? Why did you in particular, my dear brother Charles, affix your hymn and join in putting out your late hymn-book? How can you say, you will not dispute with me about election, and yet print such hymns, and your brother send his sermon against election, to Mr. Garden and others in America?' A month later the Kingswood Society was torn asunder and fifty-two followed Cennick, while over ninety remained with Wesley. From this time Wesley affirmed 'there were two sorts of Methodists; those for particular, and those for general, redemption'.

Whitefield landed in England at the time when this controversy was at its height and immediately called Cennick to London. He entered the fray by publishing his reply to 'Free Grace' along with those Articles of the Church of England that seemed to support his position, and a hymn by Dr. Watts. Cennick poured oil on the flames and the feelings even of friends were deeply stirred against one another. It was a triumph of grace that warm affection between the leaders continued unbroken, but there *were* two sorts of Methodists hereafter, and the consequences have left their impression on English (and Welsh) religious life down to the present day. In London the Tabernacle went up side by side with the Foundery and now there were rival conventicles near the scene of the open-air triumphs Whitefield and Wesley had shared together in Moorfields. In Bristol, too, the Methodists were now in separate camps. Cennick began to itinerate in Wiltshire and other parts of the country as an evangelist under Whitefield's banner. Later he became a Moravian, and many of his Societies were handed over to the Brethren, as those of Ingham had been in the North. The Societies of Howell Harris became known as Calvinistic Methodist, although that term was not used until a conference of preachers held at Waterford, South Wales, in January, 1743. George Whitefield was the Moderator of that assembly, and three clergymen and three lay preachers shared with him the task of planning the 'rounds' and the districts. This was more than a year before Wesley held his first conference in London.

Howell Harris played the part of peace-maker. He met the Wesleys in London and found them friendly and reasonable; Charles especially was 'quite loving and teachable'. This led to a correspondence between the brothers and Whitefield, who was then on a triumphant tour through Scotland; a complete reconciliation which was not again disturbed was the result. In 1743 Howell Harris reported 'revival everywhere' in Wales. The Calvinists were more successful with the dour Scottish mind and the impulsive Welshmen than with the less opinionated and more lethargic English. In Scotland it was the Presbyterian Churches that were helped by Whitefield's amazing appeal; in Wales, though the Societies were still supposed to be in association with the Church of England, a strong national Nonconformity was growing. Whitefield was no organizer, and though he was appointed as permanent Moderator of the Calvinistic Methodists whenever he happened to be in England, yet he only filled that office on two occasions, and handed it over to Howell Harris in 1749. The Tabernacle in London was the English headquarters of the same association.

In August, 1743, an attempt was made to bring the three separated fellowships together. It was John Wesley who made this effort, travelling up to London from Newcastle-on-Tyne for that purpose. He persuaded Charles to come from Land's End and John Nelson walked all the way from Yorkshire. Whitefield came from Exeter, but the Moravians held off. Spangenberg left England, and James Hutton said they could not meet unless the Archbishop of Canterbury or the Bishop of London were present. It looks as though Zinzendorf was the instrument for breaking up this reunion conference. Reunion with the Moravians seemed impossible; James Hutton, who had been Whitefield's publisher, had declined to publish Calvinistic teaching for him. He was now more concerned for the recognition of Moravian orders by the Church of England, so that he was at cross purposes with all the three leaders of the Revival. Whitefield's frequent visits to America left the direction of the Calvinistic Societies more and more in the hands of Howell Harris and the Countess of Huntingdon. When he was in Great Britain, he became the evangelist at large, and exhorted converts to join the Societies or Dissenting Churches, whichever were likely to be of most help to them.

So long as Whitefield lived, there was, in Charles Wesley's phrase, a 'quadruple alliance' between him, the Wesleys, and the Countess of Huntingdon. Whitefield and Howell Harris attended Wesley's Conference at London in 1767 and the report is that 'love and harmony reigned from the beginning to the end'. They also attended in a body at one of Whitefield's services in the Tabernacle. Thomas Olivers, in recording this incident, said: 'While Mr. Whitefield lived he was glad to confirm his love to Mr. Wesley's Societies, by preaching in their chapels, by sitting at their tables, by lying in their beds, and by conversing with them, late and early, in the most friendly and Christian manner. When he preached in Mr. Wesley's pulpits in the north of England, he several times did me the honour of making my house his home.' It is not surprising that in his will he left a mourning ring to 'my honoured and dear friends and disinterested fellow-labourers, the Rev. Messrs. John and Charles Wesley, in token of my indissoluble union with them, in heart and Christian affection, notwithstanding our difference in judgement about some particular points of doctrine'. Whitefield's body was hardly cold in his American grave before these 'particular points of doctrine' became the cause of the bitterest theological controversy Methodism ever knew.

Chapter IX

DOCTRINE

JOHN WESLEY was no philosopher; he soon displayed impatience with nice discrimination in philosophical discussion. He was, however, endowed with a singularly clear and penetrating judgement and gift of expression. Moreover, he had a deep experience of religion himself and an unrivalled knowledge of the experience of others. His practical genius and strong common sense were on the alert at all times to notice dangerous tendencies of thought. Sentimentalism was as abhorrent to him as mere convention in religion. He was also an intellectual, with an adequate knowledge of the relevant literature of theology and Church history. He tested religious experience consistently by the standard of the New Testament. What he saw clearly he proclaimed passionately, and he was never willing to surrender a truth of tested validity. He disliked controversy and yet he was an admirable controversialist, attacking principles and not persons. He was ever ready for discussion and glad to receive new light from any quarter. He met scurrilous abuse in an entirely Christian temper. Seldom did he indulge in the sarcasm that his brother Charles sometimes affected. 'I will not quarrel with you about any opinion,' he would say; 'only see that your heart be right toward God, and that you know and love the Lord Jesus Christ; that you love your neighbour and walk as your Master walked; and I desire no more. I am sick of opinions.'

Why then did his strong affirmations lead to a separation both from the Moravians and from the Calvinists? The answer is simple: after he began his missionary campaign in England, he marched straight forward without wavering. He knew the gospel that was his salvation and might be the salvation of all mankind. Anything that weakened or reduced that gospel must be resolutely set aside. If this involved the loss of friends or the purging of the Societies, the suffering involved must be accepted manfully. That it did involve deep suffering there can be no doubt, but there was never hesitation. Time has vindicated his loyalty to his deepest convictions, and we can now see how his cause must have suffered shipwreck if he had compromised with quietism, sentimentalism, or a rigid doctrine of predestination. What he dreaded most of all was what he called Antinomianism—that is, such a reaction from the bondage of law that ended not in the 'freedom of the spirit', but freedom from self-restraint and all decency. This was licence rather than liberty. There was good reason for this alarm. He met so many queer religious people in all parts of the country, who regarded emotional experiences as a substitute for a good life, that he felt it was necessary to stress the fact that Christian ethics walk hand in hand with Christian experience.

Nor could the Methodist leader tolerate the undisciplined and the unregulated life. He would have been a strong supporter of St. Paul in the excitements of the Church in Corinth when he said: 'Let everything be done decently and in order.' He was outraged by Molther's attack on the means of grace as a necessity for the seeking soul. That was the way to chaos. When the Moravians or the Calvinists talked so much about the imputed righteousness of Christ, he was anxious lest they should forget that a righteous Master demanded righteousness in His servants. Later on he reacted against the 'blood and wounds' theology of the Moravians. Though he published Zinzendorf's hymn in his hymn-book, he disliked the way in which the Moravians called him 'Papa'. Still more did he react against the familiarity with which they spoke of the 'dear Lamb' or even 'brother Lambkin'. Even George Whitefield's constant reference to 'our glorious Emmanuel' troubled him. Charles sometimes went too far in sentimental language to please the severer taste of the elder brother, who actually hesitated over 'Jesu, Lover of my soul' and 'Thou Shepherd of Israel, and mine'. He wrote in the Preface to the 1779 Hymn-book: 'We talk common sense both in prose and verse.' We may at times deplore an excess of common sense and yet be thankful that the strong, masculine mind of John Welsey kept his followers out of dangerous bypaths.

What, then, was the main road along which he travelled after he had left his early reliance on exact ritual, the fasts and festivals of the Church? His gospel was one of redeeming love for all mankind to be accepted in humble and contrite faith. This acceptance was followed by the witness of the Spirit of God to the redeemed spirit of man. It envisaged a life of perfect love as the true end of living. For forty years and more his preaching was centred on these three points. Universal redemption, the

Witness of the Spirit and Sanctification were therefore the key-words of his theology. The body of Wesleyan theology is set forth in the first four volumes of John Wesley's sermons and (more persuasively) in Charles Wesley's hymns. It is almost impossible to find theological differences between the two brothers. Charles may have doubted whether Christian perfection was possible in this life or whether it was attainable instantaneously by an act of faith; yet it was Charles who wrote:

> O glorious hope of perfect love!
> It lifts me up to things above,
>   It bears on eagles' wings;
> It gives my ravish'd soul a taste,
> And makes me for some moments feast
>   With Jesu's priests and kings.

He sees the land of promise from afar, but he does pray:

> Now, O my Joshua, bring me in,
> Cast out my foes; the inbred sin,
>   The carnal mind remove.

And again:

> This moment end my legal years;
> Sorrows, and sins, and doubts, and fears,
>   A howling wilderness.

Dr. J. E. Rattenbury says: 'Charles Wesley was not striving for practicable Christian Perfection, but for heavenly beatitude, which, as he once said, "he must die to know".'[1]

The difference here is a difference of phraseology, not of meaning. There was also a great difference of temperament between the brothers, which had its influence on expression as well as on the interpretation of Christian experience. According to Whitehead, John Wesley showed 'a too great readiness to credit the testimony of others', while Charles was 'in the opposite extreme; full of caution and suspicion'. So Charles wrote to his brother: 'When you fear the worst your fears should be regarded; and when I hope the best you may almost believe me.' This is strange when we remember that Charles had the more impulsive

[1] *The Evangelical Doctrines of Charles Wesley's Hymns*, J. E. Rattenbury, p. 299.

nature and that his brother complained of sentimentalism and namby-pambyism in some of his hymns. Yet John believed that there were no hymns equal to his brother's, when Charles was at his best. The explanation of the apparent inconsistencies in these contrasts of qualities lies in the fact that the broader mind of John was also the more tolerant and therefore more hopeful.

To all intents and purposes they were one in their theology, and if Charles ever wandered from the pathway of true Wesleyan orthodoxy he soon returned to it. One of his sermons has found a place in the standard four volumes, and it is one of the best. It is still impossible to say how many of John Wesley's hymns are mixed up with those of his brother. In considering Methodist doctrine, therefore, we must take the brothers together. Has the Christian Church ever produced so influential a manual of popular theology as *Wesley's Hymns*? They have been sung round the world by millions of people for two hundred years and, though many of them are going out of use, they are powerful still. Arius is said to have popularized his doctrines in Alexandria by writing ballads for 'Sailors, millers, and travellers'. They can hardly have been as effective in controversy as were Charles Wesley's hymns against the harsher elements of Calvinism. The Methodists were attacking the doctrine of a limited Atonement when they sang:

> For all, for all, the Saviour died,
> For all, my Lord was crucified.

Charles Wesley was the propagandist as well as the Gospel preacher when he took his stand and announced the hymn:

> Come, all the world; come, sinner, thou!
> All things in Christ are ready now.

If that is the key-note of the hymn-book and if the *Sermons* open with Salvation by Faith (preached before the University of Oxford), we may well ask whether Universal Redemption or Justification by Faith is the central doctrine of the Revival. The Evangelist preaches both doctrines at the same time. He begins like Dinah Morris, by saying that 'all the love that Jesus showed to the poor is the same love that God has for us', and he ends, with her, by saying: 'Dear friends, come and take this blessedness.' His appeal is from the grace of God to the faith of man.

The first manifesto of the Revival is based on St. Paul's words to the Ephesians: 'By grace are ye saved through faith.' Everything begins with the grace of God. Wesley preached this sermon again on his father's tombstone and doubtless in many another town and village in England. He was as firm as any Calvinist in proclaiming that religion begins with God and not with man. It is significant, too, that all the great Calvinist preachers, from Whitefield to Spurgeon, made a universal appeal, as though all men might be saved and come to a knowledge of the truth. Wesley seized on the extreme putting of the doctrine of the decrees when he set out to drive them from the field. He did not place his utterance on Free Grace among his standard sermons because it was too controversial, but he was just as trenchant when he commented on Toplady's Zanchius thirty years later as he was in his Bristol sermon:

'Call it therefore by whatever name you please,' he said. 'Election, Preterition, Predestination or Reprobation, it comes in the end to the same thing. The sense of all is plainly this: By virtue of an eternal, unchangeable, irresistible decree of God, one part of mankind are infallibly saved and the rest infallibly damned; it being impossible that any of the former should be damned, or that any of the latter should be saved. But if this be so, then is all preaching vain.' The argument marches on with increasing intensity until the charge is made against the Predestinarians: 'You represent God as worse than the devil; more false, more cruel, more unjust. . . . This is the blasphemy for which (however I love the persons who assert it) I abhor the doctrine of Predestination.' Charles Wesley's hymns against the 'horrible decree' are quite as vigorous, and there can be little wonder that Whitefield was alarmed. He professed that he said much about Election and little about Reprobation. Calvin himself was somewhat unfairly treated by the translation, 'horrible decree'; what he really said about the Almighty's fiat of salvation for the elect was that it was a decree that should be regarded with reverent dread. Wesley pushed his logic home and extracted every possible benefit from his argument. Yet in his funeral sermon on Whitefield he said: 'His fundamental point was, "Give God all the glory of whatever is good in man"; and "In the business of salvation, set

Christ as high and man as low as possible." With this point, he and his friends at Oxford, the original Methodists, so called, set out.'

Whitefield's two fundamental doctrines, said Wesley, were the new birth and justification by faith. 'These let us insist upon with all boldness at all times, and in all places.' When the leaders of the Revival came together, they said the same things. For practical purposes they might very well have continued to work together. To Whitefield, Wesley's putting of the 'doctrines of Grace' would have seemed a caricature, just as the satire of Burns would have done:

> O Thou wha in the heavens dost dwell,
> Wha, as it pleases best Thysel',
> Sends ane to heaven and ten to hell
> A' for Thy glory.

Yet Wesley and Robert Burns remained in possession of the field at the end of the day.

Father Piette dislikes the idea that Wesley agreed with Luther in his views of Justification by Faith. He would relate Wesley's account of his Aldersgate Street experience to Catholic mystics and saints in their discovery of the love of God rather than to the Reformer's faith in Christ as the gateway of salvation. He has a difficult task, since it was Luther's preface to the Epistle to the Romans to which Wesley was listening at that moment. Also he said to Archbishop Secker: 'It is the faith of our first Reformers that I preach.' Dr. Rattenbury makes a distinction between believing in faith and trusting God, and it is true that Justification by Faith became such a watchword and battle-cry at the Reformation that Lutheran theologians began to talk as if faith in their own orthodoxy was the way of salvation. Wesley never fell into this error: 'Concerning the gate of religion', he says, 'which is the true, Christian, saving faith, we believe it implies abundantly more than the assent to the truth of the Bible.' 'As soon as I saw clearly the nature of saving faith and made it the standard topic of my preaching . . . God then began to work by my ministry, as he never had done before.'

When they charged him with being a Papist or a Jesuit, he said that, while he preached justification by works, he had for ten years been (fundamentally) a Papist, but, turning on his accusers indignantly, he said: 'Oh, ye fools, when will ye understand that the preaching of justification by faith alone is overturning Popery from the foundation.' There can be no doubt that this remained his conviction for all the remaining years of his ministry. At times he would cry out against the fury of Luther's solifidian doctrine, but that was because of the extravagant utterances of that volcanic personality. In May, 1765, he wrote: 'I think on Justification just as I have done any time these seven and twenty years and just as Mr. Calvin does.' It was not merely Luther's violent language that repelled Wesley; it was the behaviour of many people he met, who were for ever crying out, 'Only believe', and attacking the Christian ideal of a holy life, as much by their example as by their arguments.

Wesley kept the General Epistles in their place, side by side with the Epistles to the Romans and to the Galatians. He was as loyal to St. James, with his definition of 'pure religion and undefiled' as he was to St. Paul when he taught 'the righteousness of God is through faith in Jesus Christ unto all them that believe'. He believed St. John when he said, 'Whosoever is begotten of God does no sin', as he believed St. Paul proclaiming, 'Through one act of righteousness the free gift came to all men to justification of life'. He remembered that it was St. Paul himself who was most alarmed at the Antinomian notion that men 'should continue in sin, that grace might abound', and cried out, 'God forbid. We who died to sin, how shall we any longer live therein?"

It was the practical question that gave pungency to the discussion over Predestination. So far as argument was concerned, the long-drawn-out debate seemed at times to be 'mere words' to Wesley. So long as the Calvinists kept to theory, logic was on their side, but it deserted them wherever they went out to preach to the unconverted. Arminian and Calvinistic Methodists both sang Charles Wesley's 'Jesu, Lover of my soul' and Toplady's 'Rock of ages'. At heart they were one, and Wesley did his best at times to state his position in terms that brought out their essential agreements. For Whitefield's benefit, he asserted his belief in Predestination and election for special service to the Kingdom of God; for a time he held that those who had entered into the Canaan of perfect love could never fall from grace. By 1755 the reconciliation between Whitefield and the Wesleys seemed to be complete, and Charles Wesley could write:

F

Come on, my Whitefield (since the strife is past
And friends at first are friends again at last).

The same year John Wesley preached and published his sermon on the Catholic Spirit from the text, 'Is thy heart right as my heart with thy heart? If it be, give me thy hand'.

All was well till after Whitefield's death, but then the controversy blazed up again over the *Minutes* of the 1770 Conference. In his wanderings, Wesley had discovered that Antinomianism had 'spread like wildfire' through the Societies, so the question naturally came up when the preachers met at London in August, 1770. They had discussed the doctrine of Predestination as early as 1745, when they came to the conclusion that the truth of the Gospel came to the very edge of Calvinism and Antinomianism by (1) ascribing all good to free grace, (2) by denying all natural free-will and all power in man precedent to grace, and (3) by excluding all merit from man even for what he has or does by the grace of God. Now they thought it was necessary to stress faithfulness as well as faith. They stated: 'We have received it as a maxim that: A man is to do nothing, in order to justification. Nothing can be more false. Whoever desires to find favour with God, should cease from evil, and learn to do well. Whoever repents should do works meet for repentance.'

They went further than this when they asked what happened to those who never heard the Gospel and asserted that he that feared God and worked righteousness according to the light that he had was accepted by God. 'Is not this salvation by works? Not by the *merit* of works, but by works, as a *condition*.' These *Minutes* fell into the hands of the Countess of Huntingdon. That good lady was no theologian and failed to see that the *Minutes* were drawn up to balance an excess. Even the present Bishop of Oxford, in his *Vision of God*, considers that Wesley accepted the Roman view of justification in these *Minutes*. It was unfortunate that Wesley had not written a preface to set out the facts he stated to Fletcher a few months later: 'I always did, for between these thirty or forty years, clearly assert the total fall of man and his utter inability to do any good of himself; the absolute necessity of the Grace and Spirit of God to raise even a good thought or desire in our heart; the Lord's rewarding no work and accepting of none but so far as they proceed from the preventing, convincing, and

converting grace through the Beloved; the blood and righteousness
of Christ being the sole meritorious cause of our salvation. Who
is there in England that has asserted these things more strongly
and steadily than I have done?' But it was too late. Selina had
shed many tears over the *Minutes*. She was convinced that Wesley
had given up 'the grand point of the Methodists, free justification'.

The battle had surged into her own sacred fold at Trevecca,
and in January, 1771, she dismissed her headmaster there, Joseph
Benson, because he shared Wesley's views. John Fletcher, who
was then Superintendent at Trevecca, resigned shortly afterwards, and the Hon Walter Shirley, a relative of Lady
Huntingdon, circulated the offending *Minutes* among Calvinist
preachers, inviting signatures in opposition to them. They invited
Dissenters, as well as members of the Established Church who
disapproved of Wesley's 'dreadful heresy', to join in the fray by
attending Wesley's 1771 Conference at Bristol in protest. The
response was poor, as Shirley was joined only by two ministers
attached to Lady Huntingdon's chapel, two students from
Trevecca, and three laymen. At the meeting of the two parties,
Shirley took a much more conciliatory line, and Wesley's preachers
signed a declaration that they abhorred the doctrine of Justification by Works 'as a most perilous and abominable doctrine'.
Wesley merely says about this meeting: 'We conversed freely for
about two hours; and I believe they were satisfied that we were
not so "dreadful heretics" as they imagined, but were tolerably
sound in the faith'.

He did not rate these theologians very highly before this, but
now the conflict had been transferred to the Press. William
Romaine, in the *Gospel Magazine*, was in full career after this
hoary heretic, and the Methodist preachers began to take up the
challenge. Wesley handed the case over to Fletcher, who produced
at intervals his *Checks to Antinomianism*, which for a hundred years
afterwards were the delight of all those Methodist preachers who
enjoyed slaying the doctrines of the decrees.[1] Wesley wrote to the
Countess with his customary directness, and the result was that
another friendship was at an end. Toplady was the ablest of the
Calvinist pamphleteers. He had published two tracts in 1769,
one of which vindicated the Church of England from the charge

[1] For a survey of the whole controversy, see *Arminianism*, A. W. Harrison, pp.
192–222.

of Arminianism, and the other was a translation of the Latin of Zanchius in defence of the Doctrine of Absolute Predestination. Wesley published an abridgement of Zanchius and added his own comment: 'The sum of all is this. One in twenty (suppose) of mankind is elected; nineteen in twenty are reprobated. The elect shall be saved, do what they will; the reprobate shall be damned, do what they can. Reader, believe this or be damned. Witness my hand, A—— T——.' For this effort Wesley was never forgiven and Toplady pursued him with scurrilous invective until he himself passed from this land of conflict to 'Where beyond these voices there is peace'.

The brothers Richard and Rowland Hill joined fiercely in the debate and by their wild utterances did more harm to their own good name than to that of John Wesley. Berridge of Everton added a spice of extravagant humour, but the whole series of abusive pamphlets is best buried in oblivion. Only Fletcher of Madeley came out of this bitter discussion without discredit. Wesley himself refused to enter the arena and when his character was attacked he merely said: 'When I devoted to God my ease, my time, my future, my life, did I except my reputation?' There is something tragic in this quarrel, though it left Wesley to go on with his constructive work with increasing success freed from the patronage of the Countess of Huntingdon and the narrowness of some of her followers. Both parties were busy in the same campaign for the salvation of their country, and the Calvinist leaders were as zealous for the good life as Wesley himself. Among them only Martin Madan strayed into the dangerous fields of practical Antinomianism, though Wesley considered that all Romaine's writings were 'brimful of Antinomianism'. Madan and Romaine, on the other hand, thought that Wesley's preachers taught 'only a dry morality'. Wesley was touched by this charge and wrote to the Rector of Pewsey: 'I think even I, to speak as a fool, can judge a little of preaching the gospel, perhaps as well as either Mr. Madan or Romaine.'

The Calvinists were almost as much disturbed by Wesley's preaching on Christian perfection as by his attacks on Predestination. All of them, without exception, attacked him on this subject. He had to warn Joseph Benson when he went to Trevecca: 'You must not even mention before her [Lady Huntingdon] anything of *deliverance from all sin. Error errorum,* as Count Zinzendorf says;

"heresy of heresies". "I will suffer no one in *my* society who even *thinks* of perfection." However, I trust you shall not only think of, but enjoy it.' Moravian and Calvinist might differ over Predestination, but they were at one in their dislike of the idea of perfect love. James Hutton was a publisher who believed that he had some responsibility for the views expressed by his authors. He would not publish books on the divine decrees and he would probably have refused to publish anything from his old friend, John Wesley, on the subject of Christian perfection. They did, however, knit up the broken fellowships, and Wesley wrote to him at the end of 1771—that year of controversy: 'After having seen above half a century of years, we are sick of strife and contention. If we do not yet think alike we may at least love alike.' He was not in the least inclined to surrender his ideal of the Christian life if every friend he had in the world criticized his teaching.

The whole aim of the Methodist movement, as he conceived it, was 'to spread Scriptural holiness through the land'. He found the doctrine of perfect love (as he preferred to call it) in the Epistles of St. John, and had become enthusiastic for it when he pored over the pages of the *Imitatio Christi* as a student at Oxford. This doctrine of holiness saved the Wesleyan theology from provincialism. It related the Methodists, not only to the New Testament, but to the saints of all the centuries and of all races. The *Christian Library* is full of the biographies of ancient and modern saints who had seen the vision of perfection, if they had not experienced perfect love. Wesley never claimed that he had himself been blessed with this experience, but believed that many of his followers had found it. His brother Charles was more sceptical; yet the ideal remained. A true Christian should be wholly devoted to God; he should love God with all his heart. He should regain the image of God and have the mind of Christ. He should 'walk uniformly as Christ walked'. 'What is the objection to all this?' he asked innocently. He was merely setting up the New Testament standard and trying to achieve it.

He thought the Church of England did no less, when it taught every member of the congregation to pray day by day in the Collect for Grace, 'Grant that this day we fall into no sin', or, in another Collect, 'that we may perfectly love Thee and worthily magnify Thy Holy Name'. How could he go on proclaiming salvation from sorrow, fear, and sin, if freedom from sin were impossible in this life? He explained carefully again and again within what limits this doctrine was true. Mortal man is limited in body and mind; he will always have to pray 'deliver us from evil'; he will always be liable to ignorance, mistakes, and infirmities; he will always be subject to temptation; nevertheless, he must cry day and night to be 'delivered from the bondage of corruption into the glorious liberty of the children of God'. He suffered much misrepresentation on this subject, yet when Edmund Gibson, then Bishop of London, heard his exposition of it, he said: 'Mr. Wesley, if this be all you mean, publish it to all the world.' Even Toplady, the bitterest critic Wesley ever encountered, wrote a hymn on desiring to be given up to God which began:

> O that my heart was right with Thee,
>   And lov'd Thee with a perfect love!
> O that my Lord would dwell in me
>   And never from His seat remove.
> Jesus, remove th' unending load
> And set my soul on fire for God.

It is difficult to believe that it would have been impossible to keep the Evangelical team together, if misunderstandings and personal prejudices had been removed.

There was less conflict over the third main doctrine of the Wesleyan Revival. The Witness of the Spirit meant to Wesley 'an inward impression on the soul, whereby the Spirit of God directly witnesses with my spirit that I am a child of God'. This doctrine sprang out of experience but was also established by Scripture. It was the source of the distinctive happiness of the new Societies. Men and women who knew that their sins had been forgiven gloried in the fact that they were the children of God. Fear and sorrow disappeared; they sang the great songs of deliverance with ecstasy and abandon. They could afford to look down with pity even on kings and princes, for they were children of a heavenly King. They enjoyed the full assurance that they had been received into God's family circle. Of course, critics ridiculed them and said they were claiming to be divinely inspired. It seemed absurd that common people should claim such intimacy with Heaven. They knew better. They were well aware of their own ignorance, not only in secular affairs, but in the deep things of God. One thing only they knew confidently, with the assurance of the blind man in the Gospels who had been to the pool of Siloam and washed at the bidding of Jesus and came back seeing. Clever leaders in his Church said to him, 'Give glory to God: we know that this man is a sinner'. It is comforting to know that dogmatic experts may be mistaken; as mistaken as the Pharisees were about Jesus. The blind man was no expert. 'He therefore answered, Whether he be a sinner, I know not: one thing I know, that, whereas I was blind, now I see.' It was the Holy Spirit of God who had worked the miracle. It was the Holy Spirit of God who gave them confidence and assurance. It was the Holy Spirit of God who sent them out to help other blind men to find the pool. In the power of that spirit they lived their lives, battled through their temptations, sang the songs of the redeemed and entered the gates of the celestial city.

This may seem a very limited programme of Christian doctrine. All the forty-four standard sermons of Wesley are concerned with the experience of salvation and practical Christianity. Methodist preaching was concentrated there. The Cross is the way of Reconciliation, faith is the means, and joy in the Witness of the Spirit is the result. It all begins in the redeeming love of God to all mankind, and it ends in the practice of the Sermon on the Mount. Wesley puts his sermons on what he calls speculative doctrines outside the four volumes that contain the preaching standards. The Trinity, the Inspiration of the Scriptures, the Future Life, the Church, and even Predestination are dealt with in later volumes. He is disappointingly orthodox except in his curious views about the immortality of animals. The catholic faith was preserved for his people, not by the constant use of the Prayer Book, but by the Hymn-book they loved so passionately and knew so well. There are hymns there for all the great seasons of the Christian year. The whole Church turns to Charles Wesley at Christmas and Easter. His hymns on Ascension Day, Whitsuntide, and Good Friday deserve to be better known by those who have not been brought up at his feet. He wrote more than a hundred hymns on the Lord's Supper. It was the Methodists who revived the frequent celebration of Holy Communion in the Church of England. They recovered the meaning of the New Testament Church in their loving fellowships. It may well be argued that the Evangelical Revival created more orthodox Christians than any popular movement of religion in the history of the Church.

Chapter X

PERSONALITIES

(*a*) ITINERANTS

THE unfortunate divisions in the ranks of the evangelical forces were not due to differences of doctrine alone; the clash of personalities counted for something. The Revival was singularly rich in men and women of strong character, whose temperaments did not always blend harmoniously. Even the wisest and best may sometimes be difficult. The leaders of the Revival suffered much from detraction and misrepresentation—even from scurrilous abuse—in their lifetimes, but when the mists of controversy had passed away their fine qualities appeared. Charges of hypocrisy, ambition, and selfishness were no longer brought against them. Of the genuineness of their enthusiasm and of their real goodness there can be no doubt. Still, wholehearted and unselfish devotion to the highest of causes may be blended with suspicion and jealousy or with a narrow-mindedness which can see one goal clearly, but is incapable of a wider vision. A truly catholic spirit is rarely found in combination with concentrated devotion.

In this combination, as in the highest qualities of judgement and leadership, John Wesley stood out head and shoulders above all the rest. Physically he was very slight. Never as much as nine stones in weight, he was certainly not the mass of whipcord of W. T. Stead's imagination. His physical achievement in more than half a century of untiring evangelism seems to us a miracle, but it was a triumph over a body disciplined to be the instrument of an iron will. J. A. Spender was repeating the views of more than one historian when he wrote: 'It has been said that the greatest Englishman of the eighteenth century was neither the great Lord Chatham, nor his son, nor Burke, but John Wesley, the heroic little man who went from village to village on his tired horse, braving insult and ridicule to preach his gospel of salvation to a multitude who had either not known or had forgotten Christianity. Certainly of no other can it be said that after two hundred years his followers in the English-speaking world number at least twenty millions, and of very few that their influence was so far-reaching in so many directions.'[1] It is true that even the

[1] J. A. Spender, *The Government of Mankind*, p. 298.

majestic figure of Chatham seems dwarfed in this comparison. They fought their battles on different arenas, but they had many qualities in common. Chatham had a world view of the first British Empire; Wesley had a world view of the Kingdom of God. Both were born leaders of men. 'No man', said a soldier of the Seven Years' War, 'ever entered Mr. Pitt's closet who did not feel himself braver when he came out than when he went in.' Most of Wesley's preachers could have said the same of their leader.

His unruffled courage in the face of most dangerous mobs comes out again and again in his story. He faced more disturbing situations created by the defection of friends or the misrepresentations of foes with the same steadiness. In executive ability in his campaigns he had, like Chatham, the qualities of a good general, while he excelled his great contemporary in meticulous regard for detail. 'Wesley lacked charm', says Birrell in his essay on Newman, comparing the qualities of the two men. But Birrell was wrong, or the testimony of many women and children is strangely at fault. Birrell came to retract that judgement when he wrote his essay on Wesley: 'Let no one deny charm in Wesley who has not read his *Journal*.' Wesley was exceedingly simple in his dealings with women and laid down some strange rules for the education of children, and yet his affectionate regard for little children (particularly in his old age) and the warm esteem with which so many of the women members of his Societies in the three kingdoms regarded him are well known. His correspondence with his women friends is particularly charming, and he remains throughout the true Father in God, without a trace of impropriety, but with a sane appreciation of the qualities of mind as well as of heart in his correspondents. That his own marriage was unhappy is one of those unfortunate accidents which are the irony of history. His wife may have been suspicious of his voluminous correspondence, but she was a difficult and jealous woman inflicted on an apostle, in the view of some of his friends, by a divine Providence that planned for him no life of domestic comfort and ease.

His preachers, for the most part, regarded him with a veneration a little this side idolatry. Surely few men can ever have won so deep a devotion from so many thousands of admirers. Old Methodists down to recent times would always mention the name of 'Mr. Wesley' with special reverence and would allow no criticism of that honoured name. 'Dr. Johnson said of him: 'He can talk well on any subject.' And again: 'John Wesley's conversation is good, but he is never at leisure. He is always obliged to go at a certain hour. This is disagreeable to a man who loves to fold his legs and have out his talk as I do.' Whitehead, who knew him intimately and saw much of him, said: 'He had the talent of making himself exceedingly agreeable in company.'

Is there any Englishman whose life is so fully open to inspection as that of John Wesley? In his *Journals* and *Diaries* we follow him, not merely through his activities during every hour of the day, but we enter into the inner sanctuary of his heart. His character stands revealed, too, in the eight volumes of his *Letters*, which have been edited with as much laborious accuracy as the Standard Edition of his *Journal*. The transparent simplicity of a fine mind appears on every page. Southey's charge of ambition as the key to Wesley's character was refuted by Watson so completely that Southey himself admitted that he had been mistaken. The King is reported to have said about Watson's reply: 'The Methodist preacher seems to have got the better of my Poet Laureate.' Ambitious for the Kingdom of God Wesley certainly was, but for himself not at all. He would not lay down the responsibilities which he believed God had laid upon him, but this was from no passion for power. It has been calculated that he gave away between twenty and thirty thousand pounds in charity, living in the utmost frugality himself. 'His liberality to the poor knew no bounds but an empty pocket', for he gave away all he had.

He had some quaint views about ghosts and witches and medical science and was apt to receive wonderful stories with rather excessive credulity. He read widely and did much to stimulate reading among his people, though he showed some strong prejudices in his judgements of certain writers. His attitude to literature, to music, art, and innocent amusements was, however, much more liberal than that of some of his evangelical contemporaries and many of his successors. All who knew him well speak of his equable and cheerful disposition. He mellowed with the years. 'So fine an old man', said Alexander Knox, 'I never saw. The happiness of his mind beamed forth in his countenance. Every look showed how fully he enjoyed "the gay remembrance of a life well spent", and wherever he went, he diffused a portion of his own felicity.' Matthew Arnold stresses his 'genius for godliness' and it is in the highest fellowship of the saints that we must leave him. He was the most efficient leader of the Church that British Christianity has ever produced and the greatest of our apostles.

His brother Charles will never be separated from him in fame, though his gifts were very different. He lacked the catholic temper of his elder brother and his prejudices were deeper. He was a good classical scholar and the brothers kept up through life a curious habit of talking to one another in Latin. Charles read less and had narrower interests than John. Few men can have known the Bible better; he turned so much of it into verse. According to the latest estimate (that of Dr. J. E. Rattenbury) he composed not less than 7,300 hymns. That would mean a composition of one a day for twenty years. He was always composing. When he reached home from one of his preaching tours, he would jump down from his horse and cry out for pen and paper to commit to writing his latest composition. He is certainly our most prolific hymn-writer and, in the opinion of many good judges, our greatest. In the early days of the Revival, he was always in the forefront of the battle. He faced the mobs with the courage of a true Wesley and with the exhilaration of a bonny fighter. He must have been a most attractive preacher, when in the right mood, enthusiastic, warm-hearted and impulsive.

We see him at his best with condemned criminals, visiting them in their cells and following them to the scaffold, singing his father's hymn:

> Behold the Saviour of mankind
> Nailed to the shameful tree!

'That hour under the gallows', he said, 'was the most blessed hour of my life.' He was rejoicing in the conversion of some who were snatched to Paradise at the last moment, like the penitent thief, yet there is a strong sense of dramatic values in his words. Is it fanciful to imagine that he was back again at that scene on his own death-bed, when he dictated to his wife the stanza beginning, 'In age and feebleness extreme', and ending:

> O could I catch a smile from Thee
> And drop into eternity![1]

[1] I owe this suggestion to my wife, whose *Son to Susanna* is sometimes a little hard on poor Charles.

Certainly the interest and concern he showed for prisoners from the days when he used to visit the jail at Oxford remained with him all his life. His last publication was a hymn-book entitled *Hymns for Condemned Malefactors*. He had the strength and weaknesses of those endowed with the artistic temperament, knowing great exaltations of spirit and many depressions.

Impressionable, he followed his brother with great devotion, though he took the lead on occasion. He was the founder of the Holy Club. He was the first to administer the sacrament to the Methodists, when they were repelled from Holy Communion in the churches in Bristol. Always a Church and State man, he became more conservative as he grew older, and the dread that the Methodists would leave the Church became an obsession with him. He also adopted a very critical attitude to the lay preachers, though his wife used to say she 'never met with persons better behaved or more agreeable in their spirit and manners'. Mrs. Charles Wesley was the daughter of a wealthy Welsh squire, who shared with her husband a great love of music and a real devotion to the cause of evangelical religion. For a time after his marriage Charles continued his itinerant labours, and sometimes his wife travelled with him. This was a strange life for Mrs. Charles and for the last thirty years of his life her husband had a settled pastorate, first to the Methodists of Bristol and then in London. His sons became famous in musical circles, and the home in Marylebone, where the last years of his life were spent, was often the scene of fashionable gatherings.

With all his humility of spirit and shrinking from positions of responsibility, Charles Wesley seemed more inclined to make friendships, in his later years, in society than among the humble Methodists. His intervention to prevent the marriage of his brother with Grace Murray nearly caused a permanent estrangement from the one whom he had idolized in earlier years. John said of these years of comparative retirement: 'While my brother remained with me, he was joyous in his spirit, and his labour saddened him not. But when he departed from that activity, to which the Lord called him, and in which he so greatly blessed him, his spirit became depressed; and being surrounded with "croakers" he often looked through the same clouds which enveloped them.' Watson dates his decline in activity to the year in which he was allowed to inquire into the characters of the preachers, because some dangerous rumours about them had been in circulation. The preachers came out of their ordeal with the greatest credit, but the inquiry 'was not conducted, to say the least of it, in the bland manner in which it would have been executed by Mr. John Wesley'. They bore him no malice and greatly admired his many excellent qualities, but they suspected his judgement, and there were occasional clashes between 'Mr. Charles' and the more independent preachers, who still bore the burden and heat of the day. His ministry became less and less active, though he interfered occasionally with his advice and, in still later years, now and then he would censure the increasing irregularity of his brother's proceedings.

John pursued his own steady course without wavering and paid little attention to his brother's criticisms. While the elder brother was growing to the end, Charles's best days were behind him. It is, however, greatly to his credit that whenever a serious attack was made on John, it was Charles who was the first to spring impulsively to his brother's side. A bitter letter written to him from the Countess of Huntingdon, written at the height of the Calvinist controversy, was found after his death docketed, 'Lady Huntingdon's last. Unanswered by John Wesley's brother'. Lady Huntingdon had been one of the most intimate friends Charles Wesley and his wife ever had. She had nursed Mrs. Charles through small-pox in very dark days in Bristol. The knife went very deep to sever a friendship such as that. After his death, his widow said that Charles was a contrast to his brother in his attitude to injuries as he was in most things. 'The peculiar virtue of John', she said, 'was forgiveness of enemies. Charles, on the other hand, could not replace his confidence where he had experienced treachery.'

He was full of fire and sensitiveness, but an odd man in many ways; 'eccentric and absent', Henry Moore calls him, adding: 'Mr. John Wesley told me, that he always dreaded his visiting him, notwithstanding their great love to each other—knowing well the derangement of books and papers that would probably ensue.' His daughter Sally could not understand this; because her father kept his accounts very accurately and his own papers were methodically arranged. Doubtless both statements are true, and Sally admitted that her father was very absent-minded. We have a pathetic picture of John Wesley preaching at Bolton soon after his brother's death and being overcome with emotion during the singing of the great hymn, 'Come, O Thou traveller unknown'. When they came to the lines,

> My company before is gone
> And I am left alone with Thee,

the lonely and desolate old man broke down altogether, burst into tears and sat down holding his face in his hands. The singing stopped and the great congregation was in tears also. Presently the preacher rose and went through to the end of an unforgettable service. It would be difficult to find a deeper comradeship between two brothers who differed widely in opinion and temperament, but whose gifts were complementary and were consecrated to the highest ends that man can serve. The only matter for regret is that the comradeship in arms was not continued to the end of the journey.

George Whitefield, on the other hand, kept up the campaign until he fell on the field of battle. For the Wesleys he had the greatest esteem, looking to John with reverence and to Charles with the warmest personal regard. After the division of the forces in Kingswood in 1741, when Cennick led his followers out of the Societies, as Wesley said, 'from this time, there were two sorts of Methodists; those for particular and those for general redemption'. When Whitefield returned from America, he was drawn into the controversy, and John Wesley says of their interview: 'He told me, he and I preached two different gospels; and therefore he not only would not join with, or give me the right hand of fellowship, but was resolved publicly to preach against me and my brother, wheresoever he preached at all." Whitefield, however, had too generous a spirit, and too affectionate a disposition to carry out this resolve. Although the Methodists continued in two camps, he was reconciled to his friends and preached regularly in their Societies in his later years, without strife. He did more than any other individual to make the message of the Revival known on both sides of the Atlantic. The problems of tradition and regard for fellowship with the Established Church that worried the Wesleys all their days meant nothing to him.

Though he was a clergyman of the Church of England, he was more often found among those who did not conform to that

Church than among those who did. He would preach 'the Gospel of the glorious Emmanuel' wherever there was a soul to be saved from sin. Presbyterianism in Scotland, Nonconformity in Wales, Presbyterianism, Methodism, and Congregationalism in the United States, Congregationalism in England are all in his debt. He was the universal awakener. He had no direct responsibility for Societies, as John Wesley had. For a time he was Moderator of those Societies that developed into Welsh Calvinistic Methodism and later worked in close association with the Countess of Huntingdon with the Tabernacle as his headquarters. But he was a bird of passage, and it is not surprising that the next generation of preachers influenced by him gave their attention to the more prosaic duties of the pastoral oversight of the flock of Christ and of reminding themselves of the duties of churchmanship.

Whitefield was a born actor and had a passion for reading plays and acting when a boy at school. He was kept from the theatre by his religious views, but he remained on the stage and in the lime-light from the moment he began his popular preaching at the age of twenty-two until his death. The surprising thing is that he was not spoilt by his amazing popularity. A naïve egoism reveals itself in the autobiography he published at the age of twenty-five, yet the youthful simplicity that led to this publication was inspired by a sincere enthusiasm for the Kingdom of God. In later years he was greatly impressed by the kindness and hospitality he received in the highest circles and shows a childish pleasure in such a surprising phenomenon. 'I am now writing in an earl's house, surrounded by fine furniture; but, glory be to free grace! My soul is in love only with Jesus.' The contrast between Whitefield and John Wesley is here most noticeable. Wesley detested amorous and namby-pamby phraseology in religion, and he had no element of toadyism in his composition. He would meet the earl and talk to him as a man and a brother, but preferred the society and service of the poor to any lingering in fine houses in high society. Still less could Wesley have written to a noble corres-pondent: 'Methinks I see your ladyship sitting in your chair and ravished with the Redeemer's beauty.' When Newman attributed to Whitefield's 'school of religion a certain general leaning towards sycophancy', he had been reading the Life of the Countess of Huntingdon. He could certainly not have made that remark after a study of Wesley's *Letters* and *Journal*. Nor could he have framed the theory that the Evangelicals' disregard for a divine priesthood was the natural concomitant of an excessive regard for the nobility.

Concerning the other end of the social scale, we find Wesley denouncing slavery as that 'execrable sum of all villainies', while Whitefield defends it. On his estate in Georgia, Whitefield was the owner of several slaves, whom he bequeathed to Lady Huntingdon in his will. Whitefield was neither scholar nor saint, but he was a singularly honest, sincere, and kindly man. He was arrested by the grace of God in his youth and lifted into the fellowship of 'Jesu's priests and kings'. The wonder of that arrest never left him. It subdued his natural egoism into humility. It led him to stretch out the right hand of fellowship to all who loved his Lord in sincerity and truth. It gave him the catholic spirit of the true Christian. It drove him forwards in one unswerving loyalty all the days of his life. If ever a man could say 'This one thing I do', of the work of proclaiming his divine Master, that man was George Whitefield. Perhaps then he, too, was of the fellowship of the saints, after all.

Howell Harris follows Whitefield, with whom he was in such full agreement, though he was in the field a little before him. He was born at Trevecca and to that place he retired in 1752, after several years of itinerant preaching in which he reached nearly every part of Wales, rousing the Principality and forming Societies everywhere. Something of his remarkable story is told in the first chapter of this book. At Trevecca he set up what has been called 'a kind of Protestant monastery' and gathered a family of nearly a hundred who lived and worked in the house, while ten families lived out in farms in the neighbourhood. His own account of it is given in Wesley's *Journal* for March 21, 1755, when Wesley preached at Trevecca. 'Before I talked with him myself', says Wesley, 'I wondered Howell Harris did not go out and preach as usual. But he now informed me he preached till he could preach no longer, his constitution being entirely broken. While he was thus confined he was pressed in spirit to build a large house, though he knew not why or for whom. But as soon as it was built, men, women, and children, without his seeking came to it from all parts of Wales, and, except in the case of the Orphan House at Halle, I never heard of so many signal interpositions of divine Providence.'

G

The Seven Years' War seemed to restore Harris to activity in the field in an unusual way. He was a strong patriot, and as there was a real danger of a French invasion, with the possibility of Roman Catholic dominance, in 1759 he accepted a commission in the Brecon militia, helping to raise a company of soldiers. Many of his Trevecca 'family' joined him, and he was stationed in different places, where he continued to preach. As he now took his stand in the open air in full regimentals, he was in less danger from the attacks of the mob than he had been when he was the evangelist of Wales. In his later years he associated chiefly with the Countess of Huntingdon and her preachers and was often to be heard at Tottenham Court Chapel. His Calvinism did not destroy his esteem for the Wesleys, and several of Wesley's preachers speak of him with affection. 'Honest Howell Harris' one of them calls him, and that seems to hit one of the characteristics of this warm-hearted and kindly man. He was an Israelite, indeed, in whom there was no guile. Two of his brothers achieve with him the distinction of a place in *The Dictionary of National Biography*. He died in 1773 and will be chiefly remembered as the founder of Welsh Calvinistic Methodism.

In Count Zinzendorf we meet another person of strongly marked character. Whitefield once said that he liked the Wesleys 'because they let the world see what they are at once. I suspect something wrong, when so much secrecy is required.' Perhaps the Wesleys erred on the side of frankness; the Moravian tendency was in the opposite direction. Zinzendorf was three years older than John Wesley. He was brought up among the German Pietists and showed signs of the most precocious piety himself from his earliest childhood. He had an estate in Saxony near the Bohemian frontier and welcomed persecuted Moravians there in 1722. It was here that their colony of Herrnhut was established. A Lutheran himself, he discovered that these 'primitive Christians' were heirs of the Church of the Brethren, who had been recognized by Luther. He wished to preserve the Moravian Church inside the Lutheran Church, and presently became anxious that the Moravians should be Christian missionaries to all the world. In 1734 he took Orders in the Lutheran Church, but was regarded as an eccentric religious fanatic in his own country and in 1736 he was expelled from Saxony as a heretic. He then founded a new colony of Moravians in Western Germany and was drawn more and more into fellowship with them until he became one of their bishops and the real leader of revived Moravianism.

His queer, mystical views often bewildered his simple followers, but they gave him unstinted adoration and devotion. He came to England in 1741 and spent a large part of the remaining twenty years of his life there. Wesley had corresponded with him in the days of his ministry in Georgia; he had also met him at Herrnhut and had listened to the Count's preaching with approval. When, however, they met again in Gray's Inn Fields there was no concord between them at all. Their curious conversation is recorded in Latin in Wesley's *Journal*. The Count was repelled both by Wesley's doctrine of Christian perfection and by the stress he laid on discipline in the Christian life. Wesley disliked the talk of Christ as the only perfection, with the implication that faith in the Redeemer gave the believer sanctification and justification together, without making demands for an endeavour after godliness. He was then disturbed by the Moravian quietism and disregard for the means of grace and clearly found Zinzendorf antipathetic.

The Moravian explanation of the inability of the two religious leaders to appreciate each other is that 'the Count was a poet and used poetic language. John Wesley was a level-headed Briton, with a mind as exact as a calculating machine.' Some of the Count's poetry was undoubtedly nonsense, and Wesley had little patience with that. Moreover, the Count talked to Wesley, as he did to Whitefield later, in the tone of a schoolmaster correcting small boys for their mistakes. Christian perfection was the error of one and Predestination of the other. The Count was hardly qualified to give lectures on theology; he had instructed his preachers that the only way to teach men to love God was to preach the Creator of the World under no other shape than that of a wounded and dying Lamb. Hence arose the 'Blood and Wounds Theology' of the Moravians. Childishly sentimental and amorous expressions of their devotion to the Lamb became common in their mystical doctrine. There is little wonder that English common sense protested against this German romanticism. Yet Wesley translated and printed the Count's hymns in his book, and five of them are still found in the *Methodist Hymn-book*. The protest against particular election, which is as strong as any that Charles Wesley ever wrote, is still popular:

> Lord, I believe, were sinners more
> Than sands upon the ocean shore,
> Thou hast for all a ransom paid,
> For all a full atonement made.

In the course of a few years, the Count made two public announcements that the Moravians and the Methodists were two distinct people and should never be confused. John Wesley's dry comment was: 'The Methodists, so called, heartily thank Brother Louis for his Declaration; as they count it no honour to be in any connexion either with him or his Brethren.' It should be remembered that some scandal had been in circulation at that time both about their financial affairs and their curious observances. The Count's influence had been a check on their evangelistic activity and he had involved them in difficulties by his ambitious settlement schemes. It should be said that he devoted his fortune as well as his life to their service, or, rather, he spent himself and all that he had for the cause of Christian fellowship.

He had no desire to make the Moravians into a flourishing Church; his ideal was the reunion of all the Churches. He secured recognition by the British Government for the Moravians in Great Britain and the colonies; he persuaded the leaders of the Church of England that the episcopacy of the Moravian Church was a true and valid one. He failed in his efforts to graft the English Moravians into the Church of England, as he failed to graft the German Moravians into the Lutheran Church. In England, they might be regarded as a true episcopal Church, but they were still Dissenters and had to license their chapels under the Toleration Act. Full of the love of Christ and zeal for the salvation of the world, Zinzendorf revived the missionary work of the Moravians, which carried them to Greenland and South Africa, to Eskimos, Hottentots, and Red Indians, to the West Indies and Surinam, to Russia and Wallachia, to the Calmucks and most degraded races of mankind. There was a touch of genius and a strong infusion of originality in Zinzendorf's strangely blended personality. He was dynamic without practical sense, humble as a penitent sinner saved by grace, but arrogant and dictatorial on occasion, emotional and imaginative in language and sentiment—even reckless in expression—and yet capable of effective and direct utterance in a crisis. He won the affection of multitudes, was heartily abused and painfully mis-represented. Still, he is a pillar in the temple of eighteenth-century Christianity. Its story is not fully told if Zinzendorf's name is omitted.

After the Count comes the Countess, 'the Queen of the Method-ists', as Horace Walpole called her. Selina Shirley was the second daughter of the second Earl Ferrers and was born in 1707. She was therefore four years younger than John Wesley and survived him by a few months, dying in June, 1791. She married the Earl of Huntingdon in 1728, and after his death in 1746 she devoted the whole of her time to the cause of the revival of religion. It was her husband's sisters who made her acquainted with the Methodists. Two of them had married clergymen; Lady Margaret Hastings became the wife of Benjamin Ingham and Lady Catherine married Sir George Wheeler, incumbent of a pro-prietary chapel in Spitalfields. The *Life and Times of Selina Countess of Huntingdon*, by a member of the houses of Shirley and Hastings, is a mine of information about peers and preachers in the eighteenth century. It may also be to the irreverent a source of a good deal of entertainment, for its thousand crowded pages and innumerable footnotes form a monument of snobbery, seriousness, and prejudice. Newman calls it an 'ill-digested and ill-arrayed volume', and complains of its lack of dates. He is satirical in the quotations he makes from its pages, but values the otherworldliness of the Countess. It would, indeed, be a mistake to approach the good lady in any light or trifling spirit. An intense Puritan, without a particle of humour in her make-up, she wins admiration by the completeness of her devotion, her benevolence, and her service for the Kingdom of God. It was the Kingdom of God rather than the Church of England that was her great concern, though she had a great love for the Church in which she had been brought up. After her own conversion, she believed that whoever preached the gospel of redeeming grace, whether he were Anglican, Moravian, or Dissenter, was a servant of God's Kingdom.

The early preaching of the Methodists roused the interest and changed the lives of the ladies of the Hastings family and through them their sister-in-law Selina. When Lady Margaret told her 'that since she had known and believed in the Lord Jesus Christ for life and salvation, she had been as happy as an angel', Lady

Huntingdon was deeply impressed. She was not satisfied until she shared the same experience. She was an early member of the Fetter Lane Society and took her husband there. Soon she made the acquaintance of the brothers Wesley, who visited her several times at Donington Hall. It was her invitation there that led John Wesley in 1742 to pay his first visit to the Midlands and, on her advice, to go north to Newcastle-on-Tyne to preach to the miners and sailors of Tyneside. Henceforth, instead of working backwards and forwards between London and Bristol, he made a great triangle with Newcastle as the apex, and so travelled all round the country. It was at the house of the Countess in Downing Street that he held his first Conference in 1744. She had an even greater regard for George Whitefield, from whom she inherited his property and responsibilities in America at his death.

She invited her friends regularly to the ministrations of her favourite preachers. It was not only great ladies like the Duchesses of Marlborough, Queensberry, and Buckingham whom she constrained to listen to the Gospel; such unlikely people as Lord Bolingbroke, the Earl of Chesterfield, and Horace Walpole were to be found listening to Whitefield or Romaine. The King himself greatly admired Lady Huntingdon and supported her protest against the worldliness of Archbishop Cornwallis so effectively that the fashionable revels at Lambeth Palace were stopped. George III thought it would be a good idea to make the Methodist leaders bishops, and when some one at Court suggested that the Countess took too much upon herself and usurped the office of a bishop, the King said that he wished he had more bishops like her. She encouraged the formation of Societies, as Wesley and Ingham did, and appointed chaplains with the idea that domestic chapels of peers of the realm were exempt from ecclesiastical jurisdiction. She was advised that the law was against her, though her difficulties might have been surmounted 'were our Bishops differently minded'. With the greatest reluctance, she was therefore compelled to license her proprietary chapels as a Dissenter in 1782. She said bitterly: 'I am to be cast out of the Church now, only for what I have been doing these forty years—speaking and living for Jesus Christ.'

Sergeant Glynn, in giving opinion on this subject, said: 'I earnestly look for reformation in some matters connected with the Established Church, to which I am conscientiously attached; and though I may not live to see any great change, yet I am persuaded the time is not far distant when Bishops will deeply lament the obstinate, headstrong tyranny which has driven so many from the Church.' She had indeed shared in other Methodist irregularities, for she was one of the first to approve open-air preaching and believed in the employment of laymen in evangelistic work before Wesley did. It was Lady Huntingdon who secured the release of John Nelson after he had been impressed for a soldier. When six Methodist students were expelled from the University of Oxford in 1768 because of their Methodism, she immediately opened her college at Trevecca for the training of ministers, who might serve either in the Established or the Dissenting Churches. The catholic spirit of her outlook was shown at the first anniversary of the opening of the college, when John Wesley, Howell Harris, John Fletcher, Daniel Rowlands, William Williams, and Walter Shirley all took part. England and Wales, Calvinist and Arminian were well represented at that festival. Alas! the concord was soon broken for the Calvinist controversy broke out the next year and she came to regard Wesley as 'the enemy of grace'.

Wesley wrote to her Ladyship one of his frankest letters. 'For several years', he wrote to Benson in November, 1770, 'I had been deeply convinced that I had not done my duty to that valuable woman: that I had not told her what I was thoroughly assured no one else would dare to do, and what I knew she would bear from no other person but possibly might bear from me.' Unfortunately the letter has not been preserved, and apparently the Countess could not 'take' it, for she was never reconciled to her old friend. When she read Elizabeth Ritchie's account of John Wesley's death, she sent for Joseph Bradford to ask if it was true that Wesley had said on his death-bed: 'I the chief of sinners am, but Jesus died for me.' When Bradford assured her of its truth and that Wesley never preached any other gospel, she confessed that she had been misinformed and broke into tears. She might easily have understood his position in 1770 but for the bondage of pet phrases and the party spirit. Berridge said with characteristic humour and penetration, 'it was a case of Pope John versus Pope Joan'. She wrote a bitter letter to Charles Wesley in which she said: 'As you have no part in this matter,

I find it difficult to blame your brother to you, while, as an honest man, I must pity and not less regard you, as you must suffer equal disgrace and universal distrust from the supposed union with him.' This was the letter to which John Wesley's brother made no reply.

John did make more than one attempt at reconciliation. To one of her letters he made no reply, but to a second (which was read at the Methodist Conference of 1771) he did. He made it quite clear that he had given up all to preach 'that great truth, Justification by Faith', and that his offending *Minutes* did not conflict with that doctrine. 'Indeed, it would be amazing that God should at this day prosper my labours as much if not more than ever, by converting as well as convincing sinners, if I was "establishing another foundation, repugnant to the whole plan of man's salvation under the new covenant of grace, as well as the clear meaning of our Established Church and all other Protestant Churches." This is a charge indeed! But I plead, Not guilty. And till it is proved upon me, I must subscribe myself, my dear Lady, Your Ladyship's truly affectionate but much injured servant.' This unfortunate quarrel is a study in psychology rather than theology. The Countess had been a real friend to Susanna Wesley and to Mrs. Charles; her association with the two brothers had been very close for more than thirty years; it was now ended. It is a real problem to know why so much bitterness was generated in this controversy. A few years later Wesley wrote to another of his old friends who had turned aside from him: 'Bitterness and wrath, yea, low, base, virulent invective, both Mr. Richard and Mr. Rowland Hill (as well as Mr. Toplady) have poured out upon me in great abundance. But where have I in one single instance returned them railing for railing? I have not so learned Christ.'

Whitefield was dead and her fellowship with the Wesleys was at an end. The Countess went on her way with other helpers. She was separated from the Church of England and, in consequence, her chaplains who also held livings were compelled to separate from her. She lost at a blow Venn, Romaine, Townsend, Jesse, and others, but she was undaunted, and sent out her preachers to the end like a high commander on the field of battle. Limited in outlook, she was yet a good soldier of Jesus Christ. Her fortune of £100,000 was laid at His feet. Newman said of her: 'She devoted herself, her name, her means, her time, her thoughts, to the cause of Christ. She did not spend her money on herself; she did not allow the homage paid to her rank to remain with herself; she passed these on, and offered them up to Him from whom her gifts came. She acted as one ought to act who considered this life a pilgrimage, not a home—like some holy nun, or professed ascetic, who had neither hopes nor fears of anything but what was divine and unseen.'

Benjamin Ingham was connected with the Countess by marriage and with the Wesleys by their early association together in the Holy Club and in Georgia. He also accompanied John Wesley on his visit to Herrnhut. He had been much impressed by the Moravians in Georgia and at Herrnhut he seems to have been preferred to Wesley by the Moravians, probably because he had already shown an inclination to leave the Church of England and to join them; also because 'his heart was better than his head', whereas Wesley seemed to allow his head to control his emotions. When Ingham returned home to Yorkshire to continue his evangelistic work there, he came more and more under Moravian influences. His Societies there should be regarded as the first fruits of Methodism in the north of England, although many of them were handed over later to the Moravians. After his marriage in 1741, he lived in Yorkshire till his death and, though Yorkshire was the chief scene of his missions, he was found helping other Methodist and Moravian preachers in other parts of the country. Whitefield and Grimshaw had a special regard for him, and Grimshaw would periodically take a preaching tour through Ingham's circuit.

His marriage caused a mild sensation in aristocratic circles. 'The news I hear from London', wrote Lady Mary Wortley Montagu from Rome, 'is that Lady Margaret Hastings has disposed of herself to a poor, wandering Methodist preacher.' Ingham was certainly a wandering Methodist preacher, but he was not particularly poor, and the marriage was a very happy one; husband and wife worked together in their high calling for twenty-seven years until her death. The Inghamite Societies were the first Methodist Societies to break with the Church of England. About 1753 he separated from the Moravians and, as the Lord's Supper was regularly administered in his Societies, they had no real association with the parish churches. Attempts were made that year, both at the Methodist Conference and at a special meeting arranged by Whitefield and Lady Huntingdon, to unite the Societies of Wesley and Ingham. Strange to say, it was Charles Wesley who favoured it, while his brother John held off. Ingham helped many causes. Both Moravianism and Methodism owed him much and Dissent also profited from his labours. The extensiveness of his work gives him his place among the leaders of the Revival, though he does not stand in the first rank. He was a very attractive and devoted minister of the Word when such men were few and far between.

John Cennick also belongs to this second rank of leaders of the Revival. He was one of the first lay preachers whom Wesley sent into the work. We have seen how he helped on the cleavage between Calvinist and Arminian in the early days at Kingswood. In October, 1760, Wesley wrote in his *Journal*: 'I visited the classes at Kingswood. Here only there is no increase; and yet, where was there such a prospect till that weak man, John Cennick, confounded the poor people with strange doctrines? Oh what mischief may be done by one that means well! We see no end of it to this day.' Probably Wesley felt this defection of Cennick the more because it marked the beginning of the divisions in the ranks of the Revival. A changeable man Cennick may have been, but his sacrificial labours for the remainder of his short life reveal few signs of weakness. After leaving Wesley, he joined forces first with Howell Harris and then with Whitefield. He faced much persecution in his open-air preaching in Wiltshire, but saw much success.

The Moravians attracted him more and more, and, after a visit to Germany, he joined their company, much to Whitefield's regret. Then in 1746 he began his campaign in Ireland, which was carried on chiefly in Dublin and Ulster practically until his death in 1755. His was a truly apostolic ministry of selfless devotion among the poorest of the poor. He forgot all controversy in the service of his Lord and the love of His people. He gathered together in Ulster no less than two hundred and twenty Societies, of which none remain. Wesley followed him to Dublin a year later and the Methodist work of evangelization began, which was destined to carry on in a much more effective way the cause to which Cennick had dedicated his life.

It is to Ireland also that we must turn for one of Wesley's best helpers. 'What man did I ever love like Thomas Walsh?' said Wesley in a letter to Benson, and in the Preface to Walsh's life, James Morgan, 'a member of the Church of England', declared about Walsh: 'Had he continued a member of the Roman communion and been as unweariedly laborious and successful in promoting the interests of Rome, as he was in promoting those of Jesus Christ, he might probably have stood fair for canonization.' Canonized he certainly was in the affection and esteem of his own people. The affectionate reverence for the memory of this young man, shown, not only by the Wesleys, but by such saints as John and Mary Fletcher, could only have been given to one of quite exceptional character.

Cennick died at thirty-six, worn out by his labours; Thomas Walsh was only twenty-eight when consumption claimed him as a victim. Hard work, violent treatment at the hands of mobs, exposure to weather cut short a life of great promise. The rustic, unpolished Irishman came like another John the Baptist to his fellow countrymen. His diary reads in places like that of a Spanish mystic. He knew the dark night of the soul, but he knew also the ecstasy of full communion. It is possible that he brought over from the Roman Catholicism of his upbringing some elements of religious feeling which gave a special tone to the expression of his evangelical experience, though there are surprising mystical visions and phrases to be found in many of the lives of Wesley's preachers. Yet Thomas Walsh was the *nonpareil*. He not only toiled for souls, for his own salvation and the salvation of those who heard him; he toiled for knowledge. A strange spiritual power accompanied his words and clothed his whole personality. When the storming crowd about him silenced his voice and he broke out into his native Irish speech in his excitement, the shouting and the tumult died away like the stilling of some great tempest into a calm.

He was as powerful in the awakening and salvation of sinners in London as in the farms and villages of his own country. At City Road, the lay preachers never occupied the pulpit when they preached there—except Thomas Walsh, who took the position as by right, none venturing to say him nay. That is a small but significant fragment of information, and we are not surprised that he dealt 'plainly and honestly' both with John and Charles Wesley. He has written a brief heroic page in Methodist history.

The love of life and learning, he said pathetically, was too deeply implanted within his heart. He could not rush at death with the joy of so many of his Methodist contemporaries, but at the end came the rapture. 'He at length burst out in transport, in a dying voice indeed, but with the joy of angels, "He is come! He is come! My beloved is mine and I am His!" ' Of his biblical learning, Wesley said: 'If he was questioned concerning any Hebrew word in the Old, or any Greek word in the New, Testament, he would tell after a little pause, not only how often the one or the other occurred in the Bible, but also what it meant in every place. Such a master of biblic knowledge I never saw before and never expect to see again.'

The idea that Wesley's helpers were a set of ignorant mechanics needs revision. Many of them were mechanics and tradesmen before they began to preach, but they were all instructed to read five hours a day if possible, and many of them became scholars. Wesley declared: 'I trust there is not one of them who is not able to go through such an examination in substantial, practical, experimental divinity, as few of our candidates for holy orders, even in the University (I speak it with sorrow and shame, and in tender love) are able to do.' In this goodly fellowship we may place John Nelson and Thomas Olivers among the leaders of the Revival. The three chosen as outstanding leaders among Wesley's many helpers represent Ireland, England, and Wales, and it would be very easy to find a Scotsman to go with them. Alexander Mather was an excellent representative of a true leader of men from the north country. It is the wealth of personality that embarrasses us as we turn over the pages of the six volumes of the *Lives of the Early Methodist Preachers*. We must accept our limitations of space.

Of John Nelson we have already spoken. He has a place of honour in *The Dictionary of National Biography*, where the Yorkshire stonemason is said to have exercised an influence on the Revival 'second only to that of John Wesley himself'. His own auto-biography deserves a place side by side with that of Bunyan, both for its contents and the strength and directness of its style. Stevens, the American historian of Methodism, considers that none of the lay preachers gave 'a more admirable example of heroism, of magnanimity, good sense, sound piety, hard work, and courageous suffering' than Nelson did. His funeral procession through the streets of Leeds to his native town of Birstall seems to have been one of the most moving spectacles ever seen in that grim town. Leeds was comparatively small in those days, but thousands followed the humble Methodist preacher to his grave 'as a grateful people follow a fallen hero who has helped to serve their country'.

Thomas Olivers may be still remembered as the author of that majestic hymn, 'The God of Abraham praise' and of several popular tunes, but before his conversion he was known as 'the cursing cobbler'. We have caught a glimpse of him and of his incomparable horse in his cool retreat from Yarmouth. He distinguished himself also in the Calvinistic controversy, and supported Fletcher in the defence of Wesley against the attacks of Toplady and the brothers Hill. Toplady began by despising this critic as a 'journeyman shoemaker, now retained by Wesley as a lay preacher, at the rate of ten pounds *per annum*'. He soon discovered that Olivers was quite equal to the task he had under-taken. When his opponents spoke of him scornfully as 'one Thomas Oliver, *alias* Olivers', Fletcher said: 'This author was twenty-five years ago a mechanic, and like one Peter, "alias" Simon a fisherman, and like one Saul, "alias" Paul a tentmaker, has had the honour of being promoted to the dignity of a preacher of the Gospel; and his talents as a writer, a logician, a poet, and a composer of sacred music, are known to those who have looked into his publications.'

Olivers shows himself to be a true Welshman in his vivid and racy autobiography. He has all the intensity of religious con-viction, the love of philosophical discussion, the ardour of the partisan which has been found so often among the children of the Principality. We can well believe that he was a most persuasive and convincing preacher. If he lacked the solid, honest Yorkshire strength of John Nelson, he had the dash and verve of the born fighter. The contrast between the two men is that between the infantryman who takes his hard pounding without flinching and the cavalryman who sweeps the enemy from the field of battle. It was with the help of numbers of such 'good soldiers of Jesus Christ' that Wesley carried on his great campaign for the soul of England. The part they played in building up a fellowship of a hundred thousand members should not be forgotten. One cannot read the story of these years without being impressed by this rich variety of personality found among this band of brothers. It is not surprising that there were some clashes and disputes, even though they had a common aim and obeyed a common call. Of this 'lovely company', however, it is John Wesley who stands out pre-eminent in leadership at the beginning, and it is the same impressive little figure that remains pre-eminent at the end.

(b) PARISH CLERGY

Wesley believed that the parochial system was unequal to the needs of a decadent Church. At its best it seemed the ideal scheme for a country in which Christianity had been established for more than a thousand years. That ideal did not merely aim at 'a gentleman in every parish', but at a man of God in every parish as the shepherd of souls, the leader of Christian worship, and the preacher of righteousness. The old ideal of such a parish priest had long been cherished:

> That Cristës gospel trewëly wolde preche;
> His parischens devoutly wolde he teche.
> But Cristë's lore, and his apostles twelve,
> He taughte, but first he folwede it himselve.

How far the eighteenth-century clergy fell short of this ideal can only be estimated from an intimate and wide knowledge of town and country. We have many records of drunken and sporting clergy and much evidence of livings held merely 'for a loaf of bread'. That there were multitudes of decent, well-meaning parish priests cannot be doubted. Wesley declared that he dare not say that one in ten of the clergy he knew were 'zealous for inward, solid virtue'. The parish churches where the fervour of evangelical faith and love glowed must have been rare indeed.

Was not Wesley right in concluding that a new life of devotion was unlikely to come to the Church of England through the comfortable occupation of livings by indifferent and incompetent incumbents? The country seemed to him to cry out for apostles, and he became one himself and stimulated many others. Early in the reign of George III, Blackstone used to go from church to church in London to hear every clergyman of note. He declared that he did not hear a single discourse that had more Christianity in it than the writings of Cicero. Romaine would pray by name for all the evangelical clergy he knew. The whole number at first did not exceed eight; before his death he could count more than five hundred. Earnest men longed for the day when there should be such a leader in every parish, but that day seemed far distant. An extraordinary mission to the heart of pagan England was needed; the harvest was plenteous, but the labourers were few. Can we be surprised that Wesley said about Fletcher: 'I can never believe that it was the will of God that such a burning and shining light should be "hid under a bushel". No; instead of being confined to a country village, it should have shone in every corner of the land.'

Wesley came back again and again to the problem of his itinerants. He disliked irregularity but could see no other way of reaching the masses of the people. He discussed the problem at length with two of the few evangelical clergy, Thomas Adam of Wintringham and Samuel Walker of Truro: 'I see the blind leading the blind and both falling into the ditch. Unless I warn in all ways I can these perishing souls of their danger, am I clear of the blood of these men? Soul-damning clergymen lay me under more difficulties than soul-saving laymen.' Walker wanted him to get some of his lay preachers ordained and settle others with Societies rather 'as inspectors and readers than preachers'. Wesley pointed out that he had thirty-four Societies in Cornwall, stretching from Devonport to St. Just, for the service of which he had only four preachers. He showed the value of his circuit system, and then went on to a new point when he argued that it was not the Lord's will 'that any congregation should have one teacher only'. He believed in the use of the varied gifts of different teachers: 'I know, were I myself to preach one whole year in one place, I should preach both myself and most of my congregation asleep.'

He believed that an itinerant ministry was a much more effective instrument of the Kingdom of God than a settled ministry. There was something in his argument as it applied to Adam at Wintringham and even to his old friend, Vincent Perronet at Shoreham. Adam and Perronet could show but little achievement in their long ministries. Henry Venn said of Adam, who was fifty-nine years in his cure, that his success was 'exceedingly small' after thirty years of Gospel preaching. The career of Walker was much shorter. He went as curate to Truro

in 1746, a worldly young man who had read a little theology and
was anxious to be popular as a preacher. He was converted by the
influence of the master of the local Grammar School, and a great
change took place both in his preaching and his popularity.
However, little by little men and women were gathered into the
fold of a living Christian fellowship. In 1754 he divided his
Society into two classes, one of unmarried men, the other of
married men and their wives, with the unmarried women. He
found, as the Moravians, Ingham, and Wesley had found, the
great value of regular meetings of these Societies. He left Truro
in ill health in 1760 and died the next year. After his death the
members of his Society were reluctant to accept the ministrations
of his successor, whom they regarded as an unregenerate man.
They therefore seceded from the parish church and formed the
nucleus of a new Independent congregation. It was probably
the doctrine of the Methodists that prevented the Society from
joining the Wesleyan group, for Walker was a Calvinist: 'Abso-
lutely a Scot in his opinions', said Wesley, 'but of an excellent
spirit.' He had attended some of Wesley's Conferences, but
differed from him on more subjects than one. He thought that
Wesley should hand over his Societies to the incumbent of the
parish, when he was an Evangelical.

Henry Venn, who was as successful at Huddersfield as Walker
was at Truro, thought the same. Wesley found it a difficult
question to decide, but ended by refusing to withdraw his
preachers from such parishes. His first care was not for
Methodism but for the service of the work of God. It was
dangerous to interfere with a real work of grace anywhere, and one
could never guarantee that a sympathetic incumbent would be
followed by another of the same character. Venn had a great
ministry at Huddersfield, but the Methodists were there before him.
Indeed, according to John Pawson, it was through Methodist
influence that Venn became Vicar there. Although the Societies
had been formed at the hazard of the lives of the preachers,
Wesley withdrew his preachers for several years at Venn's request,
'to the unspeakable grief of our Society'. However, Huddersfield
was a strategic centre to what they regarded as a dreadful
wilderness, and the Methodist preachers found their way back
without Wesley's permission. Wesley had said: 'Where there is a
gospel ministry already we do not desire to preach; but whether

we can leave off preaching because such an one comes after is another question, especially when those who were awakened and convinced by us beg and require the continuance of our assist-ance. I love peace and follow it, but whether I am at liberty to purchase it at such a price I really cannot tell.'

Venn was a moderate Calvinist and was not enamoured of Wesley's teaching on Christian perfection. To his daughter he wrote: 'I am not sorry you have heard Mr. W.—a very extra-ordinary man, but not to be believed in his assertions about perfection.' His ministry at Huddersfield lasted from 1759 to 1771, when, on grounds of health, he became Rector of Yelling in Huntingdonshire. As in the case of Walker, his removal led to the establishment of a strong Congregational Church by his followers in Huddersfield. He hoped that they would at least keep to the liturgy in their services, but in this he was disappointed. In 1768 Wesley had written to Adam of Wintringham concerning his own relation to the Church of England: 'We are in truth so far from being enemies to the Church that we are rather bigots to it. I dare not, like Mr. Venn, leave the parish church where I am to go to an Independent meeting. I dare not advise others to go there rather than to church.'

Venn was friendly with Ingham, Hervey, and especially with the Countess of Huntingdon, whom he regarded as 'a star of the first magnitude in the firmament of the Church'. Indeed, he was on friendly terms with most of the evangelical leaders of all schools of thought. His association with Clapham is important in the story of the Evangelicals in the Church of England. He was a curate there for five years before he went to Huddersfield, and it was to Clapham he retired for the last months of his life when his son was Rector there. His great friend John Thornton died there a few months before he did. It would seem as though the years he spent at Yelling ministering to twenty or thirty rustics were lost to the cause of the Revival. He preached in farmers' houses and barns in the neighbourhood, also occasionally for the Countess of Huntingdon and Rowland Hill. He was, however, only twelve miles from Cambridge and influenced several undergraduates who were to play an important part in the service of the Church. Of these Charles Simeon is of most consequence in this story; he was a friend of Henry Venn's son John, and was not only in-fluenced by them but influenced them in his turn, chiefly against

H

'irregularity'. It is significant that John Venn, who wrote his father's Life, and, still more, Henry Venn, jun., who edited it, pruned it as far as possible of all references to preachings for Dissenters and the more irregular aspects of Venn's ministry.

He was most at home with men like Whitefield and Howell Harris and with the Countess, who shared his catholic attitude to all who loved the Lord Jesus in sincerity. 'Dear Mr. Fletcher' was a special favourite with him, though he was somewhat shaken by the heat of the Calvinist controversy. Some years after its fury had died down, Fletcher and Venn stayed together for six weeks at the house of Mr. Ireland of Brislington, near Bristol. Ireland resembled John Thornton in his hospitality and in his generous support of the Methodist movement. Venn says: 'I told him [Fletcher] freely that I was very shocked at many things in his *Checks* and pointed them out to him. We widely differed about the efficacy of Christ's death, the nature of Justification and the Perfection of the Saints; but I believe we could live years together in great love. . . . He desired his love by me to all his Calvinistic brethren; and begged their pardon for the asperity with which he had written. I am persuaded, as I told him, that if he were to live with some of those he had been taught to conceive of as Antinomian and heard them preach, he would be much more reconciled to them.' The kind of Antinomianism that Fletcher opposed was well expressed by Rowland Hill in his reply to one of the *Checks*: 'David stood as completely justified in the ever-lasting righteousness of Christ, at the time when he caused Uriah to be murdered, and was committing adultery with his wife, as he was in any part of his life. For all the sins of the elect, be they more or be they less, be they past, present or to come, were for ever done away: so that every one of those elect stands spotless in the sight of God.' Probably Venn would have been a little shocked at such extravagance. He did aim at the good life, and his devotional book, *The Complete Duty of Man*, was one of the most popular religious books of the century, but Puritan rather than Anglican in its theology.

Venn's ministry at Huddersfield was in part contemporaneous with that of William Grimshaw at Haworth. Grimshaw, like Venn, was a Cambridge man, but he entered Christ's College sixteen years before Venn went up to Jesus. His conversion took place when he was curate at Todmorden and before he had made any acquaintance with the Methodists. It was in 1742 that he moved to Haworth, where he remained until his death in 1769. There he soon met the Methodist preachers and found that they were engaged in the work to which he himself was called. Ingham showed him the value of forming Societies, with a leader responsible for each class. So he became an itinerant preacher and formed Societies in the approved style. He was so irregular that his circuit soon covered a large part of East Lancashire and the West Riding. It was only his duties as incumbent of Haworth that prevented him from becoming another Wesley or Whitefield.

Charles Wesley he met in 1746 and so began a fellowship with the Wesleys, which was unbroken until Grimshaw's death. Very often they preached in Haworth Church and often, too, he shared with them the perils and adventures of open-air preaching. The Societies grew and flourished, and Grimshaw must have been a great trial to his brother clerics, into whose parishes he entered without seeking permission. It is said that they complained to the Archbishop of York, who said to Grimshaw at his next visitation: 'It has been stated to me that you not only preach in private houses in your parish, but also travel up and down and preach where you have a mind, without consulting either your diocesan or the clergy into whose parishes you obtrude your labours; and that your discourses are very loose; that, in fact, you can, and do, preach about anything. That I may be able to judge for myself both of your doctrine and your manner of stating it, I give you notice, that I shall expect you to preach before me and the clergy present, in two hours hence, and from the text which I am about to name.' Grimshaw pointed to the great congregation and begged that the order of the service might not be changed by putting the Confirmation service first, but that one of the clergy should read the prayers and he would preach at once. He preceded his sermon with such a pleading, extempore prayer and preached with such power that the archbishop said: 'I would to God that all the clergy in my diocese were like this good man.' The same evening Grimshaw said to his friends: 'I did expect to be turned out of my parish on this occasion; but if I had, I would have joined my friend Wesley, taken my saddle bags, and gone to one of his poorest circuits.'[1]

[1] Rev. A. Strachan's *Life and Times of Rev. G. Lowe*, p. 37. Not otherwise authenticated, but it sounds like Grimshaw and not unlike Archbishop Herring. A similar tale is told of Thompson of St. Gennys and the Bishop of Exeter.

The Societies that Grimshaw formed became part of Wesley's organization; he himself was named in trusts of new Methodist chapels as a holding trustee in succession to the Wesley brothers if they predeceased him; he also regularly attended Wesley's Conferences whenever they were held at Leeds. He visited classes, regularly giving tickets to the members, attended love-feasts and quarterly meetings, and constantly preached in Methodist chapels. He was equally friendly with Whitefield and probably nearer to him in his doctrinal position. It was said of him that he was more of a Calvinist after a visit by Whitefield and more of an Arminian after Wesley had visited him. There is an account preserved of a memorable service of Whitefield at Haworth in September, 1749, when there were six thousand hearers in the churchyard and a thousand communicants in the church. The Countess of Huntingdon and Lady Margaret Hastings were in the congregation. The sudden death of a man in the great crowd created a great sensation; the more so since Whitefield had just announced the alarming text, 'It is appointed unto man once to die, but after this the judgement'. Another death soon followed, and the fierce rush of emotion through the great congregation can be imagined as the undisturbed preacher went on with his message.

Grimshaw was the sort of character about whom tales are told round the countryside for generations. He was anxious that the evangelical witness should not fail at Haworth after his death, and got a Methodist chapel built there to that end. Yet he was a strong churchman and was as anxious as Charles Wesley that the Methodists should never leave the Church. He loved the Methodist preachers, listened to them with great joy, and told several of Wesley's lay helpers that he was unworthy to follow in their steps. He did not react in the same way to Dissenters, and disliked the advent of the Baptists into Haworth; yet he collected subscriptions for an Independent chapel at Halifax, though he would not preach in a building licensed for Dissenters. This great-hearted shepherd of souls was not ruled by logic; it was the power of divine love that carried him on his indefatigable journeys over the moors and mountains to the little congregations that awaited his coming. His plain, outspoken honesty and vigour of homely speech won its way to the hearts of a rough moorland people; it changed the lives of thousands who had at first opposed him. Alarming, humorous, tender, unresting, without a particle

of selfishness or pride in his make-up, he followed his own sheep
over the mountains and cared for the lambs of the flock in the
fold. Haworth to-day may be a place of pilgrimage because of the
fame of a later and more romantic name, but it is not possible to
understand the Brontës unless you have first met with William
Grimshaw. It may be that Grimshaw deserves as high a place on
the roll of national honour as the tragic sisterhood of a later
Haworth Parsonage. It was Venn who preached his funeral
sermon to the great company that had followed over the hills
from Haworth to Luddenden. His last words were: 'Here goes
an unprofitable servant.'

William Romaine was for many years regarded as being the
only well-known Evangelical who held a regular position in any
of the London churches. For nearly twenty years he was merely a
lecturer in one of the City churches or at St. George's, Hanover
Square. He did not receive preferment to a living until he was
well over fifty, when he became Rector of St. Anne's, Blackfriars,
in 1766. That so able and devout a man should find such difficulty
in finding an appropriate sphere of service in the Established
Church and should meet with such hostility in his lectureships, is
a sidelight on the religious temper of the Church of England.

Like Fletcher and Perronet, he was of Huguenot descent,
brought up with such Puritanical strictness that he was never
allowed by his father to go out of the house on Sundays except to
church. He preserved something of this morose severity throughout his life and would have been helped by that touch of humour
which enlivened Grimshaw, Berridge, and Rowland Hill. His
Calvinism grew out of an overwhelming sense of sin. 'If I had
only been in the school of Moses to learn', he once said, 'I should
with such views of sin have hanged myself long ago.' With this,
however, went an intense faith in the power of the Atonement,
'that offering of Jesus which perfecteth for ever'. He was at
Oxford with the Wesleys, but does not seem to have known them
there. His associations with them later were chiefly through their
common friendship with the Countess of Huntingdon. In 1759
we find Romaine with Wesley at the great revival in Berridge's
parish of Everton. Wesley speaks of Romaine's propriety as a
preacher, and it seems likely that the manifestations of excitement
at Everton puzzled Romaine considerably. If Wesley found open-
air preaching a cross, it was a still greater cross to Romaine. He

disliked also the growing use of hymns in religious services, and seems of the school of Howe and the seventeenth-century Puritans in many of his predilections.

We find him with Venn and Wesley in July, 1761, at the house of a niece of the Countess in Yorkshire, reading prayers while Wesley preached on 'Christ crucified, to the Jews a stumbling-block and to the Greeks foolishness'. The preacher's comment was: 'Oh, why should they who agree on this great point fall out about smaller things.' He attended Wesley's Leeds Conference in 1762, but a year later, when Wesley had trouble over the wild prophecies of Bell and Maxfield, many of the Calvinists seemed rather pleased by these disorders and attributed them to the preachings on perfection. 'Only Mr. Romaine has shown a truly sympathizing spirit', said Wesley. However, Mr. Romaine was writing at that time to the Countess about 'poor Mr. John' and fearing that the Methodist Societies were in great confusion. He made no reply the following year to Wesley's appeal to the evangelical clergy to form a union of love and service and, when the controversy over Wesley's *Minutes* broke out in 1771, he came into the field against him in the *Gospel Magazine*, of which he was then Editor. It must have been of Wesley he was thinking when he wrote to a friend the same year: 'I have done with names—great authority—and living popes—for we have an English pope. In opposition to whom I am a protestant. I protest against the merit of works and all its long, long train of errors; but I won't dispute with any pope. I will rather pray for him as I do. God open his eyes and turn him from darkness to light, from blind popery into gospel liberty.'

He wrote three books on faith that were widely read, but Wesley wrote to one of his correspondents warning her against Romaine's books, which were 'brimful of Antinomianism'. It is pleasant to find these two old associates together in friendly converse at Mr. Ireland's a few months before Wesley's death. They managed to resume friendship, but could hardly be in complete agreement in opinion. In temperament, too, they differed greatly. Romaine's manner was close and reserved and he seemed quick and irritable in conversation. He was impressive in utterance without any special grace of style; the sincerity and strength of his convictions carried his hearers along. Certainly few leaders of the eighteenth-century Evangelicals were regarded with so much esteem; his influence spread far and wide.

Vincent Perronet was named by Charles Wesley the archbishop of the Methodists. For forty years John Wesley turned to him constantly for counsel and help and never found him lacking. He was Wesley's senior by ten years and, in the opinion of one who knew him well, 'entitled to a conspicuous place amongst the brightest ornaments of the Christian Church in the last century'. He might have filled any position with dignity, but remained for fifty years vicar of the little village of Shoreham in Kent. He was blessed with a large family, all of whom were devoted to the work of God. Two of his sons became Methodist preachers and were found in dangerous places in the field. Edward Perronet is remembered to-day by his hymn, 'All hail the power of Jesu's name', and Charles Perronet was very much of a mystic and an enthusiast. Wesley speaks of him as a 'saint strangely afflicted by suffering'.

Both the brothers shared with Thomas Walsh the opinion that the Methodists should separate from the Established Church and that the preachers should regularly administer the sacraments to the Methodist people. Wesley said about the discussion of this question at the Leeds Conference in 1755: 'Here is Charles Perronet raving "because his friends have given up *all*" and Charles Wesley "because they have given up *nothing*"; and I in the midst staring and wondering at both, at one and at the other. I do not want to do anything more, unless I could bring them both over to my opinion; and I am not in haste for that.' Such are the difficulties of the moderate man. It was Vincent Perronet who first used the term, *the Methodist Church*, even in letters to Charles Wesley who must have regarded such an expression with extreme disapprobation. But Vincent Perronet believed that Methodism was raised up by God for the rapid spread of the Christian religion throughout the world. He turned his parish into something like a Methodist circuit and held a Society class weekly in his own vicarage. All his family were members of this 'Methodist Church'. For many years he saw little success in his labours and was met with much coldness and opposition. All this changed in the later years of his life and the parish was transformed. The Society grew into three classes, which met at the same hour in his house, and prayer meetings were held at many other houses in the village, including two of the three public houses. The Methodist preachers were ever welcome at that hospitable vicarage, and Shoreham came to be regarded as one of the chief centres of awakened Christianity.

What was true of Shoreham in Kent was equally true of Madeley in Shropshire after John Fletcher became vicar there. It is almost impossible to speak of Fletcher without using language which seems exaggerated. The universal testimony to the beauty and power of his character is so marked that it must be true. He was born in Switzerland and changed his name, de la Flechère, to Fletcher when he settled in England. Ordained in London in 1757, he was to be found the same day helping Wesley at the administration of the Lord's Supper at West Street Chapel. Wesley was his first spiritual guide when he came to England; then he fell under the influence of the Countess of Huntingdon and we find him writing to Charles Wesley and saying: 'We have need of you to make one in our threefold cord.' This new union was to have been between the Countess, Charles, and Fletcher. A little later he is using Perronet's expression, 'the Methodist Church' in talking to Charles, speaking of himself as a beggar receiving alms from the Methodists. He visited Berridge at Everton and then, in 1760, from the Hill family he received the living of Madeley. His induction was opposed on the grounds that he was a Methodist and not a naturalized subject. Twenty-five years of devoted labour were given to his widespread parish and every household felt the influence of his saintly character.

Three or four years before his death he married Mary Bosanquet, another of the saints of early Methodism. They had met twenty-five years before and it was a case of love at first sight, but Fletcher said: 'She was too rich for me to think of; so I banished every thought of marriage.' This decision gave Mary Bosanquet the opportunity for much social and religious work in her little communities at Leytonstone and, later, in Yorkshire. It also prepared her for the work she was destined to do at Madeley. She was a true helpmeet to her husband during the few years of their married life and a devoted servant of the Gospel after his death. They built several chapels in the neighbourhood for the Methodist Societies, kindred spirits to their friends the Perronets. They were concerned for the good training of children and provided both day and Sunday schools through their parish for this purpose. Wesley believed that Fletcher was the man pointed out by God to carry on the work after his death; but the younger man died first. Threatened for long by consumption, he had worn himself out by his toils. At one time he gave fourteen, fifteen, or sixteen hours a day to study. In his parish his visitation and pastoral duties kept him constantly at work. By constant self-denial, he was able to give generous help to the poorest of his flock. 'If I had a body full of vigour', he said, 'and a purse full of money, I should like well enough to travel about as Mr. Wesley does; but as Providence does not call me to it I readily submit. The snail does best in its shell: were it to aim at galloping like the race-horse it would be ridiculous indeed.'

The accounts of his death and the overwhelming sorrow of his parishioners and friends are deeply moving. Wesley said of him: 'Within four score years I have known many excellent men, holy in heart and life: but one equal to him I have not known; one so uniformly and deeply devoted to God. So unblameable a man in every respect, I have not found either in Europe or America; nor do I expect to find another such on this side eternity.' The graciousness of Fletcher's character, whether as seen in his charitable and catholic temper towards all men or in his unstinting service to those who needed him most, may seem alien to the vigour of his attack on extreme Calvinist tenets. He spared himself nothing in his defence of Wesley's *Minutes* against Toplady and the brothers Hill, for, like F. W. Robertson, he had wished to be a soldier before he found himself in the ranks of the Church. He went into action like a good soldier of truth and never regretted that he was called to defend the faith. Even his opponents found little to criticize in the temper of his *Checks*; of their effectiveness there is little doubt. It is significant that it was Fletcher who had the heart of the peacemaker (as he showed most powerfully on more than one critical occasion), who was the chief protagonist for universal redemption when the discussion was at its hottest. He was a great lover of his fellow men, but he loved truth above all. We may pause at Voltaire's tribute to him and yet partly understand it.

John Berridge of Everton in Bedfordshire was another of the Methodist clergy settled in remote villages. He was a scholar who occasionally preached before the University of Cambridge, but his popular, humorous style tended to lower men's estimate of his real gifts. He was an eccentric bachelor, who avoided matrimony as it seemed to him to have been a disastrous experiment with Whitefield and Wesley and to have quite spoiled 'poor Charles'. He became vicar of Everton in 1755. Wesley became acquainted with him three years later when he preached at Everton. He said: 'For many years he [Berridge] was seeking to be justified by his works; but a few months ago he was thoroughly convinced that "by grace we are saved through faith". Immediately he began to proclaim aloud the redemption that is in Jesus and God confirmed His word exactly as He did at Bristol, in the beginning, by working repentance and faith in the hearers and with the same violent outward symptoms.' The Everton revival in 1758 and 1759 spread into the neighbouring villages and was marked by the greatest excitement, trances, convulsions, and bodily contortions.

Wesley was very interested and rather perplexed, as he had been at the sight of similar phenomena under his own preaching twenty years before. He attributed some of this work to the power of God and some to the mimicry of the devil. He was more cautious about the whole question now than he had been at the beginning and used to advise his preachers 'carefully to avoid enthusiasm'. As he said two or three years later, 'the reproach of Christ I am willing to bear; but not the reproach of enthusiasm, if I can help it'. Yet he gladly welcomed Berridge as a fellow worker in the same field. We find Berridge helping Wesley at his great meeting of the London Societies on New Year's Day, 1762, when two thousand Methodists renewed the Covenant and took Communion at Spitalfields Chapel. But Berridge was a strong Calvinist and also a strong supporter of the Countess of Huntingdon. He joined in the fray over the 1770 Minutes, and enlivened the discussion by attacking Fletcher in Mr. Fulsome's Antinomian Creed. His sense of humour, however, kept him from the excessive bitterness of some of his associates, though it is remarkable that the Countess should have tolerated some of his witticisms.[1] Newman quotes at length one of Berridge's letters to her Ladyship, and comments dryly: 'What Lady Huntingdon thought of this singular style does not appear.'

Her biographer, however, was not lacking in his admiration for this singular man. He gives an attractive picture of him and then

---

[1] See, for example, The English Church in the Eighteenth Century, Abbey and Overton, II, pp. 123–4.

goes on to say: 'For twenty-four years he continued to ride nearly one hundred miles and to preach some ten or twelve sermons every week. At home, for his hearers who came from a distance, his table was served, and his stables were open for their horses; and abroad, houses and barns were rented, lay preachers supplied, and his own expenses paid out of his own pocket. His ear was ever attentive to the tale of woe; his eye was keen to observe the miseries of the poor; the law of kindness was written upon his heart, and his hand was always ready to administer relief. The gains of his vicarage, of his fellowship, and of his patrimonial income (for his father died very rich), and even his family plate, were appropriated to support his liberality.' It is Grimshaw whom he most resembles in the company of parish clergy who were also itinerants in their own locality, but his work was less enduring because he failed to build up the Societies according to the pattern of Wesley and the Moravians. His invasion of the parishes of his fellow clergy was challenged by the Bishop of Lincoln, who warned him that if he continued that practice he might find himself in Huntingdon Gaol. The bishop could make nothing of him and said that he was out of his mind and would be better or worse in a few months. Berridge gives the report of this interview himself: ' "Then, my lord," said I, "you may make yourself quite happy in this business; for if I should be better you suppose I should desist of my own accord; if worse you need not send me to Huntingdon Gaol, for I shall be better accommodated in Bedlam." ' It is gratifying to know that he did not finish his days in Bedlam. Wesley regarded him as one of the most sensible of men.

John Newton is one of the most attractive of the Evangelical clergy. He has been completely misrepresented as the evil genius of Cowper; a gloomy bigot whose morbid influence drove the poet into insanity. It is impossible to read Newton's letters without knowing that cannot be an accurate picture. We find there a man of strong common sense, kindly and genial. His letters lack the grace and charm of Cowper's, but they are very readable. So also his hymns are inferior to those of Cowper, but they do not seem out of place in the volume they published together. The true relations between the two men are given in Newton's own account. Of their twelve years together at Olney (1766–78), Newton says: 'We were seldom separated twelve hours at a time, when we were awake and at home. The first six I passed in daily admiring and trying to imitate him, during the second six I pensively walked with him in the valley of the shadow of death.' The tender and sympathetic devotion of Newton to Cowper deserved a better treatment than it has received at the hands of writers who have not grasped the quality of Newton's Calvinism. He certainly was a Calvinist, and it is not surprising that the old slave-trader should have preserved through life a deep sense of wonder at the power of God's grace in his case. 'Considering what I was in Africa and what the Lord has done for me since, my case seems an unique one in the annals of the Church', he says. He believed that his conversion was due to his mother's prayers, but, once on the way to heaven, he was never in any doubt again. 'I am in no more doubt about the way of salvation', he said, 'than of the way to London.'

Wesley met him at Liverpool in 1758 and again in 1760, and was indignant that such a man was refused ordination because of his lack of a university education. For some time Newton laboured among Dissenters, but, by the influence of the Earl of Dartmouth, he was ordained and was given the living of Olney, and, after that, of St. Mary Woolnoth in the City. He had many friends among the Nonconformists and frequently would change pulpits with Independent preachers. To a Baptist minister he wrote: 'Whether a *surplice* or a *band* be the fittest distinction of a minister, whether he be best ordained by the *laying on* or the *holding off* of hands; whether water baptism should be administered by a spoon-full or a tub-full, or in a river, or in Jordan are to me points of no great importance. I will go further. Though a man does not accord with my views of election and yet if he gives me good evidence that he is *effectually called* of God, he is my brother. If he loves Jesus I will love him: whatever hard name he may be called by and whatever incidental mistakes I may think he holds.' Wesley corresponded with him in the same spirit, but Newton had difficulty over Christian perfection. When Wesley explained that he simply meant that the Christian should give God all his heart, they agreed that such a doctrine was not so blasphemous a thing as most Calvinists believed it to be. Newton became friendly with the Thorntons, Wilberforce, Thomas Scott, and Hannah More, and so is an important name in the record of the development of the Anglican Evangelical school.

James Hervey (1714-58) was one of the Oxford Methodists. He belongs to the story of the Revival, though he never became an itinerant preacher and was content to serve within the limits of his small parish. He is remembered by his writings. Of them Tyerman said in 1873: 'Few books have passed through more editions than his have done; and after a lapse of a hundred years since this author's death, few are greater favourites at the present day.' If that was true in 1873, it is certainly not true now. No one but a specialist would now dream of reading Hervey's *Meditations among the Tombs* or *Theron and Aspasio*. His florid and verbose style is now out-moded and repels rather than attracts by its effort: 'to have the apples of gold, which are the truths of our holy religion, set in pictures of silver'. Theological arguments about justification by faith and the imputed righteousness of Christ, illustrated from the Articles and the Homilies, are not made attractive to us by genteel walks through gardens and hayfields or even by voyages down a river. These queer books had their day and, as we glance through them in our amused and detached way, we see that we have moved into a different world. Wesley criticized the manuscript so pungently that a very old friendship was shaken. 'How hard it is', he said, 'to be superficial enough for a polite audience.'

It was the 'imputed righteousness' with its tendency toward Antinomianism that Wesley attacked. It is sad to read in one of Hervey's letters, 'I can never forget that tender-hearted and generous Fellow of Lincoln, who condescended to take such compassionate notice of a poor undergraduate, whom almost every one condemned and for whose soul no man cared', and then to find that his last months were spent in replying to the same Fellow of Lincoln. His letters on the subject were published after his death and there is some question as to how far they have been 'edited'. They were certainly published against Hervey's own wish expressed when he was dying. It was one of the cases where John Wesley's frankness proved bad policy. Hervey's attack caused him real pain and weakened his influence in Scotland, where Hervey's books had a large sale.

Hervey had been troubled by the itinerant preaching of Whitefield and the Wesleys at the beginning, but remained friendly with them all until his unfortunate breach with John Wesley over *Theron and Aspasio*. He was curate of Bideford for a

time and then curate and (after his father's death) rector of
Weston Favel in Northamptonshire. This was a family living
and it was there that consumption claimed him as a victim at the
age of forty-four. Though a loyal Anglican, he seems to have been
more friendly with Dissenters than with his own people. He was
a true Evangelical, forming Societies of believers and preaching the
Gospel with a Calvinistic emphasis; a gentle, delicate man with a
most unselfish and devoted spirit. Neither his physique nor his
sense of vocation would allow him to forsake the duties of a country
parson which he did so well. Wesley might write to him, 'the
world is my parish', but his parish was Weston Favel. There
and in his writing his one task was 'to recommend his dear
Redeemer'.

Augustus Toplady (1740–78) is said by his biographer to be
'the legitimate successor of Hervey', and Toplady himself speaks of
'the seraphic Mr. Hervey'. In some respects they resembled each
other, in spite of the fact that if Toplady is ever mentioned to-day
it is either as the author of 'Rock of ages' or because of his abusive,
controversial style. He is said to have been loved by his parishioners and also to have been a pious and kindly man. One could
never guess that if he were known merely by his virulent attacks
on Wesley. It was under the preaching of one of Wesley's lay
preachers in a barn in some remote part of Ireland that he was
converted. He was slow to acknowledge this in later years. In
1768 he became vicar of Broad Hembury, near Honiton in
South Devon. Like Hervey then, he worked in a remote, country
village; like him, too, he died in early middle life. Both of them
were Calvinists who fell out with John Wesley on that very
prickly subject; but Hervey could never have indulged in
Toplady's scurrility.

In his pamphlet, *An Old Fox tarred and feathered*, he calls Wesley
'a low and puny tadpole in divinity', and in his *More Work for
Mr. John Wesley* he rakes up every possible and impossible slander
against the veteran servant of God, who had reached the three
score years and ten of man's pilgrimage and was old enough to
be Toplady's father. We do not wonder that Wesley said: 'Mr.
Toplady I know well; but I do not fight with chimney-sweepers'.
He left him to Sellon, Olivers, and Fletcher. The violence of the
attack on Wesley cannot be accounted for merely by the *odium
theologicum*. There is too much bitter, personal feeling to allow

that this heat was merely generated by questions of predestination and election. Toplady's biographer says of Wesley that 'his understanding, strictly speaking, was but ordinary. His imagination was fertile in littleness. If a prize had been given for dullness and the most superlative conceit, this gentleman might have started with a certainty of triumph'.

These judgements are so notoriously false that they raise the problem how honest men could ever have formed them. We see the eighteenth century in perspective, and at this distance Wesley's greatness, as compared with that of his contemporaries, is crystal clear. We also tend to judge them by their reaction to him. They themselves would be astonished at the judgement of posterity. Wesley himself was quite conscious of his own high calling. His judgement was so clear and incisive; his manner was imperious, though his stature was small; his frankness and courage paid little attention to the hyper-sensitive and egotistic reactions of his hearers. He was so much the embodiment of glorified common sense that his utterances must often have been infuriating to those who imagined their own sense was far from ordinary. Occasionally he could talk like a superior don to a company of undergraduates of less than average intelligence. He could certainly write a very rough letter.

Many of his fellow workers in the Revival were jealous of his amazing success, though he knew nothing of any jealousy towards them. He once wrote to the Earl of Dartmouth: 'From many little circumstances which have occurred, I have been afraid (just so far it went) that these clergymen with whom you are most acquainted were jealous of your being acquainted with me.' To Joseph Benson he wrote: 'Whatever I say it will be all one. They will find fault because I say it. There is implicit envy at my power (so called) and a jealousy rising therefrom.' Even the great Countess of Huntingdon was not entirely free from this infirmity. Wesley longed to see the whole company of Evangelical preachers and sympathizers banded together in a close fellowship of love and service. He could not understand why differences on what he considered to be secondary points should keep them apart. He never dreamed that a full and honest statement of one's own point of view could be resented. Indeed, the only way of progress was to speak out all that was in your heart and see if your brother could accept it or not. That is why he wrote his letter to fifty or sixty of the Evangelical clergy in November, 1761. That is perhaps also the reason why only three ventured to answer his letter.

It is a fine letter and stresses works as well as faith. He gives a list of those who agree on (1) Original Sin, (2) Justification by Faith, and (3) Holiness of Heart and Life, but it is too long for insertion here. (See *Letters*, IV, pp. 236 ff.)

It closes with a quotation from the *Imitation of Christ*. 'When Mr. Conyers was objecting the possibility of ever effecting such an union, I went upstairs, and after a little prayer opened Kempis on these words: *Expecta Dominum: viriliter age: noli diffidere: noli discedere; sed corpus et animam expone constanter pro gloria Dei.*'

Chapter XI

THE REVIVAL AND DISSENT

IT has been stated the Dissenters, in comparison with the Anglicans at the beginning of the eighteenth century, were as one to twenty-two; at the end of the century the proportion had increased to one to eight. These figures cannot be accepted as exact, but there is no doubt concerning the great increase in the strength of Dissent between 1700 and 1800. If the proportion of 1800 is approximately correct, it does not include the members of the Methodist Societies, as they did not regard themselves as Dissenters. In the latter part of the nineteenth century most estimates of the numbers of practising Anglicans and Nonconformists showed that the two camps were nearly equal in strength; by that time, however, the Methodists were counted with the other Nonconformists, and the residue of the population (other than Roman Catholic) was no longer regarded as Anglican.

John Wesley, in spite of his Nonconformist ancestry, had a distinct dislike for Dissent and was particularly out of favour with Baptists and Quakers. He could give generous praise to the martyrs of 1662 and speak of them as the very salt of the earth, but his rule was, 'I never go to meeting'. He was on friendly terms with Doddridge and a few other leading Nonconformists, but the bulk of the ministers in the Nonconformist Churches were strict Calvinists who regarded him with disfavour. Those who were Unitarians, or had Unitarian tendencies, were equally unfriendly. Politically, also, he was opposed to them, for he was a Tory, while they were Whigs or Radicals for the most part. Over the American Revolution, 'all the dissenters are with us', said Franklin; John Wesley, after some wavering, took the opposite side, supporting the Government. Whitefield, fortunately for himself, died before the Revolution broke out. He was no politician, nor was the Countess of Huntingdon. Both of them were on much more friendly terms with Dissent than the Wesleys were. Whitefield frequently preached for the Dissenters, and the surviving chapels that were built by his hearers are to-day Congregationalist. The Countess had the credit of establishing almost the first theological college intended solely for the training of the ministry. It was for Evangelical clergy and ministers of all denominations.

I

At the beginning of the century, Dissent was clearly a declining force. It shared in the dead, rationalistic tone that was common in Anglican circles; much of the Puritan evangelical fervour had disappeared. There were many distinguished scholars in the ranks of the ministry, and in the sphere of education Dissent played an important part. In some of the numerous Dissenting academies a higher level of research and scholarship was reached than at Oxford and Cambridge, which were at the nadir of their usefulness. The academies broke away from the hide-bound classical tradition and were more realistic in their educational methods. Science and mathematics flourished there. Priestley and Price were both ministers, and many other famous names are associated with these centres of learning. This distinction was, however, no compensation for the lack of missionary enterprise for the Kingdom of God in their Churches. It is only towards the end of the century that we come across names of apostolic quality among the Dissenting preachers.

The influence of the Revival reached Dissent, both by direct means and by raising the temperature of the whole religious life of the country. The direct influence came through the preaching of Whitefield, the Wesleys, and their helpers. A striking example may be found in the case of David Taylor, a servant in the household of Lord Huntingdon at Donington Hall, who was an early convert. He had received a fair education and began to preach in the villages of Leicestershire in 1741, being therefore one of the first lay preachers. One of his converts was Samuel Deacon of Ratby, who ministered to his neighbours and friends and formed a congregation of 'gathered souls' because of the dissoluteness and ignorance of the local clergyman. For fifty-two years Deacon was the pastor of a little church at Barton-in-Fabis, which was the centre from which new churches spread through Leicestershire and the neighbouring counties. It was not until 1755 that the Barton preachers adopted the method of baptism by immersion. The group of churches then formed themselves into a New Connexion of General Baptists. Other groups in other counties joined them until, a hundred years after David Taylor began his preaching, the Association consisted of 113 churches with 11,358 members. Taylor himself travelled occasionally with Wesley and Ingham and was very useful for a time, until he fell into a Moravian 'stillness'. Another of his converts was John Bennett, who also worked with Wesley for a time as a very effective itinerant preacher in Lancashire and Cheshire. After his marriage with Grace Murray, Bennett separated from Wesley, and his Societies became Independent Churches. Just as some of Wesley's preachers were ordained for the ministry of the Church of England, so others, who gave up itinerating, settled as ministers of Dissenting Churches.

Nonconformity also received new accessions of strength from the Evangelical clergy as well as from the itinerants. Bogue and Bennett, in their *History of Dissenters*, put the situation in their old-fashioned language: 'That the dissenters are indebted for an increase of their numbers to the good clergy as well as to the bad may be thought paradoxical, but it is a fact. Where a faithful minister has been labouring in a parish from year to year, he collects round him a company of truly devoted Christians. They love the Gospel and its ordinances; and they venerate their pastor under whose care they are training up for a state of eternal blessedness. But if he be a curate, he is removed by the rector or promoted to a living; or whatever may be his rank, he is called away by death to rest from his labours. His successor is often a man of a different spirit. Attachment to the establishment chains the people to his ministry for a season; but they no longer hear the same doctrine as before. As they would fain be pleased they eagerly grasp at anything which sounds at all like the truth, and hope that the preacher will improve. A few months' attendance, however, opens their eyes, and throws them into despair. They cannot bear the idea of quitting the church, and leaving the place where the Gospel was so purely preached. But where the love of the truth has established itself in the heart, they are constrained to seek it and to follow it wherever it may be found. The dissenting meeting is often its only sanctuary; and though, at first, their prejudices against the place may be strong, they are gradually overcome and the once zealous votaries of the church with their families become members of a dissenting congregation.'

We have seen how, in the cases of Walker of Truro and Venn of Huddersfield, their removal from their respective charges led to the formation of strong Independent Churches by their former hearers. In Venn's case Nonconformity was strengthened by his ministry, not only in Huddersfield itself, but in the neighbouring little towns and villages. Such places as Lockwood, Holmfirth,

Berry Brow, and others further afield were influenced by his ministry. If there were any Evangelical interest in the parish, church and chapel reacted on each other. The example of Whitefield's effective oratory, his emotional appeals, his freedom from the use of manuscript increased, not only the number of Evangelical preachers in the parish churches, but in the Congregational and Baptist churches. It was only in the Presbyterian churches that the cold, formal literary type of sermon prevailed. As they were largely affected by Arian theology, a great number of their congregations became Unitarian during this century and considerably decreased in size. A few imported a little of the ardour of the Methodists, and those in Northumberland, Durham and Cumberland, with some in London, kept nearer to the spirit of Scottish Presbyterianism. Elsewhere, the history of English Presbyterianism in this century is a sad story of decline.

The Independent and Particular Baptist Churches especially felt the rising tide of the streams of Gospel grace which flowed out, not from Ezekiel's Temple, but from Whitefield's Tabernacle. It was there and at the New Tabernacle in Tottenham Court Road that the greatest congregations of enthusiastic Calvinists gathered. There also that all the best-known Calvinist preachers were to be heard. The pattern of sound words was to be found there as a century later Nonconformists found it in another Temple and another Tabernacle in the preaching of Joseph Parker and Charles Haddon Spurgeon. The influences of the Tabernacle flowed out into town and countryside and the number of Evangelical preachers in the Nonconformist chapels increased, as we have seen that they increased in the parish churches during the years when Romaine prayed for them one by one. Wherever this change took place, whether in church or chapel, there was a stirring of the dry bones and the promise of 'an exceeding great army' for the Kingdom of God.

Rowland Hill was the last of the itinerating evangelists, hovering between Church and Dissent, of whom Whitefield was the type. He came from a distinguished Shropshire family and was a product of Eton and Cambridge, who held prayer meetings even when at school at Eton. He and his brother Richard preached in the villages round their home, much to the annoyance of their father, who was a baronet and a landlord of consequence. Six bishops refused to ordain young Rowland because of his 'irregularity' and the support which he and his brother had given to the cause of the six students expelled from St. Edmund's Hall, Oxford, for their Methodism in 1768. At last, in 1773, the Bishop of Bath and Wells ordained him deacon, but he could not be restrained from itinerating. It was Whitefield who kindled his first enthusiasm, but soon his admiration was given to Lady Huntingdon. Writing to his sister, he said: 'I am glad *the Head* (Selina) is much better. . . . Had I twenty bodies, I could like nineteen of them to run about for her. I could almost wish she were immortal.' At a later date his exuberant wit and liveliness was a little too much for that very precise lady, and she was constrained to keep this too popular preacher out of her sanctuaries.

Toplady tried to dissuade him from his wanderings on preaching tours in the villages, but Berridge encouraged him. It was to that group that he belonged, and he entered with zest into the Calvinistic controversy against Wesley. His disputes were partly political and partly theological, for he denounced the war with America in his sermons. His impressive appearance and commanding eloquence won him great popularity everywhere. His style can be guessed from the comments of such hearers as Sheridan and Isaac Milner. The former said: 'I go to hear Rowland Hill because his ideas come from the heart.' While the latter told him: 'Mr. Hill, I felt to-day, 'tis this *slap-dash* preaching, say what they will, that does all the good.' It was in 1782 that he secured a head-quarters in London at Surrey Chapel, the pulpit of which was open to 'pious ministers of all denominations and of every country'. The doctrine preached there was to be in accordance with the Articles of the Church of England, and the building was vested in trustees, who paid Rowland Hill £300 a year. The strength of its activities may be seen from the fact that at one time it had thirteen Sunday schools associated with it and three thousand scholars. This was supposed to be a proprietary chapel of the Church of England, but it naturally became the home of an Independent or Calvinistic Methodist congregation. He lived until 1831 and to the end would preach and speak in parish churches and meeting-houses with perfect 'irregularity'.

The true Calvinist had no doubts concerning the difference between the Elect and the non-Elect. He might not be logical in his offer of salvation to all and sundry, but he did recognize the fact that 'the Redeemer's kingdom' was spreading in a remarkable way. The *Evangelical Magazine* was established in 1793 to continue the work of the *Gospel Magazine*, but in a less controversial manner. On its editorial board Churchmen and Dissenters sat together. The Baptists Andrew Fuller of Kettering and John Rylands of Bristol, with Matthew Wilks of the Tottenham Court Road Tabernacle, were its best-known writers. In the Preface for the 1793 volume, the Editors say: 'At the beginning of this century, there were few persons of evangelical principles in the kingdom; but now, it is supposed, there are more than 300,000 Calvinist, and many others, savingly converted to God, who trust in the merits of Christ alone for salvation.' We may wonder at the precision of these calculations, but such a statement helps us to understand the background against which the lives of the Evangelical leaders were lived. When the Editors go on to add that few of these 300,000 were 'in abject poverty' or 'quite illiterate' and that therefore a good circulation could be guaranteed for the magazine, we have visions of the comfortable pews, not only in the Baptist and Congregational chapels, but in the proprietary chapels and Evangelical churches of the Establishment where the Gospel flourished. The days of opposition and persecution were over; the period of respectability had arrived. For the Wesleyan Methodists this was to come later. Though wealth had increased with them also, their strength was in the working-class congregations in the North and the Midlands; these were regarded by the Dissenters with a measure of disapproval and envy. It was a Dissenter who said of them in 1812 that 'next to the regular dissenters, they constitute the most considerable portion of those who have separated from the established church. Their separation some of them have stoutly denied. But can those who have different places of worship, different ministers dispensing all the ordinances of religion and different rules of discipline; who acknowledge no jurisdiction of the ecclesiastical rulers; who allow no interference of the State with their proceedings; who would scorn the thought of the clergyman of the parish exercising any authority over them—with the slightest shadow of propriety or truth call themselves members of the established church?'

They would indeed have hesitated at that date to regard themselves as members of the Established Church, though many

still attended the parish church on Sunday mornings and their
own conventicles at night; they hesitated still further to call
themselves Dissenters, though they were nonconforming more
and more. The actual point of separation has been fixed at
different dates by different authorities. No official declaration
of separation has ever been made by the Methodist Conference.
It would seem most reasonable to fix the date for the beginning
of separation at the time when chapels were licensed under the
Toleration Act. Wesley's New Room in Bristol was licensed as
early as 1748, and though Charles Wesley protested, he continued
to preach there. Years before, he himself had led the Kingswood
colliers from the churches where they had been refused Communion to an 'altar' of his own in an unlicensed building. That
surely was an act of separation in its way, and his continued
objection to licensing both preachers and chapels was emotional
rather than logical.

It was necessary to secure the protection of the law both for
men and buildings against the fury of the mob. John Wesley
tried to get preachers licensed as Methodists, or as members of
the Church of England and to ignore the fact that the benefits of
the Toleration Act were for 'Protestant subjects dissenting from
the Church of England'. He did not admit this until the year
before his death. Whitefield had accepted the position when his
new chapel in Tottenham Court Road was opened 'according to
the forms of the Church of England' in 1756. At first he thought
he would be safe by placing the chapel under the protection of the
Countess of Huntingdon, since the nobility had rights for private
chapels. This great new conventicle could not come under such
a definition by any straining of the law and it had to be licensed
under the Toleration Act.

The Countess herself came up against this difficulty over her
Spafields Chapel in 1779, when the minister of the parish inhibited any clergyman from preaching there. The Ecclesiastical
Courts sustained his action. She supposed that she had a right to
employ her own chaplains at any time or place, and consulted
the ecclesiastical lawyers as to whether the domestic chapel of a
peer of the realm were exempt from ecclesiastical jurisdiction or
not. Counsel's opinion was that the law was against her 'in some
points—points which would not be insurmountable, were our
Bishops differently minded'. The Countess had to give way and

said bitterly: 'I am reduced to form the finest congregation, not only in England, but in any part of the world, into a Dissenting Meeting.' Two of her chaplains seceded from the Church of England and were licensed as Dissenting ministers, while others preached for her Ladyship no more. By 1782 the separation of the Countess of Huntingdon's Connexion from the Church of England was completed. The difficult position had been cleared up by actions in the Courts. Years before, Ingham had recognized the fact of separation in his Societies by the publication of sacramental services of his own, while the Moravians had reluctantly accepted the same situation. Zinzendorf's efforts to keep their Societies within the fold of the Church of England failed. Now they were all Dissenters.

Wesley was much slower to accept the logic of the position. Indeed, he never did regard the separation as complete; strange to say, Henry Moore, commenting in 1824 on a note by Wesley on this subject, declared that at that date the people called Methodists were not separated from the Church! It would have been possible, doubtless, to have kept all these earnest and devoted orders and fellowships within the Church of England had that Church desired it. Without such action, what could the Evangelicals do but follow the guidance of Providence? Berridge wrote to the Countess in 1777 in his quaint way: 'Some years ago, two of my lay preachers deserted their ranks, and joined the Dissenters. This threw me into a violent fit of the spleen, and set me a coughing and barking exceedingly; but when the phlegm was come up, and leisure allowed for calm thought, I did humbly conceive the Lord Jesus might be wiser than the old vicar; and I did well in sending some preachers from the Methoidst mint among the Dissenters, to revive a drooping cause, and set old, crippled pilgrims on their legs again. . . . However rusty or ricketty the Dissenters may appear to you, God has his remnant among them.' With this the Countess had to be content. Non-conformity profited by the reluctance of the bishops to ordain for the ministry men who had come under the influence of the Foundery or the Tabernacle or Trevecca. There were reasons for hesitation on the part of the hierarchy, but the result was that, increasingly, the vital elements of organized religion were to be found in Methodist preaching houses and Dissenting chapels rather than in the parish churches.

The influence of the Revival on Nonconformity was even more marked in Wales than in England. At the beginning, all the leaders of the great religious awakening in the Principality were clergy of the Established Church, with the exception of Howell Harris, who was also a devoted churchman, though he was not ordained. He retained his membership in the Church until his death and loved the Church as much as Griffith Jones or Howell Davis did. Yet his labours added greatly to the growth of the Calvinistic Methodist Societies. Griffith Jones sent his circulating schools into nearly every parish, and his teachers became Methodist preachers like himself. He should be called a Methodist, for he met with Wesley and Whitefield at their Conferences and was under the same inspiration. Reading the Bible in Welsh in the schools and learning the catechism and the stirring hymns of the Revival led to the development of the national spirit and also to that zest for theological discussion, which for so long characterized the Welsh people. The flood of new idealism poured into a new Church life, independent and alive. The chapel became the centre of all the deepest interests of the community. The association of Howell Harris with Lady Huntingdon and Whitefield gave a Calvinistic colour to Welsh Methodism. The theological college at Trevecca produced a new company of preachers. When the Countess was compelled to license her chapels for worship, the chapels in Wales under her influence had to follow suit. Calvinistic Methodism had been driven into Nonconformity. The Baptist and Congregational Churches shared in the general awakening and frequently led the way. During the century the Church life of Wales was transformed. In 1700 there were only thirty Dissenting chapels in Wales, but at the end of the century there were a thousand, and soon the numbers were to reach between two and three thousand. The soul of the nation had come to life and had found its expression in Welsh Nonconformity.

Chapter XII

THE AMERICAN COLONIES

THE English people, in spite of the growth of a world-wide British Empire, remain singularly insular in outlook. This is one of the explanations of the frequent misunderstandings between this country and the United States of America. The Americans, of course, are equally isolationist; more so, in several of the forty-eight states of the Union. Still, it is strange that we persist in regarding the chapter in religious history which we are at present discussing as though it concerned this island alone. The Evangelical Revival was as potent a force in the American colonies as in the British Isles, and it had a permanent effect on the character of the American people, just as it did on our own national character. There was more excuse for misunderstanding between the two peoples in the eighteenth century than there is to-day. The Atlantic is wide and communications by telegraph and by air were then unknown. The journey by sea would have seemed to us insufferably long.

On the other hand, the colonists were more nearly related to us by blood then than they are to-day, while the prevailing use of a common speech was not then modified by newspapers in a hundred different languages. George III and his Prime Minister had some excuse for their mistakes, though, had they remembered the history of English Nonconformity and considered how many of the original colonists had gone to America with a desire to worship God according to the dictates of their own conscience, they might have proceeded more cautiously. They might also have made a better estimate of the American as a fighter, if they had thought a little about Hampden, Fairfax, and Cromwell. The fervour of seventeenth-century religion had largely died away at the beginning of the eighteenth century in the American colonies, as in England, yet Independent and Quaker and Scottish Presbyterian were all powerful forces there and counted for more than the Anglican influence in Virginia, the Roman Catholic in Maryland, or the general growth of the secular spirit.

Protestant strength was soon to find reinforcement from emigrations of Salzburghers, Moravians, and other victims of religious persecution in Europe. From these elements in colonial life there was always the possibility of religious awakening. As early as 1718 the church at Northampton enjoyed a considerable revival under the ministry of Solomon Stoddard. Sixteen years later, led by his more famous grandson, Jonathan Edwards, the same town experienced a new awakening. We are told that 'scarcely a person was to be found, old or young, rich or poor, who was not deeply concerned for his salvation, while the greatest opposers became as serious as those whom they had long derided'. Such was the effect of the preaching of justification by faith by a man of singular intellectual and spiritual power. This was a few years before the startling beginnings of the Revival in England. Connecticut and New Jersey had also received the promise of a shower through the ministry of the brothers Tennant and others. Wesley was then in the new colony of Georgia, but was ministering ineffectively to an indifferent people who had little esteem for his ecclesiasticism. Forty years later he hoped to revisit the colonies, but the War of Independence prevented him. What a change would he have discovered and what possibilities for the spread of Christ's kingdom then lay before this vigorous and hopeful nation. 'Jersey flames with religion', wrote Francis Asbury in his *Journal* in 1790. 'The work of God does revive here [Virginia], although not in the same degree that it did two years ago.' An important page of history had been written between 1736 and 1790 in the American colonies.

It may be that the story of religious changes there is quite as important as that of the political Revolution. We should pay as much attention to Whitefield and Asbury as to Franklin, Adams, and Washington if we are to understand the new republic. G. O. Trevelyan says of one phase of the American Revolution: 'Men recalled to each other's memories how Archbishop Laud said he "could find no religion in Scotland" at a period in history when, in the country which had produced John Knox and Andrew Melville, it was difficult for an unprejudiced observer to find anything else.' Whitefield played a large part in kindling the latent interest in religion into a flame. Thirteen times he crossed the Atlantic, and his preaching ministry was as much an American ministry as an English, Scottish, or Welsh one. Philadelphia was as important a corner of his parish as Moorfields or Cambuslang. Among the American Presbyterians, his own

Calvinistic theology was strengthened; the Independents of Massachusetts set him to read and re-read the writings of the English Puritans. He spent years of his itinerancy in preaching to great crowds from Georgia in the south to the valley of the Hudson in the north.

In the Seven Years' War, he sent out with his blessing soldiers who served at the capture of Quebec, but died before the development of the quarrels which ended in the separation of the colonies from the Mother Country. It was fitting that his last sermon was preached to Americans and that he was buried on American soil. No man of his time linked the two countries together across the Atlantic as Whitefield did. Ultimately Wesley was to do more, but it was through a great company of men who carried over his spirit, used his methods, and translated his ideals into action. Whitefield's campaigns met with success chiefly in Presbyterian, Independent, and Baptist circles; seldom were the Episcopalians in a sufficiently 'awakened' state to profit by his ministrations. Even seriously minded churchmen had their prejudices against this irregular preaching, even though the preacher were one of their own clergy. But his methods prepared the way for those evangelists of the school of Wesley who were to come later.

It was not until about 1760 that Methodism found its way into the Colonies. Almost simultaneously Robert Strawbridge, an emigrant from Ireland, began to exhort a few of his neighbours in Maryland, and Philip Embury, also from Ireland, in New York. There is a dispute as to priority, but converts from Wesley's Societies must have been streaming across the Atlantic in these years. There would certainly be some in the ranks of the armies that fought from Pittsburgh to Quebec. Methodist soldiers were among the chief missionaries of the Revival all over the world. Many of these unofficial labourers carried their Gospel to Canada as well as to New England. Strawbridge became an itinerant preacher of great influence, and seems to have continued in the work until his death in 1781. Embury was of the stock of the Palatines, those German Protestants who were driven out of the Palatinate by the devastations of the armies of Louis XIV. Colonies of them, which Wesley visited, were to be found in Ireland near Limerick, and some of these, including Embury, travelled in 1760 to New York. Though he landed in 1760, it was not until six years later that he began to preach in his own house, being encouraged by Barbara Heck to gather the Wesleyan Palatines together. The company grew into two classes and hired a larger room for their meetings.

In 1767 they were surprised by the appearance in their company of an English officer wearing his sword. This was Captain Webb, 'a soldier of the Cross and spiritual son of John Wesley'. He had lost an eye at the Siege of Louisberg and been wounded in the right arm on the Plains of Abraham before Quebec. Returning to England after the war, he began to preach, and was licensed by Wesley. In New York he played an important part in the establishment of Methodism, not only by his preaching, but by his generosity. John Adams, later to be President of the United States, called him 'the old soldier—one of the most eloquent men I ever heard'. Inspired by Barbara Heck, he helped to build the old chapel in John Street, the first 'Wesley Chapel' to be known by that name in the world. In 1768 Dissenters were not allowed to erect 'regular churches' in New York. To avoid legal difficulties, they built into their new house a chimney and a fire-place, and within two years of its opening there are reports of seven thousand hearers crowding into it and the area in front. Webb also founded Methodism in Philadelphia, helping also by generous contributions the building of the first Methodist chapel there. He was, too, a pioneer in the work in Delaware. He returned to England in 1772 and appealed to the Conference at Leeds for missionaries to the Colonies, taking back with him George Shadford and Thomas Rankin; Richard Boardman and Joseph Pilmoor had already been sent out in response to his urgent appeals. When the Revolution broke out, he returned home, and the rest of his story concerns Bristol, the old city from which so many of these ambassadors of the Cross sailed to America.

Of the preachers sent out by Wesley, Francis Asbury is by far the most important in the story of American Methodism. He was a Staffordshire man, born at Handsworth, near Birmingham, in 1745. When in his 'teens, he was led into the lively fellowship of the Black Country Methodists and soon began to preach. Wesley sent him out as an itinerant in Bedfordshire, Essex, and Wiltshire for four years, but he heard the call to America. At the Bristol Conference of 1771 he offered for this service and, after setting sail for the West, he never saw his native land again. For the next forty-five years he seems to have been almost continuously on the trail for the Kingdom of God. He was constantly attacked by fevers and much sickness, but with heroic endurance he preached the Gospel in the settled parts of the eastern states, down to the thinly populated colonies of the south, across the Alleghanies, and over the Mississippi into the frontier provinces of the West. His record of travelling and preaching excels even those of Whitefield and Wesley. The distances covered were so great, the dangers and difficulties so many that this long and faithful record must be almost unique in the missionary annals of the Church. It is very fitting that a statue of Asbury on his tired horse has been erected near the Capitol at Washington; what citizen of the United States played a greater part in building up the real life of the young nation?

He was a loyal Englishman, who could not take the oath of allegiance to the Government of Maryland during the War of Independence, lest he should find himself in arms against his fellow countrymen. Yet he saw the justice of the American cause and refused to leave the work to which he believed God had called him. He went into hiding for a time and was in great peril. His fellow labourers from the English Conference returned home, and he was in great depression of spirits when his closest friend, George Shadford, said good-bye, for they were as David and Jonathan to each other. It was Shadford to whom John Wesley had written when he sent him out: 'I let you loose, George, on the great continent of America. Publish your message in the open face of the sun, and do all the good you can.' Asbury's loneliness tried him severely, but he found many good friends in his new country. He believed that God's Providence would open the way before him and his faith was not disappointed. Wesley could not have found in all this English Conference a more faithful follower. Asbury carried out exactly, not only the preaching methods of his exemplar and master, but kept to all the details of the Wesleyan discipline. He set up the class meetings and band meetings and kept the love-feasts and the quarterly meetings as he had known them at home. He established circuits and convened the Conferences which had to be held at several places each year, because of the great distances. After 1792 a General Conference met every fourth year to make decisions that affected all the Societies.

For many years he kept the preachers from administering the sacraments to the Societies, exactly as Wesley had done at home.

He endeavoured to preserve a connexion with the Church of England, though it was much more difficult in the Colonies than at home. Here and there he found a clergyman in sympathy with his aims, and in Virginia one, Devereaux Jarratt, who helped him as wholeheartedly as Grimshaw did Wesley. Jarratt had been a leader in the Virginia revival before Asbury arrived on the scene. He was, however, singular among his brother clergy, who were formal or worldly men. Coke and Moore go so far as to say that the clergy of Maryland, Virginia, the Carolinas, and Georgia were, 'with a few exceptions to the contrary, as bad a set of men as perhaps ever disgraced the Church of God'.[1] Writing thirty years later, Henry Moore toned this down a little, but it was Coke (who was then dead) who had known the American clergy. Bishop Wilberforce says that in Maryland 'the scandal of ill-living clergymen had risen to a fearful height'.

In any case, they were not to be found in the frontier districts, for the Established Church was not organized for campaign. It was only in Virginia that it could be regarded as established in any sense. The Virginian Company had, in the seventeenth century, requested the Bishop of London to find and appoint the clergy there; from this request the notion had grown up that the American colonies were in the Diocese of London. No bishop was designated to these colonies by the Government at home, either for reasons of economy or from a desire to avoid religious controversy. Hence the anomaly of an episcopal Church without a bishop. Promising young men, who were sent over to England to be ordained, frequently forgot to return. The Bishops of London in succession declined to undertake the responsibility of the oversight of churches so far away from Fulham Palace. The consequence was that there was a constant shortage of clergy, and such as were found there were often quite unsuitable. Even in Virginia the Church had to fall back on the use of lay readers, and the sacraments were neglected. It is strange that the Church of England was unable to persuade the Government to see the spiritual needs of the English colonies when the Roman Catholic Church was able to supply bishops in large numbers to all the Spanish and French colonies in America. The War of Independence weakened the Church of England in America still further. All the clergy north of Pennsylvania and a majority of

[1] *Life of Wesley*, Dr. Coke and Mr. Moore, p. 447.

those in the south were on the side of the Government. After the war was over the Loyalists returned to England or withdrew into Canada. Virginia, where the Church was strongest, was left with only twenty-eight of her ninety-one clergy remaining.

It was at this moment that John Wesley acted. He had urged the Bishop of London to ordain men for America, supporting the plea of other earnest churchmen in England to the same effect. The Baltimore Conference of 1780 had pleaded for some organization of the Methodist work in the new republic that would make it as stable and efficient as it was in England. They wished Asbury to be General Superintendent, with powers over the Societies similar to those held by Wesley at home. With difficulty Asbury had persuaded the preachers not to administer the sacraments in their congregations for another year until this difficult question was settled. He had sent a full report of the whole situation to Wesley, who had followed the course of the Revolution with much interest and concern.

Early in the quarrel between the Colonies and the Mother Country, Wesley wrote to Lord North a clearsighted warning against plunging into war with the colonists, pointing out the strong points both in the American arguments and in their military potentialities. A few months later he changed his note, after reading Johnson's *Taxation no Tyranny*, and came out as a strong supporter of the Government, much to the embarrassment of the trans-Atlantic Methodists. It was no longer likely that he would go to America himself to settle the affairs of the Methodists overseas. He found in Dr. Coke the ambassador he needed. Before sending out Coke, however, he appealed to Bishop Lowth to ordain an earnest young man well qualified for such a ministry. The bishop declined, saying that there were three ministers in that country already. Previously he had refused one of Wesley's candidates because he lacked a knowledge of Greek and Latin.

Wesley's pungent letter to the bishop hardly sustains the view that his faculties were impaired when he himself decided to ordain men for America. 'Will your lordship permit me to speak freely?' he says. (This request seemed hardly necessary, as no one succeeded in preventing Wesley from speaking plainly when he was deeply moved.) 'I am on the verge of the grave and know not the hour when I shall drop into it. Suppose there were three score of these missionaries in the country, could I in conscience recommend these souls to their care? Do they take any care for their own souls? If they do (I speak it with concern) I fear they are almost the only missionaries in America that do. My lord, I do not speak rashly. I have been in America; and so have several with whom I have lately conversed. And both I and they know what manner of men the far greater part of these are. They are men who have neither the power of religion, nor the form; men that lay no claim to piety, nor even decency.'

He then went on to discuss the qualifications needed for this missionary work. He said truly that he was no despiser of learning. (He might have added that his disciple Asbury was as zealous for education and as devoted to consistent reading as he was himself.) He brought up the case of the man who had been turned down for want of knowledge of Greek and Latin and said: 'Your lordship did not see good to ordain him; but your lordship did see good to ordain and send into America other persons who knew something of Greek and Latin; but who knew no more of saving souls than of catching whales.' This was plain speaking; but, at last, Wesley had made up his mind. Since 1746 he had been convinced that he was a scriptural bishop and had power to ordain. For more than thirty years he had hesitated to exercise that right, hoping against hope that the authorities of the Church of England would find some way to help him keep his Societies within their communion. The American colonies were now free from all control by the British Government and therefore from any direction by the Established Church of England. He had come to regard the establishment of religion by the State as something of an embarrassment; the Church in America at least was disentangled from that obstacle.

His arguments were strengthened by discussion with Dr. Coke, but it is absurd to suggest, as Wilberforce does, that Coke was moved by personal vanity and surprised Wesley into a rash action. Coke himself was surprised at the daring resolution of his chief and paused before he agreed to accept such responsibility. Among the many apostolic names of this period that of Coke shines out in missionary records with a lustre equal to that of any of the leaders of the Revival. In the providence of God, he was raised up as Wesley's lieutenant just when Fletcher passed away. He found himself ill at ease in his work as curate at South Petherton and offered his services to Wesley. He became another of the

K

company of indefatigable evangelists. He placed his considerable fortune at the service of the cause, paying his own expenses of travel and contributing generously to all the funds of the Methodists. Eighteen times he crossed the Atlantic and in the United States he organized the Methodist Episcopal Church as its first bishop. Regularly he went to Ireland to preside over the Conference there; founding the Wesleyan Missions in the West Indies, in Asia and Africa, dying at last a veteran of nearly seventy years, on his way as a missionary to Ceylon, he was buried beneath the waves of the Indian Ocean.

It was this man, already a priest of the Established Church, whom Wesley, along with another Anglican 'presbyter', ordained as superintendent of the work in America on September 2nd, 1784, at Bristol. The same day Richard Whatcoat and Thomas Vasey were ordained elders or presbyters, having been ordained deacons the previous day. All these went out to America and there they transmitted their orders to Asbury and several of his helpers. Asbury himself was raised successively through the three degrees of deacon, elder, and superintendent, though he declined to accept the last order unless the Baltimore Conference approved. This consent was gladly and unanimously given by his brethren, who preferred the title 'bishop' to that of 'superintendent'. They argued that the term 'bishop' was used in the Authorized Version of the New Testament. Wesley would have preferred the less ambitious title; Charles Wesley was furious, but he was quite out of touch with the general opinion of the Methodists at home.

It was in this way that the Methodist Episcopal Church was constituted. The historian of that Church points out not only that American Methodism took precedence of the colonial Episcopal Church in its reorganization in the new republic, but that the Methodist bishops were the first Protestant bishops and Methodism the first Protestant Episcopal Church in the New World. He goes on to say that 'as Wesley had given it the Anglican Articles of Religion and the Liturgy, it became both by its precedent organization and its subsequent numerical importance the real successor of the Anglican Church in America'. This is an argument that will make little appeal to the Anglicans in England, but this chapter in the history of Christ's Church demands more attention than hitherto they seem to have given to it. The Methodist bishop was not a diocesan, he could not claim

Episcopal Ordination, and he was chosen, not by the State, but by the agreement of his ministerial brethren. The Anglican Articles were reduced in number and the Liturgy revised by Wesley, before they were adopted by the American Methodists; they have little place in the life of American Methodism to-day. By the great extension of the missionary societies, both of English and American Methodism, and the rapid growth of Methodism in the United States, it has come about that the Methodists now outnumber the Anglicans throughout the world. It is true that spiritual values cannot be reckoned by counting heads, but, if the affairs of Christ's Church are under the direction and inspiration of Almighty God, then Methodism must regard itself as blessed with something more than 'uncovenanted mercies'.

Even Bishop Samuel Wilberforce, in his somewhat bigoted *History of the Protestant Episcopal Church of America*, admits that 'the blessing of God has visibly rested' on those of the 'sects' in America who have not been guilty of a stubborn rejection of a higher teaching. 'No unprejudiced observer can doubt that His grace has wrought through them His blessed work for multitudes around them.' This is a gracious admission from one whose theory of Christ's Church almost necessitates the limitation of the grace of God to such as are in communion with Roman, Anglican, or Orthodox Churches alone. It is amusing to read Wilberforce's *History* with Newman's essay on the Anglo-American Church at one's side and compare judgements. Newman's difficulties are increased by the fact that the essay was written in his Anglican days and needed corrections, to fit in with his more restricted Catholicism, a few years later. We who have not so learned Christ are not bewildered by this mystery of the channels of the divine mercy. God, who spoke through the prophets by divers patterns and in divers manners, is quite as capable of speaking to men through an Asbury as through a Wilberforce or even a Newman.

Asbury's story continued after 1785, when he began his episcopal labours, until his death in 1816 with unabated, un-wavering devotion. It was the story of Wesley in the British Isles over again, but in a far larger theatre of war, with more romantic background and experiences. A great company of helpers was raised up, a true band of brothers, 'having', as Asbury said, 'one purpose and one end in view—the glory of God and the salvation of souls'. Their adventures and privations were as exciting and severe as any the Jesuit missionaries knew. They followed the pioneers into the most difficult areas, and the Methodist backwoods' preachers became a feature in the rapidly expanding settlements. Asbury visited the frontier evangelists almost yearly to the end of his life, often under the protection of armed men and in great suffering. He had a long battle with sickness all his days, and his allowances amounted to sixty-four dollars a year. Apostolic poverty was the mark of all the itinerants. At one Western Conference the needs of the preachers were so great that Asbury parted with his watch, his coat, and his shirts to help them. Yet there was never any lack of volunteers for this thankless mission.

Men of sterling character and strong personality were found in large numbers for this rough ministry. Their educational equipment was inadequate by Bishop Lowth's standards, but they gathered the outsiders into the fold by the thousand. Jesse Lee, who was the first Methodist preacher to venture into the hostile Calvinist territory of New England, was often saved from violence by his good temper and ready wit. Here and there the educated men of the towns tried to test his knowledge of Latin and Greek, in which he was certainly deficient; he would answer them in Dutch, which they mistook for Hebrew and let him pass as qualified for the sacred ministry. It is a pathetic sidelight on the hardships of the campaign that nearly half these early Methodist preachers in America died before they were thirty years of age. The success of their labours compensated for all their tribulations.

By the end of the century they had found their way into every state of the Union and the Church was in the midst of a great revival. Dr. Coke presided at the 1800 Conference, as he did (for the last time) at the next Quadrennial Conference in 1804. This was the period when Methodism began (to quote the words of its historian, writing in 1865) 'to advance with its triumphant banner to the front, not only of all other denominations, but of the nation itself in the ratio of increase; and thenceforward, for good or ill, lead the Christianity of the North American continent, adding to its ranks annually masses of population, which not only astonished its own humble labourers, but the Christian world, and sometimes, in a single year, exceeded the entire membership of denominations which had been in the field generations before it'. The language may sound rather flamboyant, and Methodists have been accused of too much glorying in their millions of

Church members in the United States. It has also been suggested that these great membership figures are chiefly swollen from the multitudes of negro churches in the South. It is true that Methodists and Baptists have been very effective in their approach to the coloured population of the United States, but of recent years it is the Baptists who have made the greatest advance there.

A study of the increases in Methodism in the middle years of the nineteenth century will reveal the fact that they were due chiefly to missionary activity among the white population generally, but particularly in the pioneer districts of the Middle West and South-West. Methodism also owed its increases very much less to immigration in those years than the Roman Catholic Church did. Thousands of exiles from Ireland and from the European countries were building up the great strength of Roman Catholicism in the United States decade after decade. Methodism gained but little in comparison from the continent of Europe or even from the British Isles. Its growth represented a real work of evangelism of so striking a kind that Dr. Dixon (the father of Canon R. W. Dixon, the church historian) might be forgiven for saying, after a tour through the Methodist Episcopal Church in 1848, that it was 'the greatest development of religious truth which has taken place in the history of Christianity, either in ancient or modern times'. That is an odd way of expressing what he means; but as he had just been reporting the statistics of American Methodism as having then exceeded the million in its membership, we can understand his feeling of gratified astonishment.

These figures of a century ago seem almost insignificant to-day, when the Methodist Episcopal Church has its adherents, not only in North America, but in several European countries and in its vigorous missions in many parts of Asia and Africa. Representatives to the last Oecumenical Methodist Conference, which was held at Atlanta (Georgia), were surprised to find the trams placarded with the message, 'Welcome, Methodists, to John Wesley's State'. They were still more surprised that their badges as representatives exempted them from the payment of tram fares. It seemed a long time since John Wesley had been there, but 400,000 of his spiritual children were to be found in the State of Georgia alone. Wesley had been blamed for lacking patience and for a hasty action when he sent Coke out to ordain men for the work of evangelism in the young republic. Had he waited a few months longer, the United States would have received its bishop and the work of the Church would have proceeded in a regular way. But Wesley was eighty-one when he made that decision. He could hardly look forward to many more years of waiting for the Church of England to act. He had now been waiting for some kind of sympathetic recognition for nearly fifty years. He had more reason than a notorious personage of our own times for feeling that his patience was exhausted. 'I am on the verge of the grave', he said.

It was not until June, 1785, that the duly ordained bishop of the Protestant Episcopal Church landed in America. Two years before, Samuel Seabury, formerly a missionary of the Society for the Propagation of the Gospel, having been elected bishop of the clergy of Connecticut, set out for England to seek consecration there. He had the greatest difficulty in his quest, for the English archbishops and bishops were still 'entangled' (to use Wesley's phrase) with the Establishment. Their relation to the successful rebels in the new republic was a very delicate one. Ultimately it was to the bishops of the Church of England in Scotland, who were 'not shackled by any Erastian connexion' (Bishop Berkeley's expression), that he was compelled to turn. He was consecrated at Aberdeen on November 14th, 1784, by the Bishops of Aberdeen, Ross, and Moray, about whose orders there was no question. From that point the Protestant Episcopal Church of the United States began its life anew. There was a great leeway to make up. For many years progress was slow and difficult.

A leader was, however, found in 1811, when John Henry Hobart was made Assistant Bishop of New York. He came from the old Puritan stock of New England and had been trained in a Presbyterian college, but was himself an Evangelical High Churchman. His watchword was 'Evangelical truth and apostolical order', and his own people were in some doubt as to whether he were a High Churchman or a Methodist. He succeeded in inspiring a dull and lifeless Church by his own devotion. Until his death in 1830, he followed the Methodist lead in aggression, making use of lay readers in missionary activities and creating new dioceses to complete the necessary organization. Wesley's English 'irregularities' appeared in the United States with official approval from the authentic daughter of the Church of England there. These irregularities included, not only lay readers and open-air preaching, but what seemed like extempore prayer, though it was generally the recitation of Liturgy or Collect without the use of the book.

In other ways, the influence of Methodist, Presbyterian, and Independent Churches has been reflected in the life of the Protestant Episcopal Church. It has also reacted against the multiple divisions of the Church of Christ in the United States towards a strong ecclesiasticism. It has grown steadily in the depth of its religious experience and has produced some of the strongest and best leaders of the religious life of the nation. Its influence is much greater than its numerical strength might suggest, particularly in the eastern states. We are all debtors to Phillips Brooks, whose name is still held in affectionate esteem there as here. Another bishop of the Protestant Episcopal Church, who has served nobly the real cause of Catholic Christianity, was the late Bishop Brent. He was a true leader of Oecumenical Christian movements towards reunion in the interval between the two world wars. A Church that produces such men has a character of dignity and stability, sorely needed in the life of that great people. One cannot study the history of Christianity in the United States without feeling that 'Evangelical truth and apostolical order' is a good motto still. For the interpretation of that motto, the witness of Methodist, Presbyterian, and modern Puritan is needed as well as the witness of the representatives of Canterbury and Rome.

Chapter XIII

THE EVANGELICALS

DEAN HOLE, in his *Memories*, says: 'I remember a remark made by the late Bishop of London (Dr. Jackson) that when he recalled the sad condition of apathy, indolence, and disobedience into which the Church of England had fallen, it seemed marvellous to him that it continued to exist, that it should survive such manifest indications of debility and decay. I did not share his surprise, believing that as a branch of the true Vine, it may droop, but it cannot wither, and though it may bleed when it is pruned, whether by the merciful Hand which purgeth it that it may bring forth more fruit, or by the sword of the oppressor, it can never die. Moreover, there was the remnant, the seed, the seven thousand who had not bowed the knee to the Baal of worldliness; and He who said, "I will not destroy the city for ten's sake", in His wrath thinketh upon mercy. The Evangelicals, the Wesleyans, not then severed from the Church, and devout Christians, in all grades of society, kept the lamp from going out in the temple of the Lord.' At the beginning of the nineteenth century it was the Wesleyans and the Evangelicals who kept the lamp of faith burning.

We have seen how these two groups arose and how closely they were related to each other. They were often confused under the same nickname of Methodist, until Methodist acquired a specialized meaning for one who was separated from the Established Church, and Evangelical for one who remained within it. It was often an accident which decided on which side the line a member of this school would come down. If he happened to be presented with a living, he would be an Evangelical; if he were not accommodated in that way, he would become a Methodist. There were, of course, those who resigned their livings to become Methodists and there were Methodists who held higher views of churchmanship than many Evangelicals. The question of adherence to, or separation from, the Establishment became gradually a matter of principle in the early years of the nineteenth century and soon made a clear line of division between the two parties. The Methodist followed John Wesley in making the world his parish; the Evangelical was more and more inclined to make the parish his world.

The differences in doctrine between the two parties declined in importance. The Calvinism of the Evangelicals, while strongly held by the leaders, was not universally held and tended to be modified as the century advanced. Sir James Stephen's fascinating essay on 'The Evangelical Succession' has been challenged at some points in recent years, but he is surely right in maintaining that Whitefield was the father of this school. John Newton, Thomas Scott, Joseph Milner, and Henry Venn also are all in place in this succession and lead on to the Clapham Sect, which made such great contributions to the cause of philanthropy and foreign missions. Romaine's prayer list of Evangelical clergy steadily grew during his lifetime, but Gladstone's estimate that the Evangelicals numbered one in twenty of the clergy at the end of the eighteenth century is probably too high. They were still a very small minority. They held few livings in London, but were stronger in the provinces. Yorkshire was perhaps their best area. The largest churches in Hull and York were crowded by the congregations of Joseph Milner and William Richardson respectively. The latter was Vicar of 'Belfry's' for fifty years, but Milner died all too soon in 1797. His influence, however, spread far and wide, for he was also Headmaster of the Hull Grammar School. Other churches in Hull found incumbents of the same temper and outlook. His *History of the Church of Christ* was completed by his brother, Isaac, who also wrote a biography of Joseph, whom he greatly loved and admired.

None of the Evangelicals at that time held a position of such influence as Isaac Milner, who was President of Queens' College, Cambridge, and also Dean of Carlisle. He was a Johnsonian character, a great scholar and a vivid personality. He had been a Senior Wrangler of such distinction that he was graded *incomparabilis*. He had the true scientific spirit of inquiry and the widest range of interests, from shoeing horses to making an automatic chess player. Such concern for secular matters was unusual in one who gloried in the scandal of the Cross and fought the battles of the Bible Society. Another of his conflicts was with the National Society in favour of allowing Dissenters' children in the National Schools to attend their own place of worship rather than being compelled to attend the parish church. It was with him that Wilberforce travelled in France in 1784 on a journey that led to Wilberforce's conversion. This was a shock to a father who had said, 'Billy shall travel with Milner as soon as he is of age; but if Billy turn Methodist he shall not have a sixpence of mine'. Alas! Milner took with him to read on the journey Doddridge's *Rise and Progress of Religion in the Soul* and recommended it as one of the best books ever written. Young Wilberfore read it, with the result that he went over into the camp of the 'Methodists'.

When did that term go out of fashion as applied to earnest Christians who had not left the Church of England? We get some indication of the date from a letter to Isaac Milner in 1809. He had been editing his brother's essays, the first of which was on Methodism. He consulted his friend Richardson of York about the book and received the reply: 'Though we ought patiently to bear the stigma of Methodism, we ought not to legitimate the term when applied to us, or embody ourselves, who act in an orderly way, with the proper Methodists. What was then termed Methodism is now called Evangelical Religion: would it not be better to change the title in the new edition and call it *An Essay in Evangelical Religion*?' In those years, before Keble, Newman, and Pusey began to quicken the imagination and unsteady the nerves of devout members of the Church of England, the objection to the Methodists was still based on their disorderly behaviour rather than on their sins against a true doctrine of the Church. In 1809 there was little disorderly behaviour on the part of the Wesleyan Methodists; they were becoming so restrained and respectable that they disapproved of the crowded camp meetings that led to the remarkable revival of religion known as Primitive Methodism in the next few years.

But, as Dean Hole says, 'They were fast breaking away from the Church, losing their affection for a mother who made no effort to retain it'. To be outside the Establishment was not a sin against the Holy Ghost, but it was a sin against propriety. It had almost an illegal air about it and could only be covered by a Toleration Act. That was why Sydney Smith and the Low Church representatives disliked 'the nasty and numerous vermin of Methodism' so much. At a later date Evangelicals and Low Churchmen began to fraternize in opposition to Puseyism, but before the Oxford Movement they must be clearly distinguished from each other. The Evangelical was a Methodist, who preserved his respectability by remaining in the Church; the Low Churchman was the nineteenth-century successor of the Whig Latitudinarian.

He might disguise his religious devotion under a still greater devotion to fox-hunting and port-wine drinking, but he did believe in the Establishment. The business of the Church was part of the routine of the nation that must be carried on. It was a comfortable means of livelihood for younger sons of aristocratic families, for squarsons and upper middle-class university men who had no better openings. The first article in the Low Churchman's creed was, 'I believe in the Establishment'. Even the Evangelicals began to regard the Establishment of religion as the sure safeguard against evil.

F. D. Maurice has an interesting explanation of this change of position. He went up to Oxford after a difficult struggle over his own attitude to the Church of England. He found that the Evangelicals at that time (1830) were passing into a new phase. 'They had been the great antagonists of the High and Dry School which had made the Establishment everything, the witness of the Spirit with the individual conscience nothing; they had become the most vigorous supporters of an Establishment as such— whether Presbyterian or Episcopalian signified little. They had adopted the maxim of Dr. Chalmers—that as men are fallen creatures, religion must be distasteful to them; that there will be no natural demand for it, therefore it must be recommended by all external aids and influences.' In other words, if you believe intensely enough in the doctrine of original sin, you will invoke the aid of the State to keep sinners in the way of life. Maurice himself reacted against a theology that made sin the ground of all its philosophy, believing that religion should begin with the living and holy God. 'I cannot believe that in any sense the devil is king of this universe.'

The wiser Evangelicals would not have accepted that putting of their case, but the sterner representatives of Calvinism were capable of giving a very grim picture of the utter depravity of mankind. It does, however, seem strange that those who made the omnipotence of God the centre of their system of doctrine should have found it necessary to call in the power of the State where the grace of God had failed. In the Preface of his *Life of Hannah More*, we find the Rev. Henry Thompson, the curate of Wrington, writing: 'Methodism, indeed, in the health of the church-blood that enriched its veins, has occasionally reclaimed spots from the wilderness; but the very partial success even of this wisely organized system may convince any reflective and unprejudiced mind how insufficient are any means for Christianizing a nation which are not wielded and upheld by the State.' We must try to understand why the Methodists and the Evangelicals, who were alike the product of the Revival and whose doctrines were in essential agreement, should be now so opposed to each other.

Hannah More was called a Methodist, though she regarded the separated Methodists as real opponents. She was not even a Calvinist, as many of the Evangelicals were; doctrinally she was in the same camp as the Wesleyan Methodists, as also was her friend and helper, William Wilberforce. She had been prominent in literary circles in London and had won fame by her plays when, in 1787, she turned her life wholly to religious work. When she began to write religious books and pamphlets, she reached a far greater public than she had done before this great change in her life took place. Her *Estimate of the Religion of the Fashionable World* was an immediate success and it was followed by tracts against infidelity and the French Revolution. Probably the two million circulation of her *Repertory Tracts* in 1795 constituted a record up to that date. She is, however, best remembered by the Sunday schools started by herself and her sisters in the villages of Somerset, which are so admirably described in *Mendip Annals*. She told Newton in 1796 that they had then schools in ten parishes with between sixteen and seventeen hundred scholars.

She seems to have owed a great deal to Newton for inspiration in her new way of life, and Wilberforce gave her much help and counsel. Mrs. Trimmer, also, showed her the way of advance in religious education by her experiments at Brentford. Hannah More, however, proved herself a true Evangelical by her emphasis on the new birth as the basis of all her work in education. She found the Mendip area almost completely pagan, and declared that 'the clergy of the greater part of Somerset were dead and buried'. Naturally she met with opposition and as much suspicion as all earnest workers did in those days. She dreaded being called a Methodist which, she said, was a name bestowed on any one who had a thought of a future life or was bold to carry the injunctions of Christ into practical life. With the malicious the name was synonymous with that of hypocrite. There was a great outcry when one of her teachers was suspected of using extempore prayer and instituting Monday evening meetings, which resembled a Methodist class meeting. The curate intervened and the school was closed.

The war against her tendencies to Methodism was carried fiercely to other villages at the very time when the Methodists were complaining that she was emptying the meeting-houses. She had to move with great caution, and when the report was spread that she had received the sacrament at Jay's chapel at Bath for fifteen years, she admitted that she had done so *once*, but had immediately apologized to the bishop for this offence. Her sisters were living at Bath at that time, and the preaching of William Jay was so popular that many Anglicans risked all perils to their immortal souls by listening to that devout and edifying prophet. An even greater orator was Robert Hall, who outshone himself in a visit to Bristol. 'It was transcendent,' said Hannah More, 'the reasoning of Barrow, joined to the splendour of Jeremy Taylor. Alas! I never heard him.' But sixteen clergymen were said to have been in the Baptist conventicle that evening. This gives us the situation at that time and shows how difficult it was for Evangelicals inside and outside the Church of England to work together. Hannah More's religious life was lived in the period when the scandal of separation from the Church was deeply resented, but before the rise of the Oxford Movement.

But it was Charles Simeon who was the first Evangelical leader to see clearly that attachment to the Church Establishment must be strengthened if the Revival of religion were not to end in a continuous reinforcement of the ranks of Dissent. This is well brought out by Canon Charles Smyth in his recent book on *Simeon and Church Order*. Charles Simeon, like Rowland Hill, was a product of Eton and Cambridge; like him, too, he came from the class of the higher gentry. Both experienced early conversions, the one when he was at the University and the other when he was still at school. Both became preachers whose names were known throughout the length and breadth of the land. With these likenesses, and with the fact that the central theme of their preaching was the same, the similarities came to an end. The difference lay in their attitude to the Church. Rowland Hill was never allowed to proceed to ordination as priest because of his irregularities; he remained a deacon to the end of his days. He preached in a proprietary chapel where the Liturgy of the Church of England was used, but he was in reality a Dissenter.

Simeon was fifteen years younger than Rowland Hill and was confronted by the problem of irregularity when that problem had reached a more advanced stage than it appeared to the Countess of Huntingdon and Rowland Hill. He is probably the only case on record of conversion by compulsory chapel, or rather by the compulsory reception of Holy Communion. When he was notified that the Provost of his college required him to attend the Lord's Supper in about three weeks' time, he was thoroughly alarmed. He bought and read the only religious book he had ever heard of, and cried to God for mercy. 'From that day to this, blessed, for ever blessed, be my God, I have never ceased to regard the salvation of my soul as the one thing needful.' He formed a deep friendship with John Venn (the son of Henry Venn), who was a senior student at Sidney Sussex College. This took him into the fellowship of Venn's father, who was then Vicar of Yelling, where he frequently met Berridge of Everton. Henry Venn became the guide, philosopher, and friend of Charles Simeon, as Berridge had been of Rowland Hill when he was an undergraduate at Cambridge.

Berridge would have led young Simeon into the ways of the itinerant preacher, but it was Henry Venn who kept him from that path. Perhaps the discovery that his own Huddersfield congregation had left the Church of England, and the fact that similar results had appeared from the labours of other clergy who had followed in Whitefield's footsteps, had made the old man cautious. Yet 'to the end of Berridge's life, Charles Simeon and Henry Venn used to go over and dine with him every Tuesday'.[1] They were all three of the same spirit, and the young man was destined to carry on the Evangelical tradition to a growing company of disciples. Berridge never achieved the caution which avoided every appearance of irregularity and, if Simeon did show some inclination to an extravagant and erring ministry by preaching in barns and the villages round about Cambridge, he was soon cured by being presented with the living of Holy Trinity, Cambridge, at the age of twenty-two. Here, in a large church in the middle of Cambridge, for more than fifty years he carried on his powerful ministry until, as Macaulay said, 'his sway over the Church of England was greater than that of any primate'.

He had his difficulties at the beginning, since his predecessor's

[1] *Simeon and Church Order*, Smyth, p. 195.

curate had been elected to the afternoon lectureship and he was restricted to the Sunday morning service only. It was only Methodists who held evening services at that period, but Simeon decided to try the experiment, in spite of the opposition it would arouse. It seemed to him his only chance of reaching the poorer people in his parish. He was met by the same challenge that had troubled Romaine in his London parish some years before; the churchwardens refused him access to the church. Wesley happened to be in the neighbourhood, though he never seems to have preached in Cambridge during his continuous wanderings through England. Simeon rode over to Hinxworth, Herts., and had a long talk with the 'old disciple', as he called him. Wesley's *Journal* reads: 'Mon., Dec. 20, 1784, I went to Hinxworth, where I had the satisfaction of meeting Mr. Simeon, Fellow of King's College, in Cambridge. He has spent some time with Mr. Fletcher at Madeley, two kindred souls much resembling each other both in fervour of spirit and in the earnestness of their address. He gave me the pleasing information that there are three parish churches in Cambridge wherein true scriptural religion is preached, and several young gentlemen who are happy partakers of it.' The *Journal* does not, however, tell us of the discussion of Simeon's difficulty. From other sources, we learn that Wesley advised him to 'take up the cross and persevere'.

He had already hired a small room in his parish for his evening meeting, but presently he had to go outside his parish to find a larger one. He kept up extempore preaching at this evening conventicle for six years, until he was allowed once again to make use of the church. He also turned his 'Society' into half a dozen classes and had week-night prayer meetings. There was some disorder in these meetings when he was absent through illness, and he was troubled about the question whether he should continue them. However, he felt that religious societies were a necessity if he, as their minister, were to keep his people together. He would lose them to the Dissenters if he failed to help them with their meetings for religious fellowship. He also made use of laymen and laywomen as 'under-shepherds of the flock of Christ'. In other words, his church was organized exactly as one of Wesley's churches would have been if it had been detached from a Methodist circuit. By restricting attendance at prayer meetings to those who were members of the religious societies, he believed that he was avoiding the charge of making the place 'really and truly a conventicle in the eye of the law'.

Meanwhile Wesley was being driven to license both his preachers and his preaching houses under what he called 'that execrable Act called the Conventicle Act'. The preachers were licensed, not as Dissenters, but simply as preachers of the Gospel, though it is doubtful whether that evasion complied with the terms of the Act of Toleration. Wesley met Simeon again at Hinxworth on October 30, 1787, and was again impressed by the fact that he 'breathed the very spirit of Mr. Fletcher'. His influence over succeeding generations of undergraduates was very great. His sermon notes provided a new standard for Gospel preaching in the Church of England. His ministry produced many pioneers, who, in the new missionary fervour of the opening years of the nineteenth century, carried the flag of Christ round the world. Of these none is better known or held in higher veneration than Henry Martyn. The term Simeonite became almost as common and almost as much a badge of unpopularity as Methodist had been in an earlier age. A new apostle of the Revival had arisen and from his strategic pulpit in a university town, he was able to be almost as far-ranging in his influence as the peripatetic evangelists.

His name is associated to-day with what seemed a necessary reform over a century ago, but has now come to be regarded as almost a scandal. We have seen how the problem of the continuity of Evangelical effort in a parish was complicated by the patronage system of the Church of England. When a quickening ministry was ended by the death or removal of the awakened preacher, the chances were that the congregations which had crowded the parish church would melt away under the cold and unedifying ministrations of his successor. Again and again the separated Methodists or the Dissenters gathered in the scattered flock. There is a passage in the *Evangelical Magazine* for 1793 that explains what frequently happened in such cases. It is said there that the Gospel was not preached in Farnham (Surrey) until Gunn went there as curate in 1786. Six years later the vicar dismissed him and the shepherdless sheep met in a room. A certain amount of violence followed, and the protection of the Toleration Act was sought. The result was that an Independent chapel was opened there in 1793, Wilks and other preachers from the Tabernacle coming to the opening services.

Curates could be replaced by the incumbent, but livings were in the hands of patrons, who might have no consideration for the quality of the work that had been going on in the parish. Simeon decided to raise funds to purchase livings, so that an Evangelical succession could be maintained in an Evangelical parish. It was an unsatisfactory system that made this effort to secure Gospel preaching in England necessary. Anglican writers of the time criticized severely the democratic methods of the Dissenting Churches, by which ministers were called to their charges by the majority votes of congregations, and showed how the ministry was robbed of its dignity and independence by this procedure. Dissenters replied that at least they were not left to the tender mercies of some patron who could impose on congregations men wholly unfitted for the position. Wesley found a way to avoid both evils by leaving the 'Stations' of his preachers in the hands of the Conference and changing the appointments at regular intervals, first of a year and later of three years. The preachers were not ultimately dependent on the local congregation nor even on the Circuit (though the Circuit financed them), but acted freely in the name of the whole fellowship of Methodism. It was the whole fellowship that gave its guarantee for each preacher by refusing to receive men who could not both give the assurance that they were called of God to preach and also could verify that call by the witness of 'gifts, grace, and fruit' in their labours. Simeon's trustees took upon themselves the same office as that of the Methodist Conference in guaranteeing a Gospel ministry to the *ecclesiolae in ecclesia* which they were building up. Simeon aimed at fixing 'the gospel in perpetuity' in the livings he purchased. He raised large sums of money for this purpose and was greatly helped by the Thorntons, father and son. Indeed, the Simeon Trust was constituted in 1817 on the basis of Henry Thornton's will. He had designated three trustees to administer the livings he had purchased. By 1836 the number of advowsons controlled by the Trust was twenty-one; it is now 150.[1]

Simeon's career shows how erroneous is the idea that the Evangelicals held a strong position in the Church of England at the beginning of the nineteenth century. They were still regarded with dislike in official circles. If a bishop condescended to look

[1] *Simeon and Church Order*, Smyth, p. 246 *n.*

L

on them, it was with hesitation and reserve. Some bishops had careful plans to keep Evangelical candidates back from ordination —traps to catch Calvinists they were called. In Oxford there were still colleges that would refuse admittance to known Evangelicals. Promotion to higher benefices was very rare in their case, and only Isaac Milner among their well-known leaders held any high position in the Church. It was not until 1815 that the first Evangelical bishop was consecrated—Ryder to Gloucester. The brothers Sumner followed in 1826 and 1828 to Winchester and Chester respectively. The elevation of the first three Evangelicals to the episcopate seems to have been due to their aristocratic connections rather than to their known piety and devotion. It was regarded with pleasure and astonishment in Evangelical circles. 'How delightful', said Simeon when the Hon. Dudley Ryder became Bishop of Gloucester, 'to see dignitaries in our Church thus coming forward, and disciples springing up in Caesar's household.' Which reminds one of Cowper's naïve delight over the Earl of Dartmouth as one who not only wore a coronet but prayed.

Evangelical bishops meant Evangelical clergy; preferment and ordinations were in the bishops' hands. When Palmerston was Prime Minister and his brother-in-law Shaftesbury was his adviser in ecclesiastical appointments, the opportunity of the Evangelicals at last arrived. Palmerston's bishops were by no means all of that school, but the value of this element in the life of the Church now became clear. What great achievements in the fields of missionary activity and humane service had they been able to record! Sydney Smith had sneered at the leaders as the Clapham Sect, but it was a sect that moved the world. Clapham was a pleasant village on the outskirts of London in those days. Round the Common were scattered a number of handsome villas, the homes of City merchants and prosperous professional men. To the parish church in 1792 came John Venn, the son of Henry Venn of Huddersfield fame and a man of the same spirit. His predecessor at Clapham was Dr. Stonehouse, also a strong Evangelical, as was his successor Dr. Dealtry. It was, however, the twenty-one years of John Venn's ministry, from 1792 to 1813, that constitute the golden age of Clapham.

Thackeray has given a kindly but satirical picture of that community at the beginning of *The Newcomes*. The Hermitage was a paradise 'five miles from the Standard at Cornhill, separated from the outer world by a thick hedge of tall trees and an ivy-covered porter's lodge. It was a serious paradise. As you entered the gate gravity fell on you; and decorum wrapt you in a garment of starch. The rooks in the elms cawed sermons at you morning and evening. The peacocks walked demurely on the terraces; the guinea-fowls looked more Quaker-like than those savoury birds usually do. Tommy was taught hymns very soon after he could speak, appropriate to his tender age, pointing out to him the inevitable fate of wicked children and giving him the earliest possible warning and description of the punishment of little sinners. He repeated the poems to his stepmother after dinner before a great shining table covered with grapes, pine-apples, plum-cake, port wine, and madeira surrounded by stout men in black and baggy white neck cloths, who took the little man between their knees and questioned him as to his right understanding of the place where naughty boys were bound'.

Thackeray is right about the seriousness and the good food, for the Evangelicals lived well in more senses than one. Perhaps we should speak of earnestness rather than seriousness; men like Wilberforce and women like Hannah More were not lacking in art and vivacity. The company of which they, along with Zachary Macaulay, Charles Grant, Lord Teignmouth, Henry Thornton, James Stephen, were the leaders was not a gloomy séance of sour-faced Puritans. Puritan it was in the best sense, but the popular view of the Puritan is a caricature that owes much to *Hudibras*. These were the people who did most to kill the slave-trade and emancipate the slaves; Sunday schools, Bible societies, tract societies, missionary societies, hospitals, churches owed much to their devotion. They were the salt of the earth in personal character and integrity. Henry Thornton the banker, reputed to be one of the wealthiest men in the country, lived on one eighth of his income and spent the rest on others. The inspiration of all their active and practical service was their religion. It was that of the Revival. One of the last letters that John Wesley wrote was to Wilberforce to encourage him in his attack on the slave trade. 'Go on', he said, 'in the name of God, and in the power of His might, till even American slavery, the vilest that ever saw the sun, shall vanish before it.'

So the parish church where Venn preached his earnest, learned and moving sermons was the centre from which all these great reforms flowed. We are not surprised to find that John Venn was for years Secretary of the Church Missionary Society. He was at its birth in 1799. It began, as the Methodist movement began, in a little room in Aldersgate Street, but this room was in a public house—a first-floor room in the 'Castle and Falcon'. The Baptist Missionary Society had been formed seven years and the London Missionary Society four years before. It is significant that Evangelical clergy had a share in each of these. The Baptist Missionary Society owed most in its beginnings to William Carey, but his inspiration came from Thomas Scott. 'If I know anything of the work of God in my soul', said Carey, 'I owe it to the preaching of Mr. Scott.' Dr. Haweis, Rector of Aldwinkle, and Mr. Penty-cross, Vicar of Wallingford, together with some Independent and Presbyterian ministers, were the founders of the London Mission-ary Society. Readers of the *Life of the Countess of Huntingdon* will be familiar with the names of Haweis and Pentycross. Gradually, however, the London Missionary Society came more and more into the hands of the Independents. The need for a distinctively *Church* Missionary Society was felt. Here the influence of Simeon, John Venn, Thomas Scott, John Newton, and other well-known Evangelicals appears.

They did not work through the missionary activities of the S.P.C.K. and the S.P.G., because an Evangelical missionary society must not be based on 'the High Church principle'. Considering the date, this appears to mean that they were suspici-ous of official movements under the patronage of bishops who might send any unconverted ordained men out as missionaries. So the Society began as a combination of Christian men who were seeking to extend the spiritual work of the Church abroad, without much encouragement from dignitaries. For some years progress was slow and there were many difficulties. Candidates for the field were not numerous, and the first missionaries were Lutheran clergy; then laymen were sent out. In the first fifteen years of the Church Missionary Society, seventeen of the twenty-four missionaries sent out were Germans. And of the seven Englishmen only three were ordained. These irregularities seem almost as alarming as those of Wesley had been. Strange to say, the S.P.C.K. had relied entirely on Lutherans in its missions to India. These were but the small beginnings. A great and honourable history lay before the C.M.S., and its increasing work to-day shines out as a beacon of hope to those who despise the day of small things. By the 'forties it had so won the approval of those in authority that both archbishops and many of the diocesan bishops were on its Board of management.

'The deepest and most fervid religion in England during the first three decades of this century was that of the Evangelicals.' These are the words of Canon Liddon, who could certainly be regarded as an unprejudiced witness. If the term Evangelical is extended to include those outside as well as inside the Church of England, it might even be said that the only fervid religion in England during the first three decades of the nineteenth century was that of the Evangelicals. Those within the Church began the remarkable transformation that was seen during the century in the Established Church. The Oxford Movement was not so much a reaction against Evangelicalism as a development from it. Both Newman and Manning came from the Evangelical camp. Newman has told how great was his indebtedness to Thomas Scott, the commentator, and how his love for Church history began with his reading of Milner. The leaders of the Revival were so zealous in winning 'souls for the Redeemer's Kingdom' that they lost sight of some of the wider aspects of the Kingdom. They concentrated on the Atonement as the divine method for the redemption of mankind in their preaching and overlooked the sacramental meaning of life as interpreted by the Incarnation.

It was not that the sacraments themselves were neglected. The Methodists helped to revive the practice of frequent Communion. The Lord's Supper was to them far more than a memorial feast to an absent Lord. They sang the Wesley hymns about the real presence, and believed; but it was the spiritual presence of their divine Saviour, specially manifest in the most sacred of Christian observances, which they acknowledged. The presence was not in the elements, but in the whole act of worship and communion. Few of them really believed in Baptismal Regeneration, though John Wesley hesitated on this subject. In general, they would have agreed with F. W. Robertson, who illustrated this doctrine by the allegory of the farmer who marked his sheep, not to make them his own, but because they were his own already. Some might have found a stay here because of the strength of their convictions about original sin, but all would rejoice at the Gorham Judgement of 1850, which made it clear that the Church of England was sound from their point of view.

The nineteenth-century Evangelical, however, was much more interested in conversion than in baptism. There was a real cleavage with the Tractarians here, as there was with the Ritualists on ceremony, and with both the early and later Anglo-Catholics on questions of order. The Evangelical, too, was rather starved on the intellectual and aesthetic side. He did not shine particularly in art and literature. Early Victorian ecclesiastical art makes but little appeal to us to-day, but, to the Evangelical, art was unimportant. For that matter, the Gothic revival kindles few thrills now, but the Tractarians must be given credit for thinking about beauty, whether they achieved it or not. When leaders of the Oxford Movement began to go over to Rome, the Evangelicals became alarmed. An altogether exaggerated fear of Rome and suspicion of everything but ultra-Protestant Erastianism took possession of them. They became narrow and sombre and forgot the more genial and practical temper of the best company at Clapham.

It was true that Lord Shaftesbury was carrying on, with unflagging enthusiasm, the tradition of Wilberforce in social reform. Overworked women and children in the 'Satanic mills' and mines, ragged children in the streets, boy chimney-sweeps, and other ill-treated groups of unfortunate people owed much to him. Yet he could greet *Ecce Homo* when it appeared as 'the most pestilential book ever vomited forth from the jaws of hell'. The Evangelicals in the Church of England at that time were far narrower than the Methodists outside it. They were the exponents of the strictest Sabbatarianism; they were the slowest to move from a rigid Fundamentalism in the interpretation of Scripture, the strongest opponents of Darwinism and the historical criticism of the Bible. Many of them were afflicted by Millenarianism and lurid views of prophecy. It was a dismal phase in their history and it was a pity they reacted so violently against 'Puseyism'. Together Evangelical and Tractarian might have worked out some higher conception of Christ's Church for England and for the world.

The Evangelicals, however, began to recover more of their original devotion in the later years of the nineteenth century. From the United States and Ireland came the spirit of revival quite in the old way. Later on Moody and Henry Drummond brought into the Revival Movement a more appealing humanity and the missionary fire was kindled afresh. The Cambridge Seven set out to win the world for Christ; the Universities Mission to Africa and the Student Christian Movement were born. Wider views of the Kingdom of Christ prevailed; new hopes were stirred. Such a life as that of Bishop H. C. G. Moule (1841–1920) reflects these changes in a very pleasant manner. The Evangelical still had his limitations and inhibitions, but he was more inclined to welcome new light and truth. His danger was, as Tulloch had pointed out, that he should regard Christianity as something superadded to the highest life of humanity rather than as the perfect development of that life. The generation that followed made their peace with science and greeted new discoveries as though science were the ally of truth and righteousness and not an enemy. Liberal Evangelicalism came into existence.

The Church of England at the beginning of the twentieth century was a contrast in almost every way with the same Church of a hundred years before. The day of the proud prelate and the absentee incumbent had gone. The drunken and immoral parson was regarded as a portent and a scandal. The Evangelical motto, 'spiritual men for spiritual work', had become a reality. Instead of Dissenters putting the Church of England to shame by their earnestness and devotion, the tendency was now the other way. Bishops were true spiritual leaders and fathers of truly Christian families. Churches were beautifully kept, worship was reverent, regular, and real. The Church of England had come to life. Even its divisions into High Church, Broad Church, and Low Church added to its efficiency rather than detracted from it. There was something truly catholic in its compromises. Nonconformist grievances were disappearing and the possibilities of a still more catholic development which would unite all the scattered elements of Christ's Church in England were beginning to be discussed. Then came the first world war, bringing Christians of all kinds closer together, but increasing the secular temper of the nation. Spiritual values were weakened and religion moved from the centre of the stage of national life into the wings. The glow of Evangelical ardour waned, and those forms of Church life that had placed less stress on the institutional side of religion felt the impact of the blow first of all. Still, the Evangelical had played his part in the life of the Church of England nobly and well. What that part was is studied best in the lives of members of leading Evangelical families.

Chapter XIV

METHODISM OUTSIDE THE ESTABLISHED CHURCH

AT his first Conference in 1744, Wesley asked himself the question, 'Do you not entail a schism in the Church?' His answer was: '1. We are persuaded the body of our hearers will, even after our death, remain in the Church, unless they be thrust out. 2. We believe, notwithstanding, either they will be thrust out, or that they will leaven the whole Church. 3. We do, and will do, all we can, to prevent these consequences, which are supposed to happen after our death. 4. But we cannot, with a good conscience, neglect the present opportunity of saving souls while we live, for fear of consequences which may possibly or probably happen after we are dead.' He was to learn much in the next forty-seven years, and he continued to wrestle with this problem until the latest moments of his life; but he never swerved from these governing conclusions. New facts kept emerging and his views on Church order were enlarged, but the necessity of continuing the work to which God had called him was crystal clear.

So the Societies grew, and they grew largely from the un-churched masses of the population. They were encouraged to attend the services of the Church of England 'at all opportunities' and to receive the sacraments at the hands of the Anglican clergy. Their own worship was arranged out of church hours, except in a few cases where ordained clergy regularly conducted the services and used the Liturgy of the Established Church. The fact that in their own preaching-houses (which they refused to call 'meeting-houses' lest they should appear to be Dissenters) a simple service of extempore prayer, hymns, and prayer was held, was due to the fact that it was supplementary to the liturgical service of the Church. Long prayers were to be avoided for that reason. So in 1766 Wesley said: 'I advise, therefore, all Methodists in England and Ireland, *who have been brought up in the Church*, constantly to attend the service of the Church, at least every Lord's Day.' In 1786 he allowed services in Methodist chapels during church hours in places where the clergy were 'notoriously wicked or dangerously heretical'.

But what of the growing number in the Societies who had

never had any association with the Church? As the years passed and he found helpers like Grimshaw or Berridge or Fletcher, whose livings were the centre of Evangelistic work, spreading far beyond the limits of their own parishes, he had a dream that Methodist preachers might be appointed to benefices at the head of circuits with unordained itinerants as their colleagues. By this means a Methodist order would have been created within the Church similar to the Jesuit and other orders within the Church of Rome. Wesley had not studied the life of Loyola in vain. He greatly admired his genius and discipline and was as much the general of the Methodist order himself as Loyola had been general of the Society of Jesus.

After Wesley's death, Dr. Coke revived this idea. Without any instructions from Conference, he approached the Bishop of London with the suggestion that a given number of the Methodist preachers, approved by the Conference, should be ordained and allowed to travel through the Connexion and administer the sacraments. Methodists had embarrassed the clergy in many parishes by their numbers as they thronged to the Lord's Table. There were towns in the North of England where the parish churches were not large enough to contain the number of Methodist communicants had the clergy been willing to receive them. The Methodists themselves were increasingly reluctant to attend services conducted by clergy with no apparent interest in spiritual religion, and, too frequently, with reputations far below the standards of the gospel it was their business to proclaim. Coke had discussed the question with the Attorney-General, whom he had known at Oxford, before he approached the Bishop of London. The Attorney-General approved the idea, but Coke's approach was hardly tactful. He told the bishop that 'a very considerable part of our Society have imbibed a deep prejudice against receiving the Lord's Supper from the hands of immoral clergymen'. He added that the Methodists used the term 'immoral' in an extensive sense as including 'all those who frequent card-tables, balls, horse-racing, theatres, and other places of fashionable amusement'.

The bishop agreed that the relation of the 90,000 Methodist members and half-million adherents to the Church of England was an important question, but doubted whether Coke's scheme were practicable. He said, however, that he would consult the two archbishops and report again. It is not very surprising that the Archbishop of Canterbury's reply was that they could not ordain men without inquiry as to their fitness and without control of their appointments. He naturally resented a suggestion (so he interpreted Coke's observations) 'founded on the presumption that all the regularly ordained clergy of the Church of England are immoral'. Wesley would have handled the situation in a different way, though he did once say, 'Soul-damning clergymen lay me under more difficulties than soul-saving laymen'. There was never any chance of such a scheme being approved at that time. The Church of England had no statesmen of the calibre of Wesley among its bishops to face the crisis. Perhaps it was in the Providence of God that it was so. The Methodists who remained in the Church became a powerful leaven to transform the heavy mass of well-meaning conventionality, while the Methodists who became a separated community were far more effective outside the community than they could have been within.

In many respects they were already separated when Wesley died. The licensing of his preachers and chapels had implied this. He might avoid the term 'Protestant Dissenter', but the very use of the Toleration Act meant Dissent. Wesley took a further step towards separation by his own ordinations, first for Scotland, then America, and finally England. He seemed to expect that the Societies would break up at his death, though he did his best to keep them together. By the Deed of Declaration in 1785, he constituted a Conference of a hundred of his preachers to be the legal instrument for continuing the administration of the business of the Methodist fellowship. The chosen hundred were not to assume any superiority over their brethren, nor to show any respect of persons in appointing preachers or disposing of funds. The Conference was such an admirable instrument for preserving unity that it continued in existence until 1932, when its powers were handed over to the larger Conference of nine hundred required by the Act of Methodist Union.

In 1769 Wesley had believed that at his death perhaps a fourth of his preachers would seek ordination in the Church; others would become Independent ministers, as John Edwards and Charles Skelton had done. He exhorted his preachers to keep together, form a committee, appoint a moderator, and carry on.

His arrangement of the Legal Conference was a better scheme, and the preachers formed such a band of brothers that the death of the leader whom they loved and revered bound them together more closely than ever in the determination to carry on his work. American Methodism adopted an episcopal system of government, but British Methodism has always rejected any proposals that bore any resemblance to episcopacy. Chairmen of districts and superintendents of circuits have special responsibilities and powers, but such a leader is always *primus inter pares*.

At the Conference after Wesley's death, Coke and Mather, who might have been regarded as two of Wesley's bishops, were passed by, and William Thompson was chosen President. It was significant that he was not an ordained minister of the Established Church, but one of the regular itirerants esteemed for his character, his long experience and sound judgement. There was to be no new king in Israel. An attempt in 1794 to establish a hierarchy of eight of the leading preachers was immediately rejected. A real cleavage of opinion appeared when the question was raised whether the preachers should administer the sacraments or not. John Wesley and his clerical associates had done this regularly in the Societies, and Wesley had also ordained preachers for America and Scotland with that end in view. In 1786 he also ordained missionaries for Antigua and Newfoundland, and the following year one for the West Indies and one for Nova Scotia. It was not until 1788, after long hesitation, that he ordained men for work in England. Alexander Mather was the first, and in 1789 Henry Moore and Thomas Rankin. These were three of his best-known preachers; Mather was ordained Superintendent (or bishop), Moore and Rankin as presbyters. The ordination certificate of the presbyters declares that they are qualified to feed the flock of Christ and to administer the sacraments of baptism and the Lord's Supper 'according to the usage of the Church of England'.

He was clearly looking ahead to the regular transmission of orders after his death. He declared that when he passed away the Methodists would become 'a regular Presbyterian Church'. Still, he exhorted all three to continue united to the Church of England 'so far as the blessed work in which they were engaged would permit'. He himself greatly preferred the Episcopal to the Presbyterian form of government. The 1794 Conference, which rejected any idea of Methodist Episcopalianism, also declared that the Lord's Supper was not to be given in future where the union and concord of the Society could be maintained without it. The same rule applied to baptisms. Love and harmony were to regulate action. This was difficult, since the majority strongly desired the ministrations of their own preachers at the Lord's Table as well as in the pulpit. In the opinion of John Pawson, 'Had the preachers, after his [Wesley's] death, only acted upon his plan, and quietly granted the people who desired the sacraments that privilege, no division would have taken place'. An influential minority, however, wished to go back to the arrangements carried out by Wesley during most of his ministry among the Societies. Many of these were Anglicans first and Methodists second.

The trouble came to a head in Bristol as soon as the Conference was over. Henry Moore administered the sacrament in one of the chapels, and the trustees of the other two chapel in Bristol immediately prohibited him from preaching in their pulpits. Long discussions followed which led to the Plan of Pacification of 1795. This allowed that the sacraments might be administered, where a majority of trustees and also a majority of stewards and leaders were favourable, provided the consent of the Conference were given in each case. This led to an amicable solution, since the majorities were forthcoming in increasing numbers until the practice became universal. The preachers were not, however, ordained by imposition of hands until 1836, when the Conference Ordination Service was established: until that date ordination was by the act and prayer of the President and by the public recognition of the probationers in the sessions of the Conference itself. It is of sentimental interest, at least, that Henry Moore was still alive in 1836 and took part in the ordination service.

It was surprising that there was so little disturbance in the Societies in the stormy years of the last decade of the eighteenth century. The spirit of the French Revolution had crossed the Channel and found expression in radical and republican clubs. Many Dissenters responded to the stirrings of modern democracy, while the Established Church became more entrenched in its Toryism. Methodism was conservative on the whole, but there were radical elements within it. The great majority of the members of Society were more concerned with religious than political questions. They were shocked by the popular writings of Paine, whom they regarded as a dangerous infidel. This may account for the small effect of the first Methodist schism on the great progress of Wesleyan Methodism in those years. Alexander Kilham was not satisfied with the Plan of Pacification; he wished for more popular control in the Societies. He was really a Dissenter and his methods of controversy were so much disliked that he was expelled from the ministry. Though one of the younger preachers, he had served under Wesley and had done fine work in several circuits. Although he took five thousand members and several local preachers with him, the expansion of the Societies was so great that no decrease in the parent body was reported.

The membership in Great Britain and Ireland grew year by year after Wesley's death much more rapidly than in his lifetime. Within twenty-five years the numbers increased threefold, having risen from 72,468 to 220,222. Progress in the United States was even greater, and between 1800 and 1825 the members in the Methodist Societies throughout the world increased from 188,522 to 631,252. The ministry also increased to 2,397, not including many thousands of local preachers in both hemispheres. These figures show that the great Revival of religion was sweeping on. When one remembers that these were also the years when the Evangelical influence in the Church of England was growing rapidly, when the era of social and philanthropic reform began, it becomes clearer than ever that we are here confronted by one of the greatest forces that ever shaped the character and destiny of the English-speaking people.

Whatever may have been the case with the Evangelicals in the Church of England, British Methodists were very conscious of their relationship to their fellow Methodists in the United States. In the last letter that Wesley wrote to America, a month before his death, he said: 'See that you never give place to one thought of separating from your brethren in Europe. Lose no opportunity of declaring to all men that the Methodists are one people in all the world: and that it is their full determination so to continue

> Though mountains rise, and oceans roll
> To sever us in vain.'

The American returns disappeared from the *Minutes of Conference*, but visits were paid by fraternal delegates from each side to preserve the unity and fellowship of a people who were truly one. The *Methodist Magazine* kept the people at home informed, not only of good news from fellow Methodists in America, but from the growing missions throughout the world. This magazine is still published and has had a longer continuous existence than any other in England. Its romantic stories of the adventures of missionaries in distant parts and its still more remarkable tales of 'the Providence of God displayed' had little competition in many middle-class homes. It would not only be Charlotte Brontë whose youthful imagination was kindled by 'mad Methodist magazines', but many another bright and inquiring mind. We can imagine the youthful George Eliot turning over the same strangely fascinating pages in the house of Dinah Morris.

The Wesleyan Missionary Society came into existence after the Baptist Missionary Society, the L.M.S., and the C.M.S., but the Methodists were really the pioneers of the modern missionary movement. Only the Moravians preceded them. The work of the S.P.G. and the S.P.C.K. was of another kind. Methodism was missionary by nature. Its introduction into the West Indies in 1760, into Nova Scotia in 1765, and the American colonies in 1766 marks the real beginning of Methodist foreign missions. When Boardman and Pilmoor were sent to Philadelphia in 1769, it was a conscious undertaking of world responsibility. Perhaps Coke saw this more clearly than Wesley. That remarkable little man was great only in his unquenchable faith in the greatness of the Kingdom of God and the unlimited power of God in establishing it. That confidence drove him on with unresting energy in the cause of the Gospel from the moment he met Wesley in 1776 until his body was committed to the waters of the Indian Ocean in 1814. He was the first bishop of the Methodist Church in America. He founded the missions among the slaves in the West Indies. Again and again the Methodist preachers were silenced by governors in Jamaica, in St. Eustatius, in St. Vincent; it was Coke who beleaguered the Government offices in Whitehall and even in the Hague, until he got the ban lifted.

He encouraged the missionaries in all their difficulties, and had the joy of knowing before he died that there were seventeen thousand negroes gathered into the West Indian Societies. It was a pity he did not live to see the great day, July 31, 1834, when they gathered by thousands in their chapels before midnight and at the moment of liberation rose up and sang, 'Praise God from whom all blessings flow', and then Charles Wesley's hymn, 'The year of jubilee is come'. Coke's efforts to establish Evangelical religion in France were less successful, but he stimulated the work among the peasants of Ireland and the preaching of the Gospel in the Welsh language to the people of Wales. As early as 1786 he published his design for 'A mission to Asia', but more than a quarter of a century passed before he saw his dream fulfilled. The East India Company objected to the attempt at the evangelization of India, though the Government thought of sending a bishop there.

Coke has been severely condemned because he wrote to Wilberforce offering himself for such a task and declaring his readiness to sacrifice his association with Methodism with that end in view. 'India cleaves to my heart', he said. 'I sincerely believe that my strong inclination to spend the remainder of my life there originates in the Divine will, while I am called upon to use this secondary means to obtain the end.' Needless to say, there was no hope that the Church of England would send Coke out as a bishop, but the simplicity of his offer need not be ridiculed. Coke went back to the Methodist Conference and with the greatest difficulty persuaded his brethren to undertake a mission to Ceylon and Java, if India were closed to them. They yielded to his eloquent pleading, after he had spent a night in prayer. Perhaps the fact that he was ready to spend the whole of his not inconsiderable fortune in the great cause, as he always had done, helped the decision.

He set sail on December 30, 1813, with six missionaries, two of whom were accompanied by their wives. All through the journey he was reading Portuguese, so that he could be more efficient in his work in Ceylon. It was on the morning of May 3, 1814, that he was found dead on the floor of his cabin placidly smiling. When we read the story of his labours for four continents, we can understand why Asbury, who knew him so well, said on receiving the news of his death, 'a minister of Christ, in zeal, in labours and in services, the greatest man of the last century'. His companions were almost ready to give up their undertaking under the weight of this calamity. Fortunately, they decided to go forward, and met with a remarkable welcome from Lord Molesworth, the commandant of the garrison in Ceylon. He regarded their arrival as an answer to prayer, and their services began with a parade of British troops, the Liturgy of the English Church being used. Later in the day, Lord Molesworth left a party in his own home to join the missionaries in a prayer meeting, and became the first convert, saying, 'This is the best day of my life'. Such was the beginning of the Methodist mission to Ceylon, which was to lead on to India and across the years to the moving record of the conversion of the outcaste people at the present time.

Four of the missionaries who accompanied Coke were Irishmen, and Coke himself was President of the Irish Conference. There is little wonder that the Irish Conference should consider how it could support 'our missions throughout the globe' by auxiliaries in all the circuits of Ireland. Irish Methodism has made contributions to overseas missions, both of men and money, out of proportion to its strength and numbers ever since. Where Ireland led, England followed. A little later Leeds, which was at that time the strongest centre of Methodist activity in England, took up the same cause. In the neighbourhood were Jabez Bunting and Richard Watson, who took a lead in awakening the new zeal for world evangelization, not as the concern of the few, but as the enthusiasm of the whole Church. So the Wesleyan Missionary Society came into existence at the Conference of 1818. Sixty years of missionary activity lay behind this new organization, but it was the death of Coke that crystallized out what had been so long in solution. A new chapter in the story of the Revival had begun.

Seen in the perspective of a hundred and twenty years, the story of the Wesleyan Missionary Society and of the corresponding Societies in the daughter Churches is not only one of great heroism and achievements, but a page in the history of God's Providence. In West Africa, at first tragedy seemed greater than achievement, and in South Africa, Australia, and New Zealand difficulty and success walked hand in hand. Perhaps the story of the Friendly Islands and Fiji is the most romantic of all. The first Wesleyan missionaries to Tonga arrived there in 1820. The beautiful islands of the South Seas were then the scene of cannibalism and of vice and cruelty only to be paralleled by deeds of shame of certain so-called civilized peoples of our own day. How the King of Tonga was converted, built a chapel and crowded it with more than a thousand worshippers. How the good news spread from island to island until it came to heathen Fiji. How a great revival broke out there, with scenes like those witnessed in Cornwall and Yorkshire years before, by which a thousand were added to the Church in a day. How King George became a class leader and afterwards a local preacher—a man of outstanding personality and sound judgement. How the spears of his ancestors were turned into rails for the Communion table and two clubs, formerly adored as deities, placed as pillars to the pulpit stairs. How, after a generation, the Methodist Societies in the Friendly and Fiji islands had three hundred day schools and two hundred and thirty preaching places, twenty-three missionaries, five hundred and forty local preachers and more than 15,000 communicants is a record for which a volume is needed. In the whole history of Christianity there is no better chapter of miracle and grace.

The other missionary societies born at the same time sprang out of the same awakening to newness of life and had similar triumphs to record. Even Carey, who is often called the father of modern missions, owed much to the Evangelical Revival. His awaking dates back to the Call to Prayer by the Northampton Association of Baptist Churches in 1784. 'We trust you will not confine your requests to your own societies; or to your immediate connexion; let the whole interest of the Redeemer be affectionately remembered, and the spread of the Gospel to the most distant parts of the habitable globe be the object of your most fervent requests.' These were the words which closed the Call to Prayer, and to-day they need a footnote to explain that 'Societies here mean churches; connexion means denomination'. No one who had travelled the country in company with John Wesley or the Methodist preachers would need that explanation. It may fairly be claimed that the modern missionary movement sprang directly out of the eighteenth-century Revival.

Methodism continued to expand throughout the nineteenth century with unabated vigour in every continent except South America. In England its progress was checked in the middle of the century by controversies and divisions. The growth of what we now call left-wing politics throughout Europe led to the revolutions of 1830 and 1848. All this took a milder form in England, but Radicalism and Chartism were powerfully at work. Methodism, in spite of its alleged other-worldliness, played a great part in shaping our present-day democracy. Its class leaders and local preachers were numbered by the thousand. For the most

M

part they were men of personality and excellent character, esteemed by their neighbours and gifted with great potentiality for leadership in trade unions and political clubs as well as in class meetings. They had learned to speak effectively in pulpits and Sunday schools; they were accustomed to the discussion of business in church meetings. They helped to shape the trade unions and in a later generation provided many Labour leaders.

The Conference was on the whole Conservative; its chief leaders markedly so. It still consisted entirely of the itinerant preachers as in Wesley's day. Not until 1878 was lay representation admitted, though laymen served on all the important committees at which the chief business of the Connexion was transacted. A very able group of men led the Conference, and they were chiefly concerned with preserving all that was best in the Evangelical tradition handed down from Wesley, in developing and strengthening the remarkable organization of Methodism, and in spreading the Kingdom of God far and wide. All of them were powerful preachers, and their whole lives were dedicated to the cause which they called the 'Work of God'. Head and shoulders above the rest in statesmanship, in debate, and in authority was Jabez Bunting. He was to Methodism what Rainy was to Scottish Presbyterianism in the succeeding generation; more so, inasmuch as Methodism was more highly centralized than Presbyterianism. It was Bunting who made the Conference what it was, an assembly worthy to be compared in dignity and strength with the Assembly of the Church of Scotland. It was Bunting who completed the organization of the Church and set the Missionary Society on its feet.

He was the first President of the Theological Institution and saw the first two theological colleges for the training of ministers established in London and Manchester. He strengthened the authority of the ministers in their circuits and gave the superintendents powers of rule as well as of leadership. Of his fine character and his entire devotion to the 'Work of God' there was no question, but his autocracy began to awaken opposition. In politics he was a strong Tory, and the Liberal element in the Conference and in the Societies became restless. His policy was consistently wise, but the desire for greater lay representation increased and agitations developed. A war of pamphlets, many of which were anonymous, led to the expulsion of three of the leading 'reforming' preachers from the Conference and a cleavage throughout the Societies which resulted in the loss of 100,000 members. It was a tragedy which marked the end of the confident triumphant progress of Methodism in its earliest love. Only 40,000 of those who departed found their way into the new fellowship. Feelings were strong and much tactlessness was shown in many circuits by superintendent ministers who often had good reason for provocation.

Gradually hope returned, and the 'sixties and 'seventies saw the march forward vigorously resumed. The 'eighties were the days of new forward movements and evangelistic approaches to the growing town population. Since 1849 there have been no further divisions in British Methodism. William Booth left Methodism as an individual to open a new campaign with the Salvation Army, but his was an independent venture, as had been those of the Primitive Methodists and the Bible Christians sixty years before. The nineteenth century was rampant in individualism; in the twentieth century men began to see the need for co-operation and began to talk of reunion. In 1907 the Methodist New Connexion, which dated back to Kilham's day, the Bible Christians, and the United Methodist Free Churches (who represented the various separations from the parent body in the nineteenth century) came together as the United Methodist Church. Twenty-five years later almost all Methodists in the British Isles were gathered together in the reunited Methodist Church. Weselyan Methodists, Primitive Methodists, and United Methodists were now one. The great record might have been much greater had a truly catholic spirit prevailed throughout. It may be gravely doubted whether the momentum lost during the years of secession was ever recovered.

How did the Methodism outside the Church of England compare with the Methodism within the Church during this period? There was little difference in doctrine, except in emphasis. Both stressed the conversion of the individual as the very soul of Christianity. Both waged a frontal attack on sin and worldliness. Both proclaimed the Cross and the Atonement as the way of salvation. The Evangelicals were modifying the strictness of their Calvinism and coming nearer to the Arminian position of the Wesleyan Methodists. At a later date they were even to make terms with John Wesley's views of Christian Perfection at their

Keswick Conventions. When the Clapham Sect was active in its philanthropic and missionary campaigns, it was strongly supported by the Methodists separated from the Church. There was a good deal of co-operation and friendly rivalry. For the emancipation of the slaves they worked together in complete harmony. In the pioneering days of the Missionary Societies they stirred one another up to love and good works. The Evangelicals, following the tradition of Whitefield and the Countess of Huntingdon, gained victories in aristocratic circles. The Establishment gave them a strong position and their differences from the Wesleyan Methodists were social rather than ecclesiastical.

Wesley's followers were winning their way among the middle classes and to a less degree among the working classes. The Primitive Methodists and the Bible Christians were more successful with the very poor than the Wesleyans. English religion was becoming a class question. The Wesleyans were particularly numerous among the shopkeepers, farmers, and better-class artisans. In villages, for instance, farmers and their friends might often be found in the Wesleyan chapel, while the farm-labourers met in the Primitive Methodist sanctuary. Of course, there was no clear-cut division and the situation was sometimes reversed. Primitive Methodism was also strong among the Durham miners. In some cathedral cities nearly all the shops in the High Street would be Methodist shops and a great Wesleyan congregation would gather under the very shadow of the Cathedral. In big business and in Northern factories, too, Wesleyan Methodism was prominent and grew in wealth in the prosperous years. More than ever the 'successful merchants' needed Wesley's injunction, 'Give all you can'. To do them justice, it must be said that they gave the modern Church a new standard of generosity. No Church has been better served by its laymen in money, in sacrifice and in personal devotion than the Methodist Church.

Then came a period of dangerous prosperity described elsewhere as the Mahogany Age, when Methodism was becoming wealthy and sedate. So we got our mahogany pulpits, and the preachers found their way to the mahogany tables of wealthy laymen. 'The preaching was still Evangelical, but the preacher was no longer going into the highways and hedges to constrain men to come in; otherwise William Booth might never have broken away from Methodism and the Salvation Army might never have come into existence. The well-filled family pew provided satisfactory congregations in town and country. In many ways those were delightful days for the Methodist preacher. He moved from circuit to circuit, meeting everywhere with kindly, hospitable people. The itinerant system knit the whole Connexion together into one big family. Nothing quite like it, on so large a scale, had ever been seen in Christian history. Laymen and ministers worked together in remarkable harmony. A devoted minister was received with esteem wherever he 'travelled'. He had friends in all parts of the country. It is true he never had a home of his own and travelled from one manse to another, finding similar horse-hair suites in the studies, red-plush furniture in the dining-rooms, and green rep in the drawing-rooms, but these remarkable moves were accepted as quite a normal manner of life. When the laymen began to come to Conference in 1878, the family tendency was increased. That great annual love-feast became a bewildering renewal of acquaintances, where everybody knew nearly everybody else, and friends from former circuits revived with the travelling preachers the memories of other days. It was too good to last, and the stable Victorian family life was transformed by many changes.'[1] What was true of Wesleyan Methodism, was true also of the other branches of Methodism in varying degrees.

By contrast, the Evangelical seemed less genial and less attractive at this period. He also tended to be narrower and inclined to a stricter bibliolatry, with an occasional excursion into Second Adventism. He was inclined to stand on his ecclesiastical dignity, and the Methodist often found his Evangelical and Low Church brother less friendly than the High Churchman. The Methodist, too, reacted less violently to the Oxford Movement. He was a strong Protestant, but he disliked Kensitite excesses. In Ireland, the Methodist got on better with his Roman Catholic neighbours than the Church of Ireland did. This was strange, since it was only the Methodists in Ireland who seemed to make any inroads on the Roman Catholic strength by their open-air preaching. Their successes in the middle years of the nineteenth century were obscured by the vast tide of emigration that set in for America,

---

[1] *The Methodist Church: Its Origin, Divisions and Reunion* (Epworth Press), pp. 71-2.

but the converts went to swell the numbers of Methodism overseas.

There was always a drift back to Anglicanism from English Methodism. Here social influences counted for much, though occasionally the greater dignity of worship and even the contrast of High Church doctrine won the allegiance of those who had been brought up in the simpler ways of the Methodist people. Some Methodist ministers and more sons of the manse became Anglican clergy. Not a few well-known Methodist names are found in the hierarchy of the Establishment among bishops, deans, archdeacons, and canons. There has also been a smaller return flow from Anglicanism to Methodism, almost entirely from the laity. It is generally noticed how good a Methodist a former Anglican becomes.

The Wesleyans were very stable in their theology, and in all the divisions of Methodism differences in doctrine have played no part. This may be due to the consistent emphasis on the practical side in religion and a certain lack of intellectual curiosity. Methodism has produced many biblical scholars of the first rank, but few outstanding theologians. At his first Conference in 1744, Wesley asked the question, 'Can we have a seminary for our labourers?' and received the answer, 'If God spare us till another Conference'. However, the next Conference was unable to find 'a proper tutor' and the subject was dropped. There was no Doddridge to establish for Methodism an institution like his Northampton Academy. Wesley did correspond with Doddridge about the books his preachers should read, and constantly returned to his dream of a training school for them. Kingswood did a little in this way, but the demands of the itinerant work were so urgent there was no chance to make a Wesleyan Trevecca. Failing this, he urged his preachers to read five hours a day, and in his *Christian Library* provided them with a *World's Classics* of cheap theological, devotional and historical literature.

In spite of early disadvantages in education, most of his preachers became well-read men and some of them first-class scholars. The biblical *Commentaries* of Coke and Adam Clarke, of Joseph Sutcliffe and Richard Watson had great circulations; that of Clarke exceeding in popularity even the widely read *Commentary* of Thomas Scott, so much beloved by early Evangelicals. Certainly the Bible was well studied by the Methodists of that period and the preachers were at least equipped with an accurate knowledge of the Book of books. Wesley regarded his preachers as laymen, and they continued to be so regarded for some years after his death. It was Bunting who stressed the pastoral work of the preachers and, though the 1793 and 1794 Conferences had decided that the title 'reverend' should not be used by them, the decision was reversed in 1818. From that date the Methodist preachers claimed the position of Christian ministers and, at a later date, even secured a decision in a court of law on the right to be called the Reverend A. B.

The next step was to give candidates for the ministry an adequate training. The Conference of 1823 appointed a committee of inquiry and received a unanimous report in favour of a 'seminary for our labourers', to use Wesley's term. It was not until January, 1835, that the Hoxton Academy was opened for this purpose, a poor place in a depressing district. Five years later a move was made to Abney House, where Isaac Watts had lived for thirty-six years as the guest of Sir Thomas and Lady Abney. This, too, was but a temporary home. The Centenary Fund of 1839 provided the funds to establish the first two of the theological colleges that continue to serve the Church to the present day. Didsbury College, Manchester, was opened in September, 1842, and Richmond College in the September of the following year. The course of training came to be three years in the colleges, where a 'classical' as well as a theological education was given, followed by a four-year probation in the circuits, during which the reading of the probationers was directed and examined.

This did not compare in thoroughness with the Presbyterian scheme, nor with the full training of some Roman Catholic orders, but it was better than the Anglican provision at that time. It is true that most of the Church of England clergy were graduates of Oxford or Cambridge, but their direct preparation for their life work was slender. Most of the candidates for the Methodist ministry had some experience of business before they were sent to a theological college and few of them were graduates when they were received. The older universities were then closed to non-Anglicans. Sir Richard Livingstone has pointed out recently how much of our real education begins after we have reached our majority. The students used the opportunities provided for them well and most of them in that period read consistently throughout their travelling ministry, with the result that for efficient service Methodism had a ministry equal to that of any Church. It was not until 1863 that the Evangelicals in the Church of England met the need for the theological training of the clergy. In that year St. John's Hall, Highbury, was opened, to be followed by Wycliffe Hall, Oxford, in 1877 and Ridley Hall, Cambridge, in 1881. There were also diocesan theological colleges not directly under Evangelical influence.

It was significant that the Liturgy of the Church of England was used in the Methodist college chapels at morning services, as though to set a standard for Methodist worship. It was used also in many of the larger Wesleyan chapels throughout the country. Watson, in 1830, said that the use of the Liturgy was general in foreign mission stations, and was so much increasing at home that it was probable 'that in a few years it will become the general mode of our forenoon service in all the large chapels'. Watson's prophecy has not been fulfilled. In recent years the tendency has been to give up the use of the Liturgy, though it is still maintained in many churches, from City Road downwards. This brings us to the main difference between the Methodists inside and outside the Church of England—the use of the Book of Common Prayer. Those of us who only worship according to the Prayer Book occasionally probably underestimate the influence of that great book on the lives of those who worship regularly in parish churches. With the old Evangelicals its inspiration was almost equal to that of the Bible itself. It was as much a manual of theology as of devotion. It preserved unity of belief as well as uniformity of worship.

Nonconformists were regarded as hopelessly impoverished in their religious life as well as in their worship by their neglect of the Prayer Book. There is some truth in this criticism, but those who make it should read what R. W. Dale has to say in favour of extempore prayer on the other side. Wesleyans tried to make the best of both worlds. Their order of service for Holy Communion and baptism followed that of the Church of England closely and, though the Methodist *Book of Offices* has recently been revised, it is clear that here, at least, Methodism is the daughter of the Church of England. Ignorance is the mother of misunderstanding and it would not be necessary to state these facts were it not that the ecclesiastical camps are so divided that sometimes there appears to be as much knowledge of each other's manner of life between Anglican and Methodist as between the inhabitants of Greenland and Tahiti.

Methodists may have suffered devotionally and theologically by their comparative neglect of the Prayer Book, but it should be remembered that they have had a unique devotional and theological manual in *Wesley's Hymns*. That body of doctrine, for which Charles Wesley was largely responsible, sank deeper into the heart and remained more firmly embedded in the memory, even than the General Confession or the Collects. The old Methodists were as much in danger of regarding *Wesley's Hymns* as being verbally inspired as the Evangelicals were concerning the Prayer Book. It is related of one old lay preacher that he was troubled in his conscience on his death-bed because he loved the Hymn-Book more than the Bible. He might be sure of absolution for that venial sin, because so much of the Bible went into Charles Wesley's verse. No hymns are so theological. No hymns are so biblical, and not even Keble follows the Christian year with such devotion. Still, the fact remains, that the Prayer Book and the Hymn-Book have played an important part in producing the difference in *ethos* between the descendants of the Methodists inside and outside the Church of England to-day.

That they drifted farther apart during the nineteenth century there can be little doubt. There are signs that they are coming closer together to-day. The revolutionary changes in the approach to the Bible that have taken place in the last half-century have now been accepted by Methodists and Evangelicals alike. The Methodist was more inclined to listen to the historical and scientific critics who brought about this changed outlook than the Evangelical was. Seventy years ago he might have regarded Darwin and Huxley, Wellhausen and Robertson Smith with deep suspicion, but a generation later all was changed. It was surprising how peacefully the passage was made from something like Fundamentalism to the views represented by Hastings's *Dictionary of the Bible* and Peake's *Commentary*. The old approach had almost entirely disappeared from the Methodist theological colleges at the beginning of this century, though it lingered in some Evangelical circles. Since then, the Liberal Evangelicals have demonstrated how it is possible to come to terms with modern science and with literary criticism and also to preserve a deep loyalty to the Gospel. Methodist teaching is closely akin to that of the Liberal Evangelicals at the present time. In biblical study scholars from all branches of Christ's Church have worked together and so have drawn closer to each other. The same is true in other fields of study and service. Social and ecclesiastical barriers are disappearing in these strange days. Even so unlikely an instrument as the radio is rapidly changing our outlook. Religious services tend to approximate towards a new norm as though even the Prayer Book itself were being challenged. Still, our inheritance and traditions, our loyalties and prejudices cannot be shed in a day. There are deeps of the spirit that call out across sundering straits and say to kindred souls, 'Thou art my brother'. The deepest note in the life of the true Evangelical, by whatever party name he calls himself, is, 'Who shall deliver me? . . . I thank God through Jesus Christ my Lord'.

> Love, like death, hath all destroyed,
> Rendered all distinctions void;
> Names, and sects, and parties fall;
> Thou, O Christ, art all in all.

Chapter XV

STEPS TOWARDS REUNION

In 1834 some of the bishops of the Church of England made a tentative approach to the question of the return of the Methodists to that Church. The Bishop of Exeter, in a charge to the clergy of his diocese, said: 'The great mass of Dissenters amongst us are Methodists, and of these, the far greater portion are Wesleyans—a class of Christians whom I grieve to call Separatists; for Separatists, I am bound to say, is but another name for Schismatics.' He exhorted the Wesleyans to return to the fold, since in doctrine they were in 'almost entire agreement' with the Establishment. Some exchanges of pamphlets followed, but it was clear that such an approach was not well-timed. A generation earlier it might have led to a serious discussion, though even at the beginning of the nineteenth century only a minority in the Wesleyan Societies would have called themselves Church Methodists. In 1834 they had just expelled one of their ministers for his activities over Disestablishment, and refused to be called Dissenters. Their tendencies in politics were Tory rather than Whig, and they had much esteem for the Church of England, except in those villages where squire and parson were still combined together to suppress them, if that were possible. Still they valued their class meetings, their love-feasts and their watch-nights; they appreciated the voluntary labours of their local preachers and valued their itinerant ministry so highly that they would not have listened to any suggestion of re-ordination. Separated Methodism had become strong and self-conscious and did not regard itself as schismatic. The discussion petered out and the conditions of a reunion were not frankly faced. A hundred and more years have passed, and the discussion is renewed with a deeper sense of reality. We are living in a different world. Rome *may* be *semper eadem*, but neither Methodism nor the Church of England is the same to-day as in 1834. The doctrinal standards may remain unchanged, but emphasis and interpretation have changed. We breathe a different atmosphere of political and religious life and problems have emerged of which our great-grandfathers could never have dreamed.

It is on the mission field that the discussion has become most urgent. The union of Churches in South India marches forward to its completion and North India seems likely to follow suit. Indian Christians are not interested in the difference between Anglicans, Presbyterians, Methodists, Baptists and Congregation-alists, and there is no reason why they should be. If Church union is achieved there, it must react upon the Churches at home. Chaplains in the Forces have been much embarrassed by denomi-national separations as they were in the last war, and have urged that difficulties in the way of intercommunion and united parade services should be removed. In the field of religious education at home when the old stale denominational issues recur, the more far-sighted and catholic teachers see no solution except reunion. After the last world war the Lambeth Appeal of the Anglican bishops in conference stirred the imagination and quickened the enthusiasm of an elect company. Reunion seemed likely to become an immediate concern for practical politics.

In reading through the documents on reunion issued since 1920, it is rather depressing to contrast the optimism and idealism of the Lambeth Appeal with the tentative and hesitating responses that followed. 'The time has come!' was the note of the Appeal, but twenty years have passed and little progress can be reported. The Lambeth Conference of 1931 seemed to be impressed more by the hope of closer fellowship between the Anglican and Greek Churches than between Anglican and Nonconformist at home. The approach to Constantinople was good, particularly in the days that followed the tragic experiences of the Greek Church in Russia. 'This ought ye to have done and not to have left the other undone.' There are, however, still many Anglican priests for whom the Exarch of Bulgaria looms larger than the Moderator of the Free Church Assembly; any archimandrite on the other side of Europe is of much more consequence than the Congregational minister in the next street. There is some lack of a sense of perspective here.

The old divisions of the English people from the days of Cavaliers and Roundheads down to the present time added colour and interest to our history. It was differences in religion that laid the foundations of our system of government by Court and Country Party, by Whig and Tory, by Liberal and Conservative. These differences, both religious and political, crossed the

Atlantic, with a Whig and Nonconformist ascendancy there, as
there was a Church and Tory ascendancy here. Immigration of
other races has changed the whole scene in the United States of
America, though the old religious divisions remain. The meaning
of old battle-cries and watchwords fades away and some divisions
into sects and parties have become meaningless. The Englishman,
and still more the American, has little regard for history. It is
only small nationalities that keep their historical memories alive
and, unfortunately, these are chiefly memories of grievances.
It is regrettable that great traditions are so soon forgotten.
Students and ecclesiastics may wrangle about the Fathers of the
Church, about the historic episcopate, and talk about the *una
sancta* as though it had spell-binding power. They may regard
themselves as the guardians of truth, but, for the English-speaking
people, the last three or four hundred years are of far more
consequence than the fifteen centuries that went before. In the
years that date from Queen Elizabeth onwards we find all the
creative forces that shape our lives to-day, though their origins
lie far back in the past.

La recherche du temps perdu is too boring for us. Occasionally we
may cast a fascinated glance at the strange medieval world, or the
dark ages, or the collapse of the Roman Empire, and at the Fathers
at Nicaea and their predecessors. The episcopate is historic, but its
secure diocesan history can be traced no farther back than the
second century. We see the Early Church fumbling about for a
long time before it found that admirable form of government.
The divisions of English Church life are also historic. It is nearly
three hundred years since the cleavage between the Church of
England and the Nonconformists became fixed and apparently
unbridgeable. It is more than two hundred years since the
Methodist Societies began to spring up all over the country. We
can therefore speak of our historic Nonconformity and our
historic Methodism. The Presbyterian is still more historic, and
the persistence of divisions presumes some adequate reason for so
long an existence. The lament about 'our unhappy divisions' is
an Anglican lament. What, then, are the Anglicans prepared to
do to heal the divisions which distress them so much. It seems
clear that the lead must come from the Church of England.

Many of the best minds in that Church are deeply concerned
for the future of British and American Christianity. They believe

—and rightly believe—that it has a responsible part to play in leadership for world Christianity, especially if the world war ends in a victory for the Allies over the Axis Powers. An opportunity for courageous evangelism may lie before us such as we have never seen before. If we contemplate the great areas and populations under the sway of the Soviet and Chinese Republics, we may find that our study of our own Revival of religion has something to say to us. The cell in Communism is like the Society class in Methodism. It may be that a simple form of aggressive religion in which laymen play a great part would be a more effective instrument for the Kingdom of God than an elaborate and ritualistic ecclesiasticism. Both expressions of Christianity have their value, but it would be a poor kind of reunion which would aim at the absorption of one form by the other with a view to suppressing it. We have had caution to excess. Now is the time for courage and imagination. What are the difficulties that obstruct reunion, and what are our sources of encouragement?

The difficulties are clear enough. Two or three hundred years of separation have blurred our vision of the unity of Christ's Church. In one sense, the Church was divided as soon as the disciples left Jerusalem after Pentecost. Local churches were established, separated from each other by hundreds of miles of land and sea. This inevitable geographical separation did not destroy the real unity of the Church. Nor did differences in atmosphere, in tradition of worship and government. The churches at Jerusalem, at Corinth, at Rome must all have been different. The surprising thing is that elements of uniformity soon began to appear and in the second century manifested themselves in the sphere of government as well as of worship. The unity of the Church existed before the uniformity was evolved and persisted after uniformity disappeared. Never can the Christian Church have been completely standardized. Since the Reformation in England we have known great variety and the uniformity of the Church has broken down altogether. The unity of the Church remains, but there is something more serious than geographical separation now. We have settled down on islands

With echoing straits between us thrown.

We may still be one people, but the straits that divide us are old prejudices, social distinctions, the mere inertia of history rather than differences of principle and doctrine. The Methodist is separated from the Anglican, not because they differ in belief; their doctrines may be to all intents and purposes identical. Nor are they separated because they differ in worship; their worship on Sundays may approximate very closely to each other. They are wedded to custom. A man may say, 'My father was a Methodist and I have no desire to change. If my worship is simpler than that of the church across the way, I prefer it so. Also I like the circuit system, the movement of ministers and variety of preachers'. 'Are you a member of the Catholic Church?' you ask him. 'Of course I am,' he says; 'and so, I presume, is John Smith of Trinity Church [Anglican] and all my other friends who are associated with different denominations.'

He has no sense whatever of being a schismatic. It never occurs to him that other Christians may regard him as a doubtful runner in the divine race because the whole of his side has been disqualified, their officials having been appointed irregularly. That would sound to him a piece of incredible nonsense. He may be interested in fellow Christians of other communions, but not individually so. He has no special desire to share in their fellowship; certainly not to approach their altars. He is so much occupied with the duties of his own Church that he has little time to spare for others. Certainly he does not echo the words of the Fernley Lecturer for 1873: 'What a yearning for unity pervades the Churches!' The first difficulty to be overcome, then, is that of apathy. The Methodists are not dying to come into the Anglican fold. They are still struggling with many unsolved problems that have been left them by their own union of ten years ago. It was a right thing for the scattered Methodist forces to come together into one family, and time will show the wisdom as well as the righteousness of that reunion. The process of fusion is, however, the work of years and for the moment it is problems rather than achievements that are visible.

There are many who have a wider view and find a new glow of hope for Christ's Universal Kingdom in every true oecumenical and interdenominational fellowship. Their hearts expand with joy whenever a party wall goes down. These are the watchmen who are looking for the dawn. We rejoice at pleas for action like that of Hugh Martin in his recent *Christian Reunion*; we recognize also the existence of a great mass of indifference. This is as true of

Anglicans as of Free Churchmen. We find the same parochialism joined to an even greater ignorance about the brother next door. The average Methodist is English of the English—practical, matter of fact, kindly, and direct. He is not much of a dogmatist, but is kept in the path of orthodoxy by the Bible and Hymn-Book and the old preaching standards. Whether the modern preaching is closely related to Wesley's *Sermons* or not, that body of practical and evangelical divinity is hardly ever challenged. Methodism has nearly as much variety as Anglicanism in its right, left, and centre religionists. The same spiritual, intellectual, and social influences have been at work on us all.

Even socially we are now cut from much the same cloth. In certain parts of the country attendance at the parish church still adds a little to social prestige, but the Victorian differences have gone or are going very rapidly. To-day it seems as though religious interests in England were chiefly confined to certain sections of the middle class. Modern levelling processes have brought the Churches closer together, but old snobberies and prejudices die hard. During the last war, when serving as a subaltern in a county regiment, I marched a large Wesleyan church parade to the morning service, conducted it, and then marched the parade back again. I was asked by a fellow officer if I 'went inside'. He told me there was no obligation to go inside the building with the parade, but was anxious to hear my impressions of divine worship in a Wesleyan chapel. 'I should think it was very funny,' he said. I hope he was reassured when I told him that I had not only gone inside, but had conducted the service and preached the sermon. This son of a country squire evidently knew little of Methodism. Yet we were fellow Christians who would have lived and worshipped in unity and good fellowship if we had chanced to belong to the same community. It was an accident that kept us apart.

Quite recently a rector of an important parish, who had served his Church for forty years in different parts of the country, was greatly astonished to discover that the Methodist Church issued a Book of Offices which bore a real kinship to the Book of Common Prayer. A London vicar expressed great surprise when he was told that Methodist doctrine had not really deviated from that of the Homilies and the Thirty-Nine Articles of the Church of England. He imagined that the Methodists had plunged into some wild heresies as soon as they left the sheltering precincts of the Establishment. Here was a case, not only of defective knowledge of the present Christian world in England, but a complete lack of any historical background. We are still so insular that we can barely see each other across the straits. We have a few nodding acquaintances, and friendship between the leaders in the Churches is steadily increasing, but have we yet reached the stage of complete confidence in each other?

The most hopeful step towards reunion was the brave and truly catholic declaration about non-episcopal ministries of the Appeal to all Christians from the bishops assembled in the Lambeth Conference of 1920: 'It is not that we call in question for a moment the spiritual reality of those Communions, which do not possess the Episcopate. On the contrary, we thankfully acknowledge that these ministries have been manifestly blessed and owned by the Holy Spirit as effective means of Grace.' This was explained later as meaning that 'Ministries which imply a sincere desire to preach Christ's Word and administer the Sacraments as Christ has ordained and to which authority so to do has been solemnly given by the Churches concerned—are real ministries of Christ's Word and Sacraments in the Universal Church. Yet ministries even when so regarded may be in varying degrees irregular or defective'. Many barriers go down before these statements, and one would have thought that the next step was intercommunion. If differences of doctrine and order are frankly faced, they will be seen to be of less moment than we imagined. A greater difficulty lies in sentiment resulting from the backwash of history. The less we know about the history of the past the more powerfully do the sentiments of other days, powerful even when records of fact are forgotten, cast their spell upon us. We may not be able to set out the arguments against Ship Money, or the constitutional wrangles of the Long Parliament, but we can still in spirit ride with Hampden to Chalgrove Field or charge with Cromwell and his Ironsides at Marston Moor.

If the old sentiments of hostility and conflict are now changing rapidly to cordial friendship, and if the Anglicans agree that the ministries in the Free Churches are 'real ministries of Christ's Word and *Sacraments*', why cannot Anglicans and Free Churchmen meet together at the Lord's Table? This is a real problem to Free Churchmen, and they regard the Anglican arguments

N

against it as forced and unreal. It is said that intercommunion should be the goal to mark the achievement of reunion and not a means by which to reach it. That if we join in Holy Communion when we are still divided it is somewhat hypocritical since the fellowship is broken. Surely if our hearts are truly set on Christian reunion the fellowship at the Lord's Table is at least as real as that of any Communion held in any church in the country or any given Sunday of the year. The Free Churchman is inclined to say that if we do not regard one another as sufficiently Christian to meet our Lord together in the oldest and most sacred of our Christian ways of fellowship, to go on talking about reunion is mere hypocrisy. The sooner we decide to drop the whole discussion the better. The Anglican putting of the case sounds as though intercommunion were promised as a reward for the wandering prodigal when he returns home.

As a Methodist minister, I am excommunicated in every parish church in England. The incumbent may whisper an invitation to me that I shall be welcome at Holy Communion, but I have no desire to accept his invitation when I know that he is breaking his own regulations. It seems too much like the visits of bishops to the curtained 'Nicodemus' pew in Lady Huntingdon's chapel at Bath when Whitefield or some other well-known pulpiteer was preaching. In the last war, a friend of mine, a young Methodist preacher, was refused Communion a few days before he was killed in one of the battles on the Somme. He was probably the finest specimen of Christian manhood in the battalion, an officer loved by all. That refusal seemed to me at the time a sin against divine charity; I have seen no reason to change my mind since. If our regulations choke the ministration of the grace of God, so much the worse for our regulations. The Anglican position against intercommunion or open Communion must be made much clearer before real progress towards full union can be reported. There is a long history of fencing the tables on the Presbyterian side, and Methodists were once required to show their class tickets before they were admitted even to their love-feasts, but the Free Church position to-day is well stated by Hugh Martin:[1] 'We believe this kind of "fencing of the Table" is wrong. This is the Table of the Lord. It is not the Table of the Anglican or of the Baptist. We do wrong to turn away any soul who comes in

[1] *Christian Reunion*, p. 135.

sincerity to seek communion with us and with Him at His appointed trysting place. No amount of argument can shake me from that profound conviction.'

In Conferences on Faith and Order we are accustomed to discuss reunion in theological terms. History has its place in this discussion and the creeds and symbols of former centuries are inevitably reviewed. This is all very good and necessary, but it is not here that the real difficulties arise—at least not over questions of faith. So far as the area of Christendom with which this book is concerned—that is, that part of Christ's world-wide Church renewed and created by the Evangelical Revival—it cannot be asserted too emphatically that there is no doctrinal difficulty in the way of reunion. There are no greater deviations from accepted standards of Christian doctrine in the Methodist Church than in the Anglican Church. This persistent orthodoxy for two centuries of Methodist history may be regarded either as a depressing or an inspiring fact. It is depressing if we regard it as a sign of the lack of intellectual and imaginative adventure. It is inspiring if we believe that the life of Christ's Church is guided by a wisdom greater than our own and that loyalty to Him who is the Truth may be preserved in a mixed fellowship by that Holy Spirit, who constantly tells of the things of Christ and reveals them unto us. If we could be sure that same Spirit who inspired the Revival of religion inspires now the movement towards reunion, we could confidently go forward step by step as He directs us.

One important factor in the history of the last hundred years may seem to have been forgotten in this assertion of doctrinal unity. We have overlooked the second Oxford Movement and the new emphasis on order and orders, on apostolic succession and baptismal regeneration. You cannot make a clear-cut division between Faith and Order. A scheme of Church government may be regarded with such veneration as to become of more significance than any article in the Creed. 'I believe in the threefold order of bishops, priests, and deacons' may occupy more place in one's loving adoration than 'I believe in God the Father Almighty' or 'I believe in Jesus Christ, His Son our Lord'. There has been a great change since the judicious Hooker corrected the Puritans for finding Church order too exactly defined in the New Testament. It is the extreme Anglo-Catholic now who errs where the Puritan went astray in the sixteenth century. One distinguished writer of that school even went so far as to declare that 'the things concerning the Kingdom' about which our Lord talked with His disciples in the forty days after His Resurrection were the orders in the ministry. If this is the Faith handed down to the saints that must be accepted by all within the Catholic fold, reunion is postponed to the Greek kalends. 'We have not so learned Christ.' The Jesus whom we have loved and followed seems an entirely different Person from this ecclesiastic. He was a layman Himself.

Our reading of the New Testament leads us to believe that the Incarnate Word constituted the Church through His Spirit. It is the Word of that gospel that has ever built the Church. The gifts and graces and fruits of the Spirit available for the Christian ministry are possessed by the Church as a whole. It is for the Church, under the guidance of the same Spirit, to discover its own prophets, teachers, helps, and governments. In the New Testament we see the process at work; we catch glimpses at Corinth, at Antioch, at Rome, at Jerusalem of the Church shaping its organization. This is not government from below, but from above. The highest of high Church doctrines is that which continues to lay the stress on the first person both in pronoun and adjective in the declaration at Caesarea Philippi: '*I* will build *my* church.' It is a very low view of the Church which asserts that our instruction in the Christian faith begins with the bishop sitting on his throne. That may take us back to the Ignatian Epistles, but we would prefer to go nearer to the Apostolic Church. St. Paul, at least, did not begin there. In what may very well be the earliest words of the New Testament he says: 'Paul an apostle—not appointed by men nor commissioned by any man but by Jesus Christ and God the Father who raised him from the dead.'

If order is a question of faith, Methodists are well content to accept the findings of the best Anglican scholars in the field of Church history. Westcott and Hort, Lightfoot and Hatch, Streeter, Gwatkin and Headlam are good enough names for us. As Dr. Carnegie Simpson says in a footnote in his *Evangelical Church Catholic*: 'These quotations from Bishop Westcott and Dr. Hort illustrate how easy agreement with the Anglican Church might be if we had to deal only with its great scholars.' As a contrast, consider a quotation from a recent book on *The English Church and how it works*, by Cecilia M. Ady. The book itself is a scholarly and laborious production, full of useful information. Here is the reference to Methodism separated from the Church of England: 'Wesley founded Methodist societies, that is voluntary associations of believers bound together in common worship and work for God. This is in the main the Methodist conception of the Church to-day. To speak of the Church as the Body of Christ, the divine society possessing power to bind and to loose, and in which alone the Christian life can be lived in its fullness is, from their standpoint, to use the language of metaphor rather than of reality.'

This is not meant in an unfriendly spirit, but it is a completely inaccurate statement as to what the instructed modern Methodist believes about the Church. He would agree that the words used about the Church are real, though St. Paul was using an analogy when he spoke about 'the body of Christ'. Few Christian societies in the whole history of the Church can have expressed that very doctrine more strongly than the Methodist Societies have done. There was a time when they seemed to be almost the only people in this country who had an adequate sense of fellowship in the Body of Christ. Their band meetings, their prayer meetings, their class meetings, their love-feasts, their Communion services, their circuit system, their connexional system were all part of that intense belief in their fellowship with an eternal society, part militant here on earth and part triumphant in Heaven. They knew the hymns of Charles Wesley too well not to have a sound New Testament doctrine of the Church:

> Christ from whom all blessings flow,
> Perfecting the saints below,
> Hear us, who Thy nature share,
> Who Thy mystic body are.
> Move, and actuate, and guide:
> Divers gifts to each divide;
> Placed according to Thy will,
> Let us all our work fulfil.

Or again:

> One family we dwell in Him,
>   One Church, above, beneath,
> Though now divided by the stream,
>   The narrow stream of death:

> One army of the living God,
> To His command we bow;
> Part of His host have crossed the flood,
> And part are crossing now.

and very much more to the same effect.

What had the Anglicanism of a hundred years ago to produce as a parallel to that passionate sense of fellowship in the Body of Christ? It was because there was no such consciousness of the Body of Christ in the Church of England that the Methodists left the Church; indeed, they left the Church in order to find the Church. As to the powers of binding and loosing, the charge has often been made against the Methodist class meeting that its discipline is more severe and searching than the Roman confessional. To-day, we have largely lost our class meetings in their original form, but we retain a clear understanding of what fellowship in the Body of Christ involves. It might help the cause of reunion if all of us examined over again St. Paul's teaching about the Body of Christ. This would take us back to that church of the first century of which we know most—the church at Corinth.

The twelfth and thirteenth chapters of the First Epistle to the Corinthians are of special significance for us at this time. The Corinthian church seems to have been rather disorderly; perhaps the Methodist would have been more at home in it than the Anglican. It may be that he had more need of the Apostolic injunction, 'let all things be done decently and in order'. He would certainly know what St. Paul was talking about in the twelfth chapter, and it is to be hoped that he would have a glimmering discernment of the beauty and truth of the picture of the greatest of all the χαρίσματα of the Church as set forth in the thirteenth chapter.

How far does the Anglo-Catholic's conception of the Body of Christ fit in with that of St. Paul? He would have been likely to find neither his bishops, nor his priests, nor his deacons at Corinth. This over-emphasis on orders seems to belong, as some one has said, to ecclesiastical anatomy rather than to biology. If we are thinking too much about organization when we speak of the Body of Christ, we end with a skeleton rather than with a living, breathing organism. The skeleton is important as the framework of the body, but the analogy breaks down if it is argued that there is only one possible organization for the Christian Church for all time. That diocesan episcopacy has been the form of Church government with the longest and most distinguished history is not questioned. That it may be the best form for the future organization of the Church can be conceded. What is denied is that this particular form of government concerns the *esse* and not the *bene esse* of the Church. Non-episcopal ministries 'have been manifestly blessed and owned by the Holy Spirit as effective means of Grace'. The argument for an episcopal basis for the reunited Church must be based on expediency, and not on any imaginary constitution laid down by our Lord Himself, or by the Holy Spirit's imaginary refusal to use other than episcopally ordained instruments as channels of God's grace and mercy.

It seems likely that any form of reunion reached in this country will be based on episcopacy. But as the Bishop of Gloucester pointed out in his Bampton Lectures, it would be a constitutional episcopacy. The days of the 'proud prelate' are over. 'Different elements in this conception', he says, 'have been preserved by Anglicans, Presbyterians, Congregationalists. If English Christianity were to reunite on such a basis it would not mean that the Nonconformist bodies joined an Episcopal Church; it would mean that the different fragments of Christ's Church in the land, separated and imperfect as they are, would combine together to build up a Church which would then present more adequately the full Catholic tradition.' For such an achievement, sacrifice is well worth while. Anglican leaders have expressed their willingness to receive some mark of authorization to administer the Sacraments to Free Church congregations if Free Church ministers receive reordination. This is a generous but unnecessary gesture, as no such authorization would be needed. Hugh Martin says, quite rightly, that ordination and authorization should not be confused.

Quoting one of the Puritans, Nonconformists are inclined to say that the whole idea of reordination 'hurts the mind'. If ever we achieve unity, some one's mind will have to be a little wounded. It might, however, be an honourable wound in so great a cause. If it were clearly understood that the Free Church minister was receiving no new grace in a second ordination, which he had not already received in the first, but that he was thinking of the tender conscience of the 'weaker brethren' of the Anglican Church, there ought to be no impassable barrier here. The times demand courageous and sacrificial action. The outline of a *Reunion Scheme for the Church of England and the Evangelical Free Churches of England* might very well be brought before representative assemblies of all the Churches who would consider it, and amend, accept, or reject it. The widespread apathy on the subject would disappear if once proposals came into the sphere of practical politics. The younger generation finds little meaning and no value in our divisions. It seems hardly worth while to waste time on discussions over the Federation of the Churches as a stepping-stone to reunion. As V. F. Storr said, 'federal unity would overcome our divisions by recognizing them'.

But we cannot afford to lose sight of our fellow churchmen in America. W. Adams Brown says that 'one reason why the movement for corporate union has followed a course in the United States different from that which it has assumed in Great Britain and on the Continent has been the comparatively small representation within American Christianity of Catholic Christianity of the non-Roman type. Whereas in Great Britain the Church of England contains many Christians who would call themselves Catholic rather than Protestant and on the Continent the Orthodox Churches include a very substantial number of the total number of Christians, the number of such Christians in the United States is comparatively small. The Orthodox Churches altogether comprise only 998,087 members and the Episcopal Church, the only body which includes a party which definitely calls itself "Catholic", includes scarcely more than one-thirtieth of the total number of American Protestants. There is thus no large body of Christians (aside from the Roman Catholics) who feel at home in the Catholic type of piety, and union, so far as it is a living issue, presents itself as primarily a Protestant question'.[1]

The Americans are accustomed to large numbers and they report a total Church membership of 60,630,990. We cannot plan a scheme for reunion on a numerical basis. In our survey of the extension of the Evangelical Revival to the American colonies, we have seen the promise of the huge growth of Nonconformity across the Atlantic. This fact must be considered. It is not easy to fit it in with views of Christ's Church which imply that there is neither reality nor the promise of permanence in any non-

[1] *Church and State in Contemporary America* (1936), p. 212.

episcopal body. The 'Catholic' views with which we are so familiar in this country are altogether too parochial. It is clear that they constitute the chief problem for the Anglican Church in any scheme of reunion. If the Free Churches of this country and the Church of England came together in a real fellowship, the Anglican compromise would be thrown out of balance. The Anglo-Catholic should, however, take courage. He would find a new field for fresh conquests. Nonconformity has a sense of sacramental and institutional values in its Church life and latent possibility for much enlightenment in 'Catholic' doctrine. After all, *Magna est veritas et praevalebit.*

NOTES ON AUTHORITIES

ONE of the charms of J. E. Neale's *Queen Elizabeth* is the absence of footnotes and references. It may seem an impertinence to excuse one's own deficiencies by a reference to one of the best biographies of our time, written by one of the most finished scholars among our historians. Still, he has set an example, and it is but natural that lesser fry should follow in his steps. We have become accustomed to expect in any serious study that 'a neat rivulet of text should meander through a meadow' of footnotes. Perhaps forty years of spasmodic reading in the literature and history of the Revival may be a guarantee that judgements have not been formed hastily nor without authority.

Is any Englishman better known from day to day, and almost from hour to hour in his mature years, than John Wesley? The eight volumes of his *Journals* and the eight volumes of his *Letters* have been edited in the Standard Editions with equal labour and loving accuracy by Curnock and Telford respectively. These, along with his *Works*, give us all we need to know. Of his too numerous biographers, Tyerman is still the most important, while the standard biography is that by J. S. Simon in five volumes. Tyerman was an indefatigable collector of pamphlets and manuscripts about the Revival. Hard words have been said about his style and his opinions, but all who have followed him have been glad to make use of his material. His works include *The Life and Times of Samuel Wesley* (1866), *The Life and Times of John Wesley* (3 vols., 1871), *The Oxford Methodists* (1873), and *The Life of George Whitefield* (2 vols., 1876).

The first Life of John Wesley appeared in the year he died, and was written by John Hampson jun., one of his preachers who left him because he and his father were not included in Wesley's list for the Legal Conference. He became Vicar of Sunderland and allowed a certain acerbity to appear in his three volumes of memoirs. Wesley's literary executors were Dr. Coke, Henry Moore, and John Whitehead, M.D. Unfortunately, disputes arose between them, and Coke and Moore rushed out their volume in 1792 to catch the market. It is entitled *The Life of the Rev. John Wesley, A.M.: including an Account of the great Revival of Religion in Europe and America, of which he was the first and chief Instrument*. Whitehead followed with two volumes on John and Charles Wesley in 1793 and 1796. He was inclined to support the attitude of Charles Wesley towards the lay preacher, though he was a lay preacher himself. None of these books is quite satisfactory, but Southey did better with his 1820 biography. Southey's book is not such a classic as his *Life of Nelson*, but it had a literary quality that was lacking in its predecessors. It is, however, rather dull and suffers from imperfect sympathy. In 1824 Henry Moore tried again and his two-volume work is the best that Wesley's literary executors were able to produce. Richard Watson produced a shorter Life in 1831, which corrected some of Southey's mistakes.

Of other books on Wesley those of Isaac Taylor, *Wesley and Methodism* (1851), and Julia Wedgwood, *John Wesley: A Study in the Evangelical Reaction of the Eighteenth Century* (1870), are still worth reading for their independent approach. The latter should be compared with Père Maximin Piette's *La Réaction de John Wesley dans l'évolution du Protestantisme* (Second Edition, 1927). This interesting study by a Belgian Franciscan has since been translated into English. The historical approach to Wesley through Protestant history on the Continent is valuable, but, while enthusiastic for Wesley, Father Piette is rather strongly anti-Lutheran and anti-Anglican. This volume is selected out of the mass of recent Wesleyan literature as important by the Historical Association. The only other book that has that honour is G. Elsie Harrison's *Son to Susanna* (1937), which is a study of Wesley in his relation to women. This gives us the most vivid and lifelike picture of John Wesley that we have, though it catches Charles Wesley at an unfortunate moment. It should be compared with Rigg's *Living Wesley*, which appeared as long ago as 1875.

For Wesley's early career, Richard Green's *John Wesley, Evangelist* (1905) is valuable, and J. E. Rattenbury's *Wesley's Legacy to the World* (1928) and *The Conversion of the Wesleys: A Critical Study* (1938) give the best interpretation of the secret of the Revival published in recent times. His Fernley-Hartley Lecture for last year on *The Theology of Charles Wesley's Hymns* is also a very full and careful study of doctrine as the Methodists learnt it in song. Methodists overseas have also made notable contributions to this subject. From Australia came W. H. Fitchett's *Wesley and His Century* (1925), a picturesque story, as might be expected from the author of *Deeds that Won the Empire*. The best American biography is that by Winchester, though Umphrey Lee has made useful contributions to the story. Bishop McConnell's recent Life is disappointing, but Professor George Croft Cell in *The Rediscovery of John Wesley* (1934) has found in the message of the Revival an answer to modern humanism. This is a strong defence of the value of Wesleyan theology. From Canada came *England: Before and After Wesley* by J. W. Bready (1938), which is too much a study in black and white. It should be modified by J. H. Whiteley's *Wesley's England*, which appeared in the same year, or by any of the numerous social histories of the period. The most readable one-volume study of John Wesley is that by C. E. Vuilliamy (1931); Marjorie Bowen's *Wrestling Jacob*

(1937) has some good chapters, but lacks both sympathy and an adequate knowledge of the subject.

For Charles Wesley we must still depend on Thomas Jackson's two-volume biography, published in 1841, and the *Letters and Journals of Charles Wesley*, which were edited by the same writer and appeared in 1849. Shorter lives have been written by John Telford, D. M. Jones, and Dr. F. L. Wiseman. The *Poetical Works of John and Charles Wesley*, in thirteen volumes, were edited by Dr. Osborn in 1868; most of this voluminous output is from the pen of Charles Wesley. The *Proceedings of the Wesley Historical Society* have added much to our knowledge of detail in the fifty years of the Society's existence and some of its work reappears in the notes to the Standard Editions of the *Journal* and *Letters*. We come back in the end to Simon's five volumes on John Wesley which appeared between 1921 and 1934. They represent the reading of a lifetime and, if they err a little on the side of idolatry, they give us the fullest picture of the life and work of one of the greatest of Englishmen.

There are many histories of Methodism, but two mid-Victorian histories that have gone out of fashion provide much material. These are, from this country, Dr. George Smith's *History of Wesleyan Methodism* (1857) and, from the United States, Abel Stevens's *History of Methodism* (1878), both in three volumes. Another three-volume history is that of *Irish Methodism* by C. H. Crookshank, which appeared in 1885. Stevens also published a one-volume *History of American Methodism*. Of even more value are the numerous local histories and the long list of biographies from those of Adam Clarke down to that of Hugh Price Hughes by his daughter. Perhaps Benson's *Life of Fletcher* and Mrs. Fletcher's *Life* edited by Henry Moore should be specially mentioned. The six volumes of the *Lives of the Early Methodist Preachers* are still our best document for the romance of the Revival. Any one interested in theology could still enjoy Fletcher's *Checks to Antinomianism*. If any one is fortunate enough to possess the Christmas numbers of the *Methodist Recorder* issued year by year from 1892 to 1907 he will have an unrivalled collection of anecdotes, histories, and legends of Methodists in all parts of the country which gives an authentic picture of a past now rapidly receding from our memory. There is nothing that remotely represents it in the journalism of our day. The *Methodist Magazine* of an earlier period preserved something of this tradition, but the gold was imbedded in much intractable material.

Methodism in America and in the overseas mission stations has also a lengthy bibliography. The best introduction to the study of American Methodism is through Tipple's *Heart of Asbury's Journal* (1904) and the records of the pioneer preachers, such as *The Autobiography of*

Peter Cartwright (1856). Studies of the lives of individual missionaries, too, are the best means of kindling interest in the story of the modern movement for the evangelization of the world. The excellent *History of the Wesleyan Methodist Missionary Society*, by G. G. Findlay and W. W. Holdsworth (five vols., 1905), should be compared with the *History of the Church Missionary Society*, by Eugene Stock (three vols.), for a study of Methodist and Evangelical working in a common cause on parallel lines.

The religious histories of the period fit varying movements of thought and action into their context. The relevant volumes in Macmillan's *History of the Church of England* are by Overton and Relton for the eighteenth century and F. Warre Cornish for the nineteenth century. Canon Overton, from an Anglican standpoint, made as full a contribution to the study of the Evangelical Revival as Tyerman did from the Methodist standpoint. His volume on Wesley is a sound estimate, and his book, *The English Church in the Nineteenth Century, 1800–1833*, which appeared in 1894, is really a continuation of the studies represented in the valuable two-volume *English Church in the Eighteenth Century* (1878 and 1881), in which C. J. Abbey collaborated. Abbey also produced the two-volume *English Church and its Bishops, 1700–1800* in 1887. For the same period, John Hunt's three volumes on *Religious Thought in England* (1870–3) is a good survey of religious literature between the Reformation and the end of the eighteenth century. Corresponding to the nine volumes of *The History of the Church of England* we have from a Nonconformist angle Dr. John Stoughton's *History of Religion in England*, which was reissued in eight volumes in 1901. The Dean of Exeter (then Master of the Temple), S. C. Carpenter, produced in 1933 a very readable volume on *Church and People, 1789–1889*. This is a history of the Church of England from William Wilberforce to *Lux Mundi*.

For the Evangelicals, *A History of the Evangelical Party in the Church of England* by S. R. Balléine (1908) is a good introduction, while Sir James Stephen's delightful essays on the 'Evangelical' Succession, William Wilberforce, and the Clapham Sect keep their interest although they were written a century ago. They first appeared in the *Edinburgh Review*, but are now conveniently found in the second volume of the *Essays in Ecclesiastical Biography* (1907) in Longman's Silver Library. Baring-Gould's *The Evangelical Revival* (1920) is a prejudiced and foolish book in many ways, though it has some good stories. He says that Wesley owed his success 'largely to his powerful voice and his graceful attitudes'! Was he thinking of Whitefield? G. W. E. Russell has written more entertainingly, but with real sympathy.

Here, as in the study of the Methodists, it is the biographies that are most rewarding, though some of them are intolerably long and verbose. A beginning might be made with the two volumes of that queer book, *The Life and Times of Selina, Countess of Huntingdon*, by a member of the houses of Shirley and Hastings (1840). It is packed with references to preachers and aristocrats and an Index to this formless mass has fortunately been provided by the Wesley Historical Society in their *Proceedings*, Vol. 5. The author was Aaron Crossley Hobart Seymour. The best Life of Whitefield is still Tyerman's, and A. D. Belden's *George Whitefield, the Awakener* (1930) adds nothing to it, though it is well produced and has the benefit of an Introduction by Ramsay MacDonald. For Howell Harris, the Life written by H. J. Hughes in 1892 is the best, though Morgan's *Life and Times of Howell Harris* should be mentioned; a more recent life in Welsh has not been translated. Toplady's Life is included in the large single volume of his *Works* which is found in its most convenient form in the 1850 Edition. It is strongly anti-Wesleyan in tone and keeps up the Calvinist vendetta against the Arminians. John Newton is best studied in his *Letters*, but we have several Lives of Hannah More. Those by Thomas Roberts and Henry Thompson give us the spirit of the times, particularly the latter book, as Thompson was curate of Wrington, where Hannah More lived and was buried. The *Mendip Annals* is an attractive little book and describes the Sunday schools set up by this devoted lady and her sisters in the Somerset countryside. Also the *Letters of Hannah More to Zachary Macaulay* are still readable.

Other biographies of note are *The Life of Henry Venn*, by his son, John Venn, edited by his grandson, Henry Venn, in 1839; the Life of that good but dull man, William Romaine, by W. B. Cadogan, and that of Rowland Hill, by Edwin Sidney; and especially the *Life of Isaac Milner*, D.D., F.R.S., by his niece, Mary Milner. This is a weighty volume, but it shows the Evangelicals struggling into recognition as an important 'party' in the Church of England. Many of the Lives of Victorian Evangelicals provide useful material, though they are too numerous to mention here, as are those of the Methodist preachers. For the latter it may be convenient to turn to the Bibliography of the second volume of the *New History of Methodism*, edited by Eayrs, Townsend, and Workman in 1907.

The Moravians may be studied in the *Memories of James Hutton*, by Daniel Benham (1856), and the *History of the Moravian Church*, by J. E. Hutton (Second Edition, 1909). Spangenberg's *Life of Zinzendorf* was translated into English by Samuel Jackson in 1836. A more recent study is that by W. G. Addison on *The Renewed Church of the United Brethren, 1722–1930*, which appeared in 1932.

This greatly abbreviated introduction to a bibliography should be supplemented by tracts, pamphlets, etc. For the eighteenth century we have excellent lists in Richard Green's *Wesley Bibliography* (1896) and *Anti-Methodist Publications* (1902). Dr. Osborn published in 1896 a *Record of Methodist Literature from the Beginning*, but no one has yet struggled to survey the nineteenth-century collections.

The literature on reunion, also, is assuming large proportions. Bell's *Documents on Christian Unity* reveals something of the scope of this movement in recent years. The present Bishop of Gloucester's 1920 Bampton Lectures on *The Doctrine of the Church and Reunion*, appearing, as they did, at the same time as the Lambeth Appeal, made the difficult problem appear capable of solution. Reports on the great Conferences at Edinburgh (1910 and 1937), Stockholm, Lausanne, Tambaram, Oxford, and Amsterdam helped in the good cause. Contrasted points of view are represented by H. L. Goudge, *The Church of England and Reunion*, and, quite recently, Hugh Martin, *Christian Reunion: A Plea for Action*. So far as this country is concerned, the movement has crystallized in the *Outline of a Reunion Scheme for the Church of England and the Evangelical Free Churches of England* (S.C.M. Press, 6d.). 'Though only a small pamphlet', says Hugh Martin, 'it is one of the most significant Christian documents of the last three hundred years.'

Printed *in* Great Britain
By The Camelot Press Ltd
London *and* Southampton